MOTHERING
THE UNION

MANCHESTER
1824

Manchester University Press

EUROPE IN CHANGE SERIES EDITORS: *Thomas Christiansen and Emil Kirchner*

already published

The formation of Croatian national identity
A centuries old dream
ALEX J. BELLAMY

Committee governance in the European Union
THOMAS CHRISTIANSEN AND EMIL KIRCHNER (EDS)

Theory and reform in the European Union, 2nd edition
DIMITRIS N. CHRYSSOCHOOU, MICHAEL J. TSINISIZELIS,
STELIOS STAVRIDIS AND KOSTAS IFANTIS

German policy-making and eastern enlargement of the EU during the Kohl era
Managing the agenda?
STEPHEN D. COLLINS

The European Union and the Cyprus conflict
THOMAS DIEZ

The changing European Commission
DIONYSSIS DIMITRAKOPOULOS (ED.)

Reshaping Economic and Monetary Union
SHAWN DONNELLY

The time of European governance
MAGNUS EKENGREN

An introduction to post-Communist Bulgaria
EMIL GIATZIDIS

The new Germany and migration in Europe
BARBARA MARSHALL

Turkey: facing a new millennium
AMIKAM NACHMANI

The changing face of federalism
SERGIO ORTINO, VOJTECII MASTNY AND MITJA ŽAGAR (EDS)

The road to the European Union, volume 2
Estonia, Latvia and Lithuania
VELLO PETTAI AND JAN ZIELONKA (EDS)

The road to the European Union, volume 1
The Czech and Slovak Republics
JACQUES RUPNIK AND JAN ZIELONKA (EDS)

Europe and civil society
Movement coalitions and European governance
CARLO RUZZA

Two tiers or two speeds?
The European security order and the enlargement
of the European Union and NATO
JAMES SPERLING (ED.)

Recasting the European order
JAMES SPERLING AND EMIL KIRCHNER

Rethinking European Union foreign policy
BEN TONRA AND THOMAS CHRISTIANSEN (EDS)

Institutional and policy-making challenges to the European Union
in the wake of eastern enlargement
AMY VERDUN AND OSVALDO CROCI (EDS)

The emerging Euro-Mediterranean system
DIMITRIS K. XENAKIS AND DIMITRIS N. CHRYSSOCHOOU

Roberta Guerrina

MOTHERING THE UNION

Gender politics in the EU

MANCHESTER UNIVERSITY PRESS
Manchester and New York

distributed exclusively in the USA by Palgrave

Published by Manchester University Press
Oxford Road, Manchester M13 9NR, UK
and Room 400, 175 Fifth Avenue, New York, NY 10010, USA
www.manchesteruniversitypress.co.uk

Distributed exclusively in the USA by
Palgrave, 175 Fifth Avenue, New York, NY 10010, USA

Distributed exclusively in Canada by
UBC Press, University of British Columbia, 2029 West Mall, Vancouver, BC, Canada V6T 1Z2

British Library Cataloguing-in-Publication Data
A catalogue record for this book is available from the British Library

Library of Congress Cataloging-in-Publication Data applied for

ISBN   0 7190 6584 4 *hardback*
EAN   978 0 7190 6584 2

First published 2005

14 13 12 11 10 09 08 07 06 05   10 9 8 7 6 5 4 3 2 1

Typeset in Minion with Lithos
by Action Publishing Technology Ltd, Gloucester
Printed in Great Britain
by Biddles Limited, King's Lynn

Contents

Preface and acknowledgements   *page* vii

Introduction: equal rights, maternity and work–life balance
in Europe   1

1 Feminist interpretations of equality, difference and motherhood   17

2 The development of women's rights in Europe: equal pay, equal
   treatment and constitutionalism   39

3 Reconciliation between work and family life: a concrete move
   towards establishing substantive equality as a working principle
   for the Union?   65

4 The European Court of Justice: ruling on gender   86

5 The family-friendly discourse in Italy: mothering, the family and the
   nation   114

6 Between the family and the market: the case of the UK   129

   Conclusions   150

   Bibliography   159
   Index   177

PREFACE AND ACKNOWLEDGEMENTS

Scholarly interest in the issue of gender has been growing steadily over the last ten years. This surge of interest is reflected in the growing number of publications in mainstream politics journals. Yet this is an area of study that is still all too often on the fringes of political debates about the future of Union. In this context, I would like to thank the editorial board of the Europe in Change series at Manchester University Press for giving me the opportunity to contribute to this growing area of research and debate.

I began to research this project nearly ten years ago. Since then, feminist discourses on women's employment, equality and mothering have evolved. Particularly notable is the shift in feminist research from a focus on motherhood and difference to an analysis of fatherhood and masculinity. Although the analysis presented here looks at mothering and the social construction of motherhood as reflected in employment legislation, it is important not to underestimate the impact of social pressures on the social construction of fathering. The analysis of these two functions is not mutually exclusive, as they are currently constructed in opposition to one another.

The book deals with feminist theories, EU policies and national case studies. The reason for including such an array of issues and debates is to draw the reader's attention to the impact of European social polices on the construction of gender power hierarchies. The discussion of EU policies also provides an overview of the historical background to the development of women's rights in Europe and sets out the general context for the discussion and analysis of current developments in this field such as the Charter of Fundamental Rights, the Draft European Constitutional Treaty and the 2003 Commission Proposal for a Directive on Equal Treatment for access to goods and services. This shift in focus signals a move beyond the narrow scope of employment rights. This optimism, however, needs to be curtailed by the reality of EU politics and the continued focus on the market citizen.

Earlier elements of this research were presented at various conferences, seminars and symposiums, including the British International Studies Association Annual Conference, ECPR joint session in Edinburgh and the Association for Research on Mothering Symposium on Becoming a Mother. I would like to thank all participants for their constructive feedback and comments on my work. In particular, I would like to thank Thomas Christiansen, Marysia Zalewski, Catherine Hoskyns and Ben Tonra for their comments on an earlier version of this project.

A special thanks also goes to Babu Rahman, for his emotional support over the years. Finally, I would like to dedicate this book to Rosanna Guglielmo whose life has been an inspiration and provided me with the resolve to complete this work.

Introduction: equal rights, maternity and work–life balance in Europe

The process of demographic transition experienced by European states over the last thirty years is starting to have an impact on the long-term objectives of economic and social policies. In this context, the decline in birth rates, increased female participation in education and the official labour market, changes in employment patterns, and the ageing of the European population have become important markers of socio-economic change. The values that underpin this transition are also reflected in various changes in the policy environment. In terms of women's employment rights, the impact of demographic trends on government policy and discourse has become evident in the last decade of the twentieth century. A marked a shift in policy discourse from equal opportunities to work–life balance, also known as reconciliation between work and family life or family-friendly policies, is perhaps the single defining characteristic of this change in policy environment. At the same time, the European market has also undergone a process of evolution under the banner of European integration. The Treaty of Maastricht (1992) is a particularly important landmark in this process as it signals the launch of the Single European Market, the creation of the European Union and, in terms of social policy, it marks the establishment of a European social dimension.

The overall aim of this book is to investigate the scope of maternity legislation and family friendly policies in the European Union. The wider context of analysis is the development of equal rights as part of a European social dimension. In particular, this book is concerned with the influence of values and beliefs about women, equality, politics, and employment on the scope of equal rights and maternity provisions. Given this background, the analysis presented here will endeavour to answer the following questions: What are the stated objectives of family-friendly policies? Which values transpire from the analysis of maternity rights? And, how do gender power hierarchies shape the overall aim of policies for the reconciliation between work and family life?

In other words, this book aims to uncover the values that underpin the policy-making process and their impact on policy outcomes.

The analysis of various policies falling under the broad umbrella of reconciliation between work and family life is particularly important in order to understand the position of women in society and the official labour market. However, by focusing specifically on maternity rights it is possible to uncover the role of social values in relation to women's role as primary carers. In this context, it is interesting to note that there are two elements to maternity legislation; the first is health and safety, and the second deals with women's employment rights. Although the stated purpose of maternity rights is to protect women's position and role in the official labour market, they also implicitly endorse a specific understanding of mothering based on the assumed special nature of the mother–child relationship. Maternity legislation therefore includes specific conceptualisations of woman, mother, worker, and employment, which have also been the focus of several debates since the onset of second wave feminism.

The critique of maternity legislation and family-friendly policies thus seeks to challenge traditional conceptualisations of women's role in society and the official labour market. The categorisation of maternity legislation as an equality issue, as well as a health and safety concern, draws attention to the impact of gender relations, and specifically women's role as carers and mothers, upon the ratification and implementation of employment policy (Conaghan, 1993; Grecchi, 1996: 71–6; McGlynn, 2001). The analysis conducted here will highlight how equal rights, and maternity provision as part of this policy area, are not only about protecting women's health and safety, but also seek to reaffirm women's role and position in the public as well as the private sphere. Such awareness is important for the overall conceptual framework of the book, which questions the division between public and private, as well as formal and substantive equality. The implications of this critique are twofold. Firstly, it draws attention to the continued importance of gender analysis in the field of employment and social policy; secondly, it challenges traditional assumptions about gender, gender roles and the construction of woman. In this way, it highlights the weakness of current policy discourses and approaches to this particular field.

In the process of addressing the overall aim of this research, I will therefore ask the following questions: how have public–private divisions and the current gender order influenced the scope and reach of maternity legislation and family-friendly policies? And what concept of equality does the principle of reconciliation between work and family life espouse? These questions provide the basis for my investigation, as they challenge the foundations of equal rights legislation. In other words, by posing these questions this book will challenge the validity of an equality approach founded upon traditional dichotomies and hierarchical structures.

Key issues and concepts

The analysis presented here will address some of the primary concerns of three feminist approaches engaged in the equal rights debate. Three issues or concept will provide the conceptual framework for this discussion. Firstly, it is important to engage in the debate about the meanings and principle of equality. Secondly, it is necessary to evaluate the continued presence of a division between public and private, and its impact on the application of the principle of equality. Particularly important in this context is the impact of the public–private dichotomy on the division between formal and substantive equality. Finally, the analysis presented here requires a comprehensive assessment of the social and political values associated with the concept of motherhood and the social construction of 'woman' through the process of mothering. The analysis of these issues will also be supported by a more general discussion of gender power hierarchies and gender divisions of labour.

As some of the most extensive endorsements and critiques of these concepts have come from the feminist 'camp', I shall start by engaging with theoretical discourses about the meaning and limits of these concepts. Feminist theories will thus inform the argument presented here. However, as feminism is not a homogeneous movement or epistemology, a comprehensive analysis of the legislation must begin with a discussion of feminist theories vis-à-vis the concepts of equality, difference and woman (Bacchi, 1990; Elam, 1994; Elshtain, 1992; Enloe, 1990; Evans, 1995; Landes, 1998; Phillips, 1987; Scott, 1994; Whitworth, 1994).

These concepts were chosen amongst the vast array of issues tackled by feminist debates as they provide important insights into the application, or lack of application, of the overarching aims of maternity rights and family-friendly policies. In this context, they raise challenging questions about the interaction between gender values and the policy-making process and, in doing so, they highlight how traditional assumptions about women workers shape equal rights and maternity legislation. The application of feminist discourses to the analysis of European and national policy structures for the reconciliation between work and family life will thus draw attention the impact of gender power hierarchies on social and economic policies.

As outlined above, one of the central themes addressed by this book is the pervasive nature of the public–private dichotomy. Various feminists have criticised Western political elites for creating a false division between the political and the familial spheres, which has in turn crystallised the separation between substantive and formal equality (Cavarero, 1990; Cornell, 1992; Enloe, 1990; Grecchi, 1996; Hoskyns, 1985; Lacey, 1993; Phillips, 1987; Whitworth, 1994). It is in this context that feminist scholars and activists have sought to challenge the public–private dichotomy, representations of gender roles, and the overall gender order that structures contemporary social, political and economic relations.

Nicola Lacey (1993: 98–100) argues that the distinction between the public and private sphere is founded upon assumptions and beliefs about gender roles and the gendered division of labour. As she further argues, 'the importance of the public/private dichotomy lies in the fact that the cultural construction of the public sphere in which universal reason holds sway implicitly marginalizes or is inhospitable to women'. This book will apply Lacey's (1993: 96, 98–100) argument to the analysis of maternity and equal rights policies. Thus, it will discuss how the distinction between formal and substantive equality is the by-product of policy-making structures that are gendered and maintain gender divisions of labour through the separation of the political from the domestic sphere.

Clearly, this analysis underpins any evaluation of the impact of gender power hierarchies on the policy-making process. It is by taking on board the values embedded within these discourses that we become aware of the process through which assumptions and expectations about women's roles and functions in the private have come to define women's position in the public sphere (Cavarero, 1992; Flax, 1992; Pateman, 1989; Pateman, 1991). The analysis of maternity rights and family-friendly policies thus becomes instrumental to uncover how gender norms and power hierarchies permeate the seemingly neutral spheres of politics and economics. As it will become clear through the evaluation of the empirical evidence presented here, these provisions not only *protect* women's position and rights in the official labour market, but also *regulate* the relationship between women's participation in the official labour market and women's role as carers.

Given this background, a likely conclusion is that the scope and reach of maternity rights and family-friendly policies are representative of a social, economic and legal framework that seeks to maintain these same gender divisions of labour. The way in which European labour market policies have achieved this unstated objective is by regulating women's employment in the public sphere without acknowledging the impact of traditional gender roles and responsibilities in the domestic sphere. These considerations are important because they highlight the biases entrenched in a legislative framework founded upon male standards of work and worker (Bridgeman and Millns, 1995: xx, xxiii). The persistent distinction between women's public and private responsibilities thus serves to reaffirm the current gender order (Conaghan, 1993: 80, 71–2). As Rivka Polatnick (1983: 24) explains, the differentiation between carer and breadwinner alters the balance of power within the family unit, ultimately reinforcing gender power hierarchies.

Another important theme addressed by this book is that of equality. More specifically, the analysis of the division between formal and substantive equality is key to understanding the role of the legislation in promoting women's rights as workers and citizens. Catherine Hoskyns (1985: 74–6) argues that there is a difference between substantive and formal equality. This difference, she argues, is important because it influences the scope and reach of equal rights legislation. The distinction between substantive and formal equality is based upon the difference between legal rights and the impact of such rights on women's status in the public and the private sphere (Grecchi, 1996: 46–7; Hervey and Shaw, 1998; Hoskyns, 1985, 74–5). In other words, it is the difference between legal equality on the one hand, and what is necessary to achieve equal status and recognition in employment and everyday life on the other. This dichotomy is very important with reference to maternity legislation, because of the very nature of the issues targeted by maternity rights. If maternity legislation only aims at providing a framework for equal rights in the official labour market then, it implicitly ignores the impact of gender power hierarchies on women's choices about employment and mothering. In this context, maternity legislation therefore *protects* women formal rights, but fails to *promote* women's rights as equal members of society and the labour force (Bakker, 1988; Bland, 1985: 23; Conaghan, 1993; McGlynn, 2001b; Millns, 1996: 167–9, 172; Paul, 1992: 30–6; Ross and Schneider, 1992: 18–19; Smart and Brophy, 1985: 15–16; Wynn, 1999).

The argument presented here revolves around the application of the principle of substantive equality to social and economic policies. It is important to move away from a narrow understanding of equality based on the principle of equal opportunities, to a more holistic approach to women's employment rights in order to challenge gender power hierarchies in the family and the official labour market. It is in this context that the concept of substantive equality thus raises important questions about the construction of equality, difference and women at the European and national level.

Given the theoretical context outlined above, the last issue to be addressed here is that of the centrality of motherhood to the European socio-economic order. More specifically, this book will seek to uncover the values and norms attached to the practice of mothering and in so doing evaluate the importance of women's caring role for the long-term survival of European welfare structures. Starting from Nancy Chodorow's (1978: 3, 34) claim that 'women's mothering as an organisation of parenting is embedded in and fundamental to the social organisation of gender', the analysis presented here will evaluate the role of the legislation in sustaining gender divisions of care work as embedded in parenting roles. The analysis conducted by Chodorow (1978: 3, 10–39) illustrates the extent to which women have been associated with the social function of reproduction in Western society. For Chodorow, traditional values and norms about motherhood and mothers exemplify the pervasive nature of gender divisions of labour. Linda Birke (1986) also discussed the interrelation between nature and society, whereby biological experiences are shaped by social structures and influences.

Clearly, not all women share the same experience of motherhood and maternity (certainly not all women are, will be or want to be mothers). However, the importance of motherhood in defining gender structures reflects Western representations of women's role in society and the relation-

ship between gender roles on the one hand and economic and political structures on the other. The analysis of the role of mothering, therefore, shows the
overwhelming importance of gender in shaping women's social and political
identity (Brannen and Moss, 1991: 5–6).

Given these considerations it is possible to conclude that, in as far as the
legislation reflects socio-political trends, it also encompasses specific representations of women and their role in society. It thus provides a framework
through which gender power hierarchies can be maintained and reinforced.
In this context, maternity legislation poses an important challenge to employment legislation as a whole. Whereas Western political elites have
traditionally considered motherhood and mothering to be private or domestic affairs, with little or no relevance to the official labour market, maternity
legislation regulates the effect of this 'private' function upon women's
employment practices (Bock and Thane, 1994: 12–13; Cavarero, 1990: 225,
229; Held, 1983: 8–9; Lacey, 1993: 94; Lovenduski and Randall, 1993: 266–9;
Richardson, 1993: 8–16). Given this background, the analysis of the relationship between mothering and maternity legislation draws attention to three
considerations outlined above. Firstly, it highlights the persistence of gender
division of labour in the family. Secondly, it emphasises the division between
employment in the official labour market and unpaid labour in the private
sphere. And finally, it helps to deconstruct the concepts of worker and mother
(Beechey, 1988: 52–5).

The structure of the book

The book comprises three main sections. The first focuses on the feminist
debates on equal rights. The second provides an overview of the European
framework. And the third provides an insight into the impact of EU policies
at the national level.

The first section looks at feminist discourses on equality, difference and
the construction of the concept of woman. The equal rights debate in feminist theory, as categorised for the purpose of the analysis presented here,
fulfills two important functions. Firstly, it addresses important questions that
have been at the centre of various feminists debates since the onset of the
second wave feminist movement (Pascall, 1997: 20–9; Whitworth, 1994).
Secondly, it will establish the overall analytical framework of this book. As
outlined previously in this introduction, it is possible to uncover how the
legislation constructs the public and the private sphere through the analysis
of feminist approaches to the role of the legislation in promoting women's
rights and equality. The application of specific feminist lenses (Peterson and
Runyan Sasson, 1993: 1–3; Poole, 1997) to the analysis of the case studies will
further disclose the values entrenched within maternity legislation and equal
rights policies.

Section two outlines the main developments in the field of women's rights in the EU. This section is important because it provides the overarching framework for the establishment of a transnational equality agenda. This discussion will provide a historical overview of the main developments in this policy area from the Treaty of Rome (1957) to current debates about the position of gender in the EU Charter of Fundamental Rights and the negotiations for a European constitution. The analysis will then turn to a detailed discussion of the progressive widening of the European equality agenda. In particular, it will consider the impact of the introduction of the principle of reconciliation between work and family life for European social policies. As part of this discussion, this section will evaluate the strengths and weaknesses of this principle within the context of feminist discourses on equality and gender divisions of labour. Finally, this section will assess possible interpretation of EU law in this field through the analysis of European Court of Justice (ECJ) rulings and opinions.

Section three provides some necessary information to measure the success of EU policies at the national level. The discussion of the case studies of Italy and the UK will draw attention to the difference between theory and practice in the application and the implementation of the principle of reconciliation between work and family life.

Having highlighted the bases for the analytical framework and the overall issues driving the analysis presented in this book, I will now discuss the content of the chapters, and how they fit together to provide a comprehensive analysis of the scope and limitations of family-friendly policies in Europe.

Theoretical framework: the equal rights debate
The equal rights debate in feminist theory provides the conceptual framework for the analysis of the empirical data presented in this book. More specifically, the exchange between equality, difference and post-structuralist feminism will uncover some of the main issues affecting the position of women and mothers in contemporary society. These feminist approaches were chosen for the following reasons: equality and difference offer conflicting conceptualisations of the power of legislative structures as agents of women's emancipation, whereas post-structuralist approaches provide a framework for the deconstruction of the concepts of gender, gender roles and motherhood.

The discussion presented here focuses on diverging interpretations of women's role as mothers and workers presented within contemporary feminist theorising. More specifically, feminist debates on equality and difference provide an interesting spectrum of interpretations of the concepts of woman and mother, and the relationship between women's role as carers and workers (Bacchi, 1990: 108–33; Bock and James, 1992; Cavarero, 1992: 45; Evans, 1995). In this context, whereas equality feminists focus on equal rights in the public sphere as the basis for the achievement of equality, difference feminists strongly criticise the assumption that legal or formal equality will lead to extensive social changes (Whitworth, 1994: 12–16). Difference feminists' critique of women's role in the social order uncovered the predominance of the public–private dichotomy, as well as introducing the concept of women's *different* needs (Cavarero, 1992: 45; Evans, 1995: 5). On the other hand, equality feminists' constant pressure and lobbying for the development of equal rights policies in the public domain has led to significant improvements in working conditions and statutory rights available to women. These considerations highlight the main contributions of this debate to feminist understanding of the position of women in contemporary Europe. Firstly, the equal rights debate draws attention to the continuities in gender dynamics by emphasising women's lack of status in the official labour market and the family. Secondly, it has succeeded in highlighting the presence of 'gender based relations of domination' in current employment practices and the legislation that is supposed to regulate them (Flax, 1990: 45).

The continued reliance on male norms and standards of work is further evidence of the power of gender hierarchies in the European labour market (Flax, 1992: 193). Equality feminism's blindness to such dynamics ultimately undermines the radical potential of this approach's work and analysis. On the other hand, although difference feminism has come to be associated with a wide-reaching critique of maleness and the use of male norms as standards, its focus on women's *different* needs ultimately reinforces the same standards it seeks to criticise. This is the case because for women's needs to be *different* there has to be a *normal* standard for them to be compared to (Conaghan, 1993: 76).

Although the equality–difference debate provides a useful starting point for the analysis presented here, these two approaches have only limited reach. Whitworth (1994: 22–3, 67) discussed at length the key tenets of the equal rights debate, only to conclude that post-modern and critical approaches can help feminist researchers to deconstruct the environment within which gender actually develops. In doing so, these approaches help feminist theorising to move beyond the binary oppositions entrenched within the equality–difference debate. In a similar fashion, the introduction of post-structuralist feminism to the analysis presented here will allow me to problematise the values underpinning the legislative and policy-making framework at the European and national level. The advantage of post-structuralist feminism is that in the process of assessing the role and function of mothering, it also challenges gender relations and gender identities. This feminist approach will therefore enable me to question the usefulness of assuming the existence of a 'universal woman'. Moreover, it will provide me with the necessary tools to evaluate the impact of gender values associated with the social function of reproduction on the legislative process (Whitworth, 1994: 20–3).

To summarise, although all three approaches provide important insights in the analysis of maternity legislation, the equality and difference approaches are based on a modernist understanding of feminism and woman (Whitworth, 1994: 20-1). What this means is that despite having developed an extensive critique of gender inequalities, equality and difference must operate within the constraints of mainstream social discourses (Flax, 1990: 175, 177–8). This focus in turn limits the radical potential of feminist analysis. Post-structuralist deconstructions, on the other hand, challenge the very foundations of gender. However, post-structuralism can also become overly pre-occupied with the deconstruction of woman, power, identity and politics and, in so doing, lose 'sight of the political imperatives which inform feminism' (Whitworth, 1994: 23). Despite these weaknesses, post-structuralist feminism is important for the analysis conducted here as it challenges enduring constructions of society as an unchangeable entity. The main difference between these approaches can thus be summarised as follows: whereas the latter seeks to deconstruct universalising categories, the former are founded upon essentialised values about a true nature of women/mothers (Grant, 1993).

Despite the various weaknesses embedded within each approach outlined above, these theories provide important insights into how beliefs about male and female roles in society determine gender divisions and women's employment choices. Birke's (1986: 32) analysis of women's role as carers in the reproductive process also provides interesting insights into how gender power hierarchies are constructed and maintained. Evidence of the division of labour in the family is the predominance of the male breadwinner model as the organising principle of social and political relation in Europe. For Birke (1986) women's association with the function of care is a key factor in understanding sexual oppression and relations of domination in the family. This book will apply this conceptual framework to the examination of the scope and reach of maternity rights and family-friendly policies. In doing so, I will discuss how gender values have permeated political and legal structures, thus bringing to light the relationship between gender, culture, politics and work.

Specifically within the framework of maternity rights, Linda Birke (1986: 32) discussed at length the impact of gender divisions of labour on the development of health and safety legislation. She argued that, as women are perceived primarily in terms of the reproductive process, and more vulnerable to their surrounding environment, there has been an incremental development of health and safety policies directly targeting women. The same can be argued with reference to the development of maternity rights. As maternity legislation has developed in a socio-political and economic context that is not immune from gender power hierarchies, it then follows that these values have become entrenched within those policies aimed at *protecting* the position of women in the reproductive process.

To conclude, I will make use of various concepts arising from the analysis of each feminist approach in order to highlight the limitations of maternity legislation and family-friendly policies. In this context, the legacy of equality feminism will allow me to discuss the impact of the legislation in fostering equality of opportunities. Difference feminism, on the other hand, will allow me to introduce an important analysis of women's needs and position in the official labour market. Finally, through post-structuralist feminism I will be able to deconstruct the concepts of mother, woman and workers, as embedded in the legislation. This final analysis will therefore provide the necessary tools for a detailed discussion of the scope of maternity rights and the principle of reconciliation between work and family life in terms of the impact of gender and gender relations.

The European framework

As explained in the previous section, theoretical discourses play an important role in shaping the basis for the analysis of policy developments at the European and national level. By applying the feminist framework outlined above I will be able to discuss the scope and reach of family-friendly policies, thus challenging the values upon which they were developed.

The analysis of the development of women's employment rights in the European Union is a challenging and important task. As much of the current literature on European integration highlights, the process of Europeanisation whereby policy-making and decision making power is transferred from the national to the European level draws attention to the power and influence of this organisation in the fields of social and employment policy. Moreover, the interaction between the interests of member states' governments and those European institutions highlights the complexities that underpin socio-political and economic relations and that ultimately are transposed in women's employment rights. Although member states retain much influence in the policy-making process of the EU, its unique institutional structure makes this organisation more than the mere sum of its parts (Cairns, 1997; Hoskyns, 1996; Rees, 1998). It is for all these reasons that the EU has been often used as a framework of analysis for the development of women's rights and equality in Europe. The same rationale applies to the analysis of maternity rights and family-friendly policies.

This section is made up of three chapters. Chapter 2 provides an overview of the development of women's rights in the EU. It traces the establishment of equal opportunities, as a European policy area, from the introduction of Article 119 (Treaty of Rome) to current debates about constitutionalism in Europe. Particular consideration will given to the analysis of the initial association of the principle of equality with equal pay (Hantrais, 2000; Hoskyns, 1996: 45; Warner, 1984: 142–3). The chapter then goes on to discuss the expansion of equal rights from equal pay for equal work, to work of equal value and equal treatment. It will look at the 1976 and 1986 Directives on Equal Treatment, and will evaluate whether the principle of equal treatment broadened the scope of European equality policies (Hoskyns, 1994: 226–8;

Rees, 1998: 29–34). The chapter then goes on to assess the changes brought about by the institutionalisation of the principle of mainstreaming and the consolidation of equality of opportunities as one of the main aims of European integration. As part of this analysis, I will engage with current debates about the role of gender and/or feminist contributions to current debates about constitutionalism and democracy in the EU. This is phase three in the development of the European equality agenda.

This detailed survey of the development of women's rights in the EU has a dual function. Firstly, it provides an overview of the aims of European integration and the biases of its policy-making process. Secondly, it questions the overarching aims of the European equality agenda and its position within the policy hierarchy of European integration. This overview provides the necessary background for the evaluation of the aims and policy outcomes of the fourth phase in the development of women's rights in the EU.

Chapter 3 turns to look at the development of reconciliation between work and family life as one of the main policy objectives of the European equality agenda. This chapter will focus predominantly on five policy initiatives: the 1992 Pregnant Worker Directive (92/85/EC); the 1992 Childcare Recommendations (92/241/EC); the 1993 Working-Time Directive (93/104/EC); the 1996 Parental Leave Directive (96/34/EC); and the 1997 Part–time Worker Directive (97/81/EC). These policies represent the bulk of EU initiatives on work–life balance. Of particular interest for the analysis conducted here are the 1992 Pregnant Worker Directive and the 1996 Parental Leave Directive because they seek to tackle the relationship between production and reproduction. In the context of the analysis presented in this book, this chapter provides some important insights into current socio-economic and political trends. In the first place, the issues examined in this chapter raise important questions about the overall aims of the European equality agenda. Secondly, they help us to understand the influence of gender power hierarchies on the policy-making process. Finally, they draw attention to the complex web of interests that influence EU politics and policies.

The last chapter in this section looks at the application of the principle of reconciliation between work and family life through the analysis of European case law. There are several reasons why it is both useful, and imperative, that a comprehensive analysis of women's rights takes into account the role/influence of the ECJ in this process. First of all, it is an influential actor in EU politics. The impact of its rulings on the establishment of a powerful supranational legal order has been widely documented. More specifically within the context of women's rights, the ECJ has proved to be a complex and, at times, controversial actor. On the one hand, it has been an important ally of the women's lobby, in as far as its rulings have promoted a wider reaching interpretation of the rights established within EU law. On the other hand, it has proved to be very conservative when the question of gender divisions of labour in the family has arisen.

Taken together these chapters will show the continued reliance on gender norms by policy actors in Europe. One of the major criticisms that can be raised against European equality policies, and implicitly the European equality agenda, is their reliance on employment rights and formal equality as their operating principle. The focus of most EU policies discussed in these chapters is on employment and, more broadly, the public sphere, as if this were the only way to achieve emancipation and gender equality (Buckley and Anderson, 1988: 3; Burrows, 1993: 51; Guerrina, 2001; Guerrina, 2003b; Rees, 1998). What emerges from this discussion is the persistence of a dualism between public and private. The impact of this division on national equal rights policies has been widely documented; what the analysis presented here shows is how this bias has been reinforced by the addition of the European level to the policy-making process. Aside from promoting only a narrow interpretation of equality, it also serves to engender another division between the overall aims of equal rights policies and their application at the national level (Conaghan, 1993; Pringle, 1998).

The national framework: the case studies of Italy and the UK

The case studies of Italy and the UK were chosen for their unique approach to social policy and equal rights. These factors have often been used by various scholars to define and/or chart their membership to welfare regimes. (Duncan, 1995; Esping-Andersen, 1990; Lewis, 1992b; Sainsbury, 1994). In this context, Italy has been categorised either as a conservative corporatist welfare state or a strong male-breadwinner state, whereas Britain has been placed either in the neo-liberal and market oriented welfare model or in the strong male-breadwinner category (Gomá, 1996: 213; Lewis, 1992b; Pringle, 1998). Regardless of which model is applied to the categorisation of these two case studies, they represent different social, political and economic frameworks within which equal rights have developed. More importantly, they abide by different categorisations of the importance of the family as provider of care and support network for the welfare state. These case studies will thus fulfill a triple function. Firstly, they will allow me to assess the impact of EU policies on the national sphere. Secondly, they will bring to light the relationship between women's (care) work in the private and the long-term survival of the European social model. Finally, they will provide a framework of reference and comparison for the analysis of gender power hierarchies in Europe.

Briefly, the analysis of the case study of Italy begins with a general discussion of the function of the family in Italian society and the position of women in the Italian economy. Some attention will be given to the impact of the Fascist regime on the development of a conservative ideology of mothering as embedded in the idea of *focolare domestico* (domestic hearth) (De Grazia, 1992; Maugeri, 1991; Ranti, 1991; Weber, 1981). This chapter then goes on to consider the development of maternity rights and family-friendly policies, with particular emphasis on the 1971 Maternity Law, the 2000 Mothering and

Fathering Law and the 2001 Legislative Decree for the Protection of Mothering and Fathering. Sections three and four will discuss the impact of EU policies and ECJ rulings on the development of women's employment rights. The chapter will conclude with the analysis of three key issues: firstly, it will evaluate the role of the legislation in maintaining the division between public and private; then, it will assess the legal developments outlined in section two through the lenses of the substantive equality discourse. To conclude, it will look at the impact of the legislation in maintaining traditional gender power hierarchies and the ideology of mothering outlined in section one. This analysis is particularly important because this is a country in which the employment market is strongly based upon full time employment, and male values and structures are readily accepted as the norm (Del Boca, 1988; European Labour Force Survey, 2003: 75–6; Rubery *et al.*, 1999: 201–3).

The UK has also proved to be an interesting and challenging case study for the analysis of reconciliation between work and family life. Its history of intense labour and union movements, as well as its adoption of a laissez-faire approach to economic and employment policy, make this country a particularly interesting case study. The social impact of liberal ideology on British society is widespread and is particularly evident in the rigid division between the public/political/economic sphere and the private/familial/domestic sphere (Carter, 1988; Lacey, 1993; Tilly and Scott, 1987). It is for these reasons that it is important to look at how women's rights have developed within a framework that revolves primarily around the market and market forces.

The chapter begins with a discussion of feminist debates about equality and difference, and post-Second World War conceptualisations of what Teresa Rees (1992) defines as the *ideology of the family*, or what Elizabeth Roberts (1988) calls the *domestic ideology*. Section two then looks at the position of working mothers in the employment market. This section outlines the development of equal rights from the 1970 Equal Pay Act to the 2002 Employment Act. The chapter then considers the complex relationship between UK governments and European institutions. In particular, it looks at how fears of a British veto led to a change in Treaty base for the 1992 Pregnant Worker Directive. On the back of this discussion, this section will also assess the impact of the Parental Leave Directive on the introduction of reconciliation between work and family life as a policy objective in the UK (Anon., 1992; Conaghan, 1993; James, 2001).

Three questions will drive the analysis presented in these chapters: What are the employment arrangements available to working mothers? What are the key features of women's employment patterns? And finally, what are the biases transpiring from the legislation under analysis? In order to provide a comprehensive overview of these issues, these chapters will cover a range of themes, the most important of which are: 1. The role of the family as the locus of socialisation and provider of care; 2. Women's participation in the official labour market; 3. The development of women's employment rights and the introduction of the principle of reconciliation between work and family life in their respective equality agendas; 4. The impact of EU policies on the development of women's employment rights at the national level.

These considerations have important implications for the reach and scope of the legislation available to promote women's substantive equality in the official labour market. By identifying some basic assumptions about gender that provide the foundation for the legislation, these chapters will show how the legislation, and more generally employment structures, are responsible for maintaining gender power hierarchies. Ultimately, the aim of this discussion is to uncover various questions and puzzles that arise from the analysis of the relationship between gender and politics on the one hand, and national and European political structures on the other.

Preliminary conclusions

This book sets out to discuss the aims of maternity rights and family-friendly policies in the EU. In the process of evaluating the scope and reach of the legislation, the analysis presented here seeks to show how maternity policies and equal rights legislation serve to promote a narrow understanding of the principle of equality. These considerations are based on feminist reflections on equality, difference and the concept of woman, which highlight different ways of interpreting the scope of the policies under discussion. Through the application of this theoretical background to the analysis of current policies in this field, the book argues that maternity legislation, and more generally family-friendly policies, have been founded upon an intricate set of power relations that define sexual divisions of labour in the family and the official labour market.

Given the context outlined above, the contributions of this book are threefold. From a theoretical point of view, it highlights the continued importance of the equal rights debate in feminist theory. The evidence presented here shows how beliefs about equality, difference and women continued to be disputed concepts. Moreover, the analysis of different feminist approaches to these issues also highlights the contextuality of feminist debates and arguments about the role of the state and international organisations in promoting women's rights. From a policy-making standpoint, the analysis presented in this book should lead to an increased awareness of the role of gender and gender power hierarchies in shaping women's employment choices. This single realisation has important implications for the scope of maternity and family-friendly policies. As the analysis of the empirical data will show, although the rhetoric associated with this particular policy area seeks to encourage greater gender equality in the distribution of unpaid care work, the reality of women's position in the labour market and the family ultimately works against this objective. These contributions draw attention to the importance of using post-structuralist feminism as a tool for deconstructing the basis of equal rights legislation and the legislative process. Although Kristin Waters (1996: 285) criticised post-structuralist feminists for disempowering feminist politics, this book shows how challenging traditional conceptualisations of 'woman' can help us to understand how gender power hierarchies influence the legislation and the policy-making process. Only by questioning the meaning of 'woman' and 'mother', will feminist and policy-maker be able to bridge the gap between formal and substantive equality.

Some important considerations emerge from the application of this conceptual framework to the analysis of EU and national family-friendly policies. First of all, it draws attention to the role of gender divisions of labour in defining the scope and reach of maternity and equal rights legislation. Perhaps one of the most significant issues arising from the analysis of maternity policies in particular is the focus upon *protection* rather than *promotion* of women's rights. As Lucy Bland (1985: 23, 38–40) explained, historically this bias has been used to limit the reach of equal rights and prevent the achievement of substantive equality. The analysis of current developments in the area of maternity rights highlights a continued reliance of gendered assumptions of care, protection and work. As a matter of fact, much of the official literature on workers' rights focuses on the need for greater protection from hazardous agents. This is clearly an important development in the area of workers' rights. However, for equal rights policies to include a broader concept of substantive equality, policy-makers and employers must not use concerns over health and safety to limit women's access to the official labour market. As discussed in the introduction of this chapter, maternity rights must encompass both a protective and equality element. However, if the legislation's primary focus is health and safety, then it fails to challenge social norms about care work. In other words, if the focus of maternity rights is on protecting the position of women in the reproductive process, then far from promoting women's rights, these policies limit the reach of equal rights by narrowly defining equality in terms of formal equality.

A second issue arising from the analysis presented in the book is the continued reliance on male norms of work. It is important to note that the 1992 Pregnant Worker Directive attempts to move away from this assumption by stating that maternity leave is not comparable to sick leave. Unfortunately, it falls short of this objective when it uses the standard of sick leave to establish the right amount of compensation for workers undertaking maternity leave. Another example of the bias present in the legislation revolves around the terms of compulsory maternity leave. This is a particularly sensitive issue as the legislation has to balance the need to protect women's health and safety on the one hand, with women's equal rights in the official labour market and social representations of mothering on the other (Hoskyns, 1994: 229–30; Romito, 1993: 583).

To conclude, the analysis presented here endeavors to develop a gender sensitive approach to the examination of the policy outcomes at the European and national level. In so doing, it highlights the persistence of a gap between substantive and formal equality. In terms of maternity rights and family-friendly policies, this book will show the limitations of current policy development by drawing attention to the biases implicit in policy processes that ignore either the links between public roles and private duties, or the power of gender hierarchies. Finally, despite the focus on the official labour market and the public sphere, the claims of this book fall far beyond the reach of formal rights. The focus on the employment market arises from the consideration that within the current economic and political framework economic independence remains a necessary requirement for emancipation (Lovenduski and Randall, 1993: 47). In this context, it is thus important to address the current limitations of the legislation available to promote women's rights within all arenas of society.

1

Feminist interpretations of equality, difference and motherhood

The issues of equality and difference are central to any analysis of the role of family-friendly policies in constructing and constraining gender relations in contemporary Europe. They have been at the centre of feminist debates since the onset of second wave feminism at the end of the 1950s. Lack of consensus as to importance of biological differences has given rise to a wide range of exchanges between different theoretical approaches, and has been identified as a way of differentiating and making sense of contemporary feminist discourses (Scott, 1994: 362). At the heart of this debate is one of feminism's most fundamental questions: what kind of consideration should be given to sexual difference in public policy discourses?

The aim of this chapter is to evaluate feminist contributions to contemporary debates about equality and equal rights. This analysis will establish an analytical framework for the critique of the principles underpinning the concepts of work–life balance, reconciliation between work and family life, and family-friendly employment structures. Starting from the assumption that current policy discourses on women's employment and work–life balance are not separate from wider social considerations about family structures and gender divisions of care work, the analytical framework developed in this chapter will provide the necessary tools for a gender sensitive evaluation of the overall objectives of this new policy area. More specifically, the analysis of equality, difference, and the concept of woman/mother will allow me to raise an array of questions about the overall implications of the current shift in policy discourse towards reconciliation between work and family life.

It is important to note that this chapter will not come to a conclusion as to which feminist approach holds the greatest explanatory power; rather it seeks to discuss how each approach accounts for the relationship between equal rights legislation and women's participation in the official labour market. All sides to this debate have made useful contributions to women's

struggle for equal recognition and academic understanding of women's position in Europe. By looking at these approaches, I will construct a
comprehensive analytical framework for the analysis of family-friendly policies in Europe.

The chapter is divided into four sections. Section one will briefly outline
the key tenets of the equal rights debate, thus providing an introduction to the
overall context within which equality, difference and post-structuralist feminisms have been developed. Section two will evaluate the contributions of
equality feminism and its relationship with liberal feminism. It will present
different conceptualisations of equality, ranging from equality as sameness to
equality in difference. This section will also engage in a discussion of the
difference between formal and substantive equality, two concepts that underpin the analysis conducted throughout the book. Section three will explore
the concept of difference and the contributions of radical feminism to current
debates about the role of women in contemporary European society. Finally,
section four will assess the contributions of post-structuralism to feminism
and its understanding of 'woman'. In this section, the concepts of woman and
mother will be problematised, thus challenging traditional assumptions about
the naturalness of motherhood and mothering. More specifically, the introduction of post-structuralist deconstructions will challenge the link between
mothering and the social function of care, a critique that is essential to foster
a comprehensive re-elaboration of gender roles and power hierarchies.

The equal rights debate

> What exactly is the relationship between sexual equality and equal rights? Are
> equal rights and opportunities what in the end feminism is about?
>
> (Phillips, 1987: 3)

Anne Phillips draws attention to the substantial amount of debate currently
taking place about the best way of promoting women's rights in cotemporary
European society. Despite media misrepresentations of feminism as a homogeneous movement, the persistent lack of agreement over the importance of
sexual differences has been the defining feature of first and second wave feminism (Phillips, 1987: 5). As such, the equality–difference debate can be seen
as the driving force of twentieth-century feminist discourses. The question
that remains to be addressed, however, is whether this debate is still relevant
for the analysis of gender in the twenty-first century. As the discussion of
family-friendly policies will show, this debate remains particularly useful for
the analysis of maternity rights and the development of a policy framework
for the reconciliation between work and family life.

The equal rights debate, as outlined in this chapter, will expand the
analytical reach of the equality–difference debate by adding a post-structuralist dimension. Each one of these approaches has, in its own way, challenged

traditional assumptions about women's position in society and the processes that contribute to the construction of gender identities. Each approach has thus raised a different set of questions and challenges which, when brought together, present a comprehensive overview of the role and function of gender power hierarchies in Europe. In this context, their contributions can be summarised as follows: whereas equality and difference have questioned women's relationship to social structures and the impact of this relationship on women's position in society, post-structuralist feminism challenges the very nature of what it means to be a woman (Bock and James, 1992; Phillips, 1987; Scott, 1994; Whitworth, 1994).

Judith Evans (1995: 3, 7) synthesises the complexities of this debate, arguing that feminist analysis should engage with all different conceptualisations of equality and difference with the aim of constructing a new concept: equality in difference rather than sameness. This new principle of equality, in turn, would be particularly useful in revealing the kind of power hierarchies that underpin the relationship between gender and public policy. Equality in difference would thus allow scholars and policy-makers alike to acknowledge the social, political and economic forces that shape gender structures and define the scope of family friendly policies. Elam (1994: 7) summarises the current state of the debate as follows:

> For some feminism means equal pay, abortion rights and partnership in a law firm. For others, feminism means a celebration of women as separate and distinct from men. To others still, feminism is a subversive ideology used to undermine authority and create alternative power structures. There is no thematic identity to 'woman' in these various arguments, which doesn't mean that feminism ought not to support them all in different context.

Within this framework, feminist debates about equality and difference are a useful analytical tool for the analysis of public policy discourses, as they generate important insights into the assumptions that underpin contemporary policies aimed at advancing the position of women in the official labour market (Cavarero, 1992: 27; Evans, 1995: 3; Flax, 1992: 194–5).

Despite the overwhelming contributions of this debate to our understanding of gender relations, it is also important to draw attention to the weaknesses of each approach and of the debate as a whole. The main limitations of the equality–difference debate arise from the binary opposition of man and woman, equality and difference. This kind of dichotomisation is based upon a division between public roles and private duties, another pillar of feminist analysis and an important tool for the critique of family friendly policies in Europe.

In many ways, the discussion of the public–private dichotomy mirrors the division between equality and difference in as far as it is based on divergent assumptions about the role and function of social structures in defining women's position in society and the official labour market. This chapter will thus consider three questions: What is the public–private dichotomy? How does it affect gender structures and relations? And finally, who are the main actors in shaping and maintaining gender power hierarchies? This discussion draws attention to the interaction between each theoretical approach and its tools of analysis. Just as gender operates across the public–private divide, so equality and difference are mutually defined. As Scott (1994: 256–7) points out: 'equality is not the elimination of difference, and difference does not preclude equality'. In this context, post-structuralist feminism enriches the debate by questioning the underlying principles that construct these binary oppositions (Barret and Phillips, 1992; McDowell and Pringle, 1992; Scott, 1994).

This chapter will now turn to feminist interpretations of three key concepts: equality, difference and woman/mother. As the aim of each section is to introduce the analytical tools for the discussion of family-friendly policies that will take place in the rest of the book, it will present the case for and against each approach. And, in doing so, it will outline how each concept, and related theoretical discourse, can be used in the analysis of social policy developments.

Equality

The aim of this section is to assess the strengths and weaknesses of the concept of equality and its application to the analysis of family-friendly policies and the principle of reconciliation between work and family life. In order to do this, the section is divided as follows: first, it will explore various definitions of equality; it will assess the strengths and weaknesses of each definition, and how it can be applied to the analysis presented in this book. Then, it will explore the legacy of liberal feminism to the analysis of this concept. This discussion will draw upon the analysis of the public–private dichotomy and will provide a brief overview of the weaknesses of this particular interpretation for the discussion presented here. Following this particular path, this section will outline the historical links between the concept of equality and the development of equal rights policies. Finally, I will present an alternative understanding of this concept as embodied in the principle of substantive equality, and will thus make the case for this expanded version of the equality principle.

Defining equality
The concept of equality has long been associated with feminism and the struggle for women's rights. However, it is not a concept that can be easily defined, as it can be attributed a number of meanings depending on the context in which it is used. Bock and James (1992: 4) summarise the ambiguity associated with the operationalisation of this concept as follows: equality has been interpreted

'sometime as the right to be equal, sometime as the right to be different'. Arguably, in the context of women's rights, equality is both. In order to understand better this complexity, it is possible to formulate three questions that will help us to define its scope and its applicability: 1. What is the standard by which equality is measured? 2. Who falls within the scope of equality? 3. What are its theoretical limitations, and how do they affect its policy effectiveness? (Bacchi, 1990: xv–xvi; Bryson, 1992: 168; Evans, 1995: 14)

Maggie Humm (1989: 62–3) defines equality as a principle 'based on the idea that no individual should be less equal in opportunity or human rights than any other'. This interpretation of equality it is based upon the principle of equal opportunities, and it is by and large uncontroversial. It is, however, also a very limited vision of equality. Hoskyns (1985) expands this definition, arguing that it is possible to differentiate between formal and substantive equality. According to Hoskyns, formal equality corresponds to women's legal rights, and thus Humm's initial definition; whereas substantive equality refers to the ability of equal rights policies to promote social change and assert women's voice in social and political affairs. I will return to this discussion later, for now suffice to say that the latter definition of equality draws attention to the interaction between gender hierarchies and socio-economic structures (Bacchi, 1990: 174–5; Flax, 1992: 205–6; Kitzinger, 1996: 92–6; Tiessalo, 1996).

Equality as equal rights

Historically, the main advocates of equality have been liberal feminists. This standpoint has thus become synonymous with the campaign for formal equality. As Humm (1989: 62–3) explains, liberal feminists have been campaigning 'for the granting of the full equality of formal rights to women as the solution to women's subjection'. Sameness is the basis for this standpoint, according to which if women are given the opportunity, they will be able, and willing, to behave like men in order to participate and absolve their responsibilities in the public sphere. Over the years, this approach has proved to be very influential and has lodged itself at the heart of second wave feminism. Moreover, it has been the driving force behind a much wider-reaching movement known as equality feminism (Evans, 1995; Whitworth, 1994: 15–16; Zalewski, 1993: 116–17).

Given this background, Juliet Mitchell (1987: 24) summarises the tenets of equality feminism as follows: 'biological differences between men and women obviously exist, but it is not these that are the concern of feminism'. As this quote highlights, true to its liberal foundations equality feminism has sought to downplay the socio-political and economic significance of sexual differences. The reason why equality feminism has been reticent to recognise the significance of sexual differences is because historically they have been used to justify sexual discrimination and the exclusion of women from the public sphere (Bryson, 1992: 4). It is on these grounds that this feminist standpoint rejects the political importance of those values traditionally asso-ciated with women and the feminine. Such values, they argue, should not shape public relations, and have no influence over women's attainment of formal equality (Bryson, 1992: 4; Humm, 1989: 118–19; Pateman, 1992; Whitworth, 1994: 12–16).

One of the main exponents of equality feminism is Jean Bethke Elshtain, who defended the power of the principle of equality as part of feminist thought as well as mainstream political discourse. She claims that equality has been greatly misunderstood and unfairly criticised, as it remains 'a powerful term of political discourse and an instrument for social change and justice, one of the strongest weapons the (relatively) powerless have at their disposal in order to make their case and define their claims' (Elshtain, 1992: 124). She accepts the rhetoric of liberal feminism, according to which equality needs to be achieved from within mainstream social, political and economic struc-tures. As she further explains, 'grappling with those powerful terms of political discourse in the West is an unavoidable task' (Elshtain, 1992: 124). Zillah Eisenstein (1993) also comes to the defence of liberal feminism, claim-ing that this standpoint has a much greater potential to challenge various forms of oppression currently defining women's lives than is commonly perceived. Both of these contributions draw on one of the main strengths of this approach: equality, as principle and practice, draws its power and influ-ence from the fact that it keeps open the lines of communication with mainstream theories and politics.

This brief overview of equality feminism emphasises how, true to its liberal foundations, this feminist standpoint accepts the division between the public and the private sphere. In doing so, its political agenda focuses on the achievement of equality in the public rather than a comprehensive critique of gender power hierarchies. The founding assumption is that social values and standards are gender neutral. In this context, equality becomes tantamount to formal equality. Its failure resides in its resistance to acknowledge that liberal equality is based upon male standards of work and participation in the public sphere. As a consequence, this position is blind to this bias and it actively ignores anything that may be classed as women's needs. However, what is even more significant is that formal equality becomes a vehicle through which male norms are reinforced. It is on these grounds that equality feminism has been subject to wide reaching criticisms which have sought to redress the inequalities created by the binary opposition of public and private, care and work, man and woman (Bacchi, 1990: xv, 105; Douchet, 1995: 277–80; Evans, 1995: 3; Hoskyns, 1996: 197; Pascall, 1997: 57–8; Rees, 1998: 32; Showstak Sasson, 1992: 165).

Formal vs substantive equality

Catherine Hoskyns (1985: 74) argues that 'the extent to which the provisions which do exist are taken up and used, can make the whole difference between laws which assert a formal equality only, and those which begin to tackle the substantive problems which create inequality in the first place'. The distinction between formal and substantive equality is thus an important analytical tool by which to judge the achievements of the current legislation.

Critiques of formal equality have been advanced by Anne Showstack Sasson (1992) and Carole Pateman (1989). Both scholars claim that formal equality encompasses the failures of 'liberal patriarchalism' and therefore has the effect of maintaining the public–private dichotomy. From this perspective, legal structures reflect the current gender order, and codify women's position in society. The persistent underdevelopment of the necessary infrastructure for a successful family-friendly policy framework is testament to such dynamics.

The concept of substantive equality, on the other hand, widens the remit of equality feminism by challenging some of the basic assumptions of liberalism and liberal feminism. The basis for this principle is the recognition that the personal and the political sphere are joined and mutually reinforcing (Pateman, 1989: 131). It is a call for a new policy agenda that seeks to redefine the very foundations of the employment relationship. Along these lines, the concept of substantive equality can also be used to mediate between the position of equality and difference, therefore allowing feminists and policy-makers to maintain a commitment to women's legal rights, whilst expanding the actual scope of the legislation in question. The radical potential of this concept lies in a combination of its applicability to the current socio-legal framework, thanks to the persistent appeal of the principle of equality, and a challenge to traditional gender power hierarchies embedded in the shift from formal to substantive rights.

Equality feminism: some general considerations

The analysis of the public–private dichotomy poses a serious challenge to the concept of formal equality. This position rests on the assumption that women's roles in the private will not interfere with employment in the official labour market. The private is ignored and silenced, even though the socio-economic system upon which this position is based is heavily reliant on women's role as carers in the family. What this paradigm fails to consider is that it is women's work in the private that exonerates the state from its obligations towards individual needs. It thus ignores the power dynamics that define the relationship between these two spheres of social life and the impact they have on women's position in society. By focusing on the public sphere and formal equality, this feminist standpoint fails to recognise the importance of women's roles in the private upon their participation in the official labour market. More specifically, by dismissing the impact of gender power hierarchies upon which the traditional family is based, equality feminists have ignored the power dynamics that shape the policy-making process.

Critiques of formal equality have shown how a narrow interpretation of this principle not only reproduces the gender order upon which it is based, but also prevents women from fully participating in the public sphere and thus taking full advantage of their rights (Bacchi, 1990: xv). Jane Flax (1992) provides an alternative vision that bridges the gap between formal and substantive equality as well as the public and the private sphere. She claims that by focusing on the principle of justice it is possible to overcome the shortcomings of the concept of equality. As she explains, 'understood as a process, justice is one way the individual manages the strain of being simultaneously public and private, alone and in relation to others, desiring and interdependent' (Flax, 1992: 205). The concept of justice, Flax goes on to argue, allows feminists to reconcile divergent agendas: 'justice requires a unity of differences, mutuality, incorporation, not annihilation of opposites and directions'.

This position opens the way to a new feminist critique of the public–private dichotomy. Susan Moller Okin (1989: 111, 125) challenges this binary opposition by using the concept of justice to assess relations within the family. Justice, she argues, cannot be achieved without serious consideration for the power relations present within the family. As defined by Moller Okin, the concept of justice exposes the kind of gender hierarchies upon which the traditional family is based, highlighting the impact of gender divisions in labour upon women's position in society and their participation in the official labour market. This analysis, thus, expands the reach of the concept of equality by recognising the impact of socio-economic structures on women's opportunities to take advantage of their legal rights.

To sum up, equality feminism's focus on formal equality at the expense of difference has important implications for the type of equal rights policies it seeks to endorse and promote. The danger entrenched within this position is its outright dismissal of the importance of sexual differences the repercussions of which ultimately fall beyond the scope of scholarly debates about the nature of feminism. As Hare-Mustin and Marecek (1994: 63) explain, 'minimising differences also has consequences for understanding gender'. By ignoring sexual differences, equality feminists fail to consider the impact of gender roles and divisions of labour on women's participation in the public sphere. In other words, they fail to acknowledge the existence of women's needs. Ultimately this blindness to women's role in the family and the reproductive process limits the scope of the principle of equality, because women seeking to participate in the public sphere still have to face these obstacles; and gender power hierarchies remain essentially unchallenged (Hare-Mustin and Marecek, 1994: 63; Rees, 1998: 15–8). Equality feminists therefore not only ignore the political importance of sexual difference, but they also downplay the economic and social impact of such differences and divisions. In doing so, equality feminism fails to challenge the social structures that continue to be used in order to justify and excuse sexual discrimination in the workplace. This last point is particularly important, as the costs associated with maternity and parental leave are still seen by many as valid justification for discrimination against women, particularly during their reproductive years. These issues will be considered in greater detail in chapters 4 and 5 (Bowers and Moran, 2002; Bowers *et al.*, 2003; Bryson, 1992: 167–8; Gill and Monaghan, 2003; Rees, 1998: 21, 120–45; Valentini, 1997).

Despite the weaknesses outlined above, the principle of equality remains a powerful tool for the advance of women's rights. Moreover, the concept of justice and substantive equality provides an alternative to traditional conceptualisation of equality, and can ultimately be used as a conceptual and policy-making tool. So powerful is this concept, that its outright dismissal would cause a silencing of the cause of women's rights in mainstream circles. To conclude, the analysis presented in this section highlights the need to develop this concept so that it encompasses the complexities that define women's position in society and the choices women have to face with reference to employment in the official labour market. The next section of this chapter will turn to the main critics of equality and liberal feminism: the difference paradigm.

Difference

As Anne Phillips (1987: 3) explains, 'when people first hear of feminism they often assume it denies sexual difference. Yet, as long as women bear children there is at least one inescapable difference between the sexes'. The concept of difference is another source of dispute amongst feminist scholars and, as with equality, there is no homogenous position on this issue and its impact on the policy-making process (McDowell and Pringle, 1992: 14). This theoretical standpoint starts from the assumption that the recognition of difference is a positive and necessary tool for emancipation. In this context, whereas equality feminists have sought to downplay the relevance of sexual differences, difference feminists elevate them to iconic status.

According to Maggie Humm (1989: 51) 'defining difference has been the single greatest contribution of second wave feminism to theory'. More specifically, the analysis of difference is the legacy of radical feminism to the feminist movement. From this standpoint, sexual oppression/domination becomes a cross-cultural phenomenon that extends beyond gender relations in as far as it affects all aspects of society and social transactions (Zalewski, 1993: 118). As Whitworth (1994: 16–17) summarises:

> much of the way in which society is reorganised supports patriarchy, and this affects not only the ways in which the world actually operates, but even the ways we think about the world.

Whitworth's analysis highlights the main tenet of difference feminism: gender relations are all-encompassing and permeate every aspect of social structures and social relations. From this position, it is therefore impossible to achieve equality feminism's ultimate goal of gender neutral social relations.

Defining sexual difference and women's needs

Sexual differences, and the values ascribed to them, have been at the heart of social debates about the position and role of men and women in society. The revolution brought about by this approach is a substantial re-evaluation of difference, whereby it is seen as an important and essential part of society. Instead of denying the differences in men's and women's roles in the social function of reproduction and social dynamics at large, difference feminism exalts the importance of such differences and endeavours to achieve recognition for women's contributions as women.

According to Adriana Cavarero, another key exponent of difference feminism, the institutionalised equalisation of men and women is possibly the greatest weakness of current equal rights policies. As she explains:

> Modern law has in fact included women as equal to men, as if women despite female sexual difference, were men. Modern law is therefore (as both theory and history show) completely modelled on the male subject and can take in women only by homologizing them with the male subject which operates as a basic paradigm. (Cavarero, 1992: 37)

Cavarero's analysis provides some important insights into the social, political and economic dynamics that influence the policy-making process and structure women's participation in the official labour market. An example of this is the way in which maternity and pregnancy have traditionally been dealt with by employment legislation. The assumption that maternity and pregnancy should be treated on a par with disabling illness highlights the implicit bias of socio-economic structures in favour of the male worker. More importantly, it draws attention to the persistence of a norm that is based on value-laden assumptions about male participation in the public sphere. Difference feminism emerged as a critique of this bias, and the main claim associated with this position is a call for recognition of women's difference and women's needs (Cavarero, 1992: 37; Evans, 1995: 4).

Along similar lines, Hare-Mustin and Marecek (1994: 63) argue that dismissing sexual differences also 'draws away from women's special needs and from differences in power and resources between women and men'. Whereas equality feminism dismissed the political and economic importance of motherhood and mothering for fear that it could be used to excuse discrimination against women, difference feminism focused on women's special needs as mothers. From this perspective, current efforts to devise a gender neutral framework for the reconciliation between work and family life ignore the unique needs of a mother who has recently given birth (Bryson, 1992: 167–8; Hare-Mustin and Marecek, 1994: 63).

Bryson (1992: 167–8) claims that the struggle for sex-blind or gender-neutral legislation has led many feminists to deny the political importance of sexual difference. Thus, equality feminism has been reticent to campaign for any rights that acknowledge these differences, such as maternity rights. Hare-Mustin and Marecek (1994: 63) reiterate this point, claiming that,

> giving birth is, paradoxically, both an ordinary event and extraordinary one, as well as the only visible link in the kinship system. The failure of the work place to accommodate women's special needs associated with childbirth represents beta bias, in which male needs and behaviours set the norm, and women's unique experiences are overlooked.

Celia Kitzinger's (1996) examination of the links between the public and the personal sphere confirms these conclusions, arguing that the public and the private are interdependent and mutually reinforcing. It follows that sexual differences, understood both in terms of biological differences as well as gender roles, have a direct impact on women's access to the official labour market. What emerges from this analysis is further confirmation of the shortcomings of the equality approach, which portrays motherhood and pregnancy as personal and private issues that rest outside the scope of equal rights legislation. From the position of difference, on the other hand, it is possible to conclude that an in-depth analysis of motherhood, maternity and pregnancy is central to our understanding of women's condition in contemporary Western/European society, and the impact of policy-making on gender power hierarchies.

The critique of equality as sameness that has been developed by the difference paradigm raises three important issues. Firstly, the male worker continues to be accepted as the norm against which all workers must be judged. More importantly, this bias has permeated equal rights legislation, diminishing its potential to bring about radical change in the current gender order. Secondly, the recognition of difference implies the acceptance that women's different needs must be catered for. Maternity and pregnancy are particularly good examples of this assessment as they are conditions experienced solely by women. And finally, this analysis draws attention to the fluid nature of gender boundaries.

As mentioned above, the discourse of sexual difference was developed extensively by radical feminism. From this position not only should sexual difference become the centre of feminist analysis, but it should also be exalted for introducing a whole new set of values into the political realm. Women's roles and functions should therefore be valued exactly because they are different from men. Given the contributions of this theoretical approach to the equality–difference debate, it is essential to summarise its main tenets.

Pratica e pensiero della differenza sessuale (philosophy and practice of sexual difference) and radical feminism

The difference paradigm is clearly a structural approach to the analysis of women's position in society, and patriarchy is one of the key concepts that have been used by its exponents. More specifically, this approach seeks to shed light on the links between patriarchy and sexual relations of domination, which are identified as instrumental to understand social relations and women's position in society. In this context, this paradigm is indebted to the radical tradition, much like equality is to liberal feminism. Two writers that have been particularly influential are Carole Pateman and Adriana Cavarero. Given their contributions to this approach, I will now outline their basic positions and their contributions to our understanding of women's position in society.

Carole Pateman's (1989) groundbreaking book, *The Sexual Contract*, sought to highlight the patterns of oppression that define contemporary Western society. She argues that the sexual contract permeates all social, economic and political relations, and as such it is a defining feature of contemporary society. Its foundations are to be found in the hierarchy of relations within the family, and its ultimate outcome is women's oppression. As she summarises: 'The sexual contract is an integral part of civil society and the employment contract; sexual domination structures the workplace as well as the conjugal home' (Pateman, 1989: 136–7, 142).

For Pateman, in order to understand inequality and oppression in the workplace it is essential to have a good grasp of the dynamics of the sexual contract. All the more so, as she believes that discrimination in the official labour market and the public sphere is only one feature of the struggle for the recognition of women's contributions in society. More importantly, this particular argument draws attention to the importance of gender structures in the policy-making process. As she further explains, ignoring the role that social structures and the sexual contract play in society and the policy-making process implicitly accepts and reinforces gender power hierarchies. Unlike exponents of the equality paradigm, Pateman identifies sexual oppression as a problem inherent to all socio-economic relations, and reflected in the aims of social policies and equality legislation.

Another exponent of difference feminism is Adriana Cavarero (1992: 45) who summarises the thinking of difference feminism as follows:

> thinking in terms of sexual difference (*il pensiero della differenza sessuale*) is thus not simply a philosophical exercise, but the inaugural act in a political project that assumes women to be subjects capable of freedom and self signification.

From this position, equal rights legislation becomes a concession, as well as an extension, of 'relations of domination', and consequently should be dismissed as a tool for the emancipation of women (Flax, 1992: 45).

Thinking about sexual difference has been a central feature of the Italian feminist movement, which represents perhaps one of the most extensive elaborations of this paradigm. The position of the *pensiero della differenza sessuale* questions traditional representations of womanhood without discounting the importance of 'feminine' values. The primary aim of this theoretical approach is to increase women's self-awareness (Bock and James, 1992: 5–6). In Caldwell's (1991: 112) words, 'mothers too are women'. There are two steps in this process. First, there is the 'theoretical investigation of the implications for women of finding themselves in the role of daughter or mother'; and secondly, there is the 'examination of its manifestation in relations between women' (Caldwell, 1991: 113). Teresa Mezzatosta (1992: 29–30) has argued that this particular interpretation of womanhood will allow women firstly to challenge, and consequently to overcome, oppressive social and gender structures. In this way, this approach aims at allowing women to develop a well-balanced identity that reconciles the old with the new.

This approach is very interesting because it focuses on women's recognition of the self, or self-consciousness, with particular emphasis on language, space, and social practice (De Lauretis, 1994: 17–18). According to De Lauretis (1994: 19) this movement signified the development of a framework that 'valorised women's interactions with one another'. This approach can thus be summarised as a movement of women searching for strength through contact and interaction with other women. This growth in self-consciousness was to be based on the recognition of women's role, position and function in society (Valentini, 1997: 46–51). In turn, this recognition was not founded on a hierarchy of values, but on an increased appreciation for women's norms and roles. Self-consciousness should lead to a reaffirmation of women's value as women. As such, this approach is a critique of equality as sameness and the increased reliance by the economy and the state on women's double presence or dual burden (Balbo, 1978).

Critiques of difference and radical feminism
Despite the clear contributions of this paradigm to feminist theory and practice, it has also been the subject of extensive criticism, not all necessarily coming from the liberal/equality camp. These critiques have focused on two key issues: the homogenisation of the concept of woman, and its implicit acceptance of social dynamic and structures.

The first criticism raised against this paradigm argues that its focus on sexual difference has caused it to assume that women are a homogenous group and to overlook the impact of differences between women in their experience of oppression. This criticism concentrates on the assumption that there is a common experience of oppression and patriarchy, leading to the conclusion that the experience of sexual domination is a universal norm.

Although sexual oppression is a central feature of Western society, women's experience of it is filtered or mediated by many social and cultural factors, such as race, class, ethnicity and sexuality. The importance of these socio-economic structures should not be underestimated, as they interact with gender in order to define a woman's identity and her perception of gender structures and patriarchal relations. As Barbara Johnson (1980: x–xi) explains, 'the differences *between* entities ... are shown to be based on a repression of differences *within* entities, ways in which an entity differs from itself'. In other words, the difference paradigm is founded upon an assumption about the essence of woman, which in turn defines all other social relations (Bacchi, 1990: 101, 104, 231–2; Elam, 1994: 31; McDowell and Pringle, 1992: 47).

Elam (1994) goes as far as to argue that the analysis of the heterogeneous nature of the category of woman is as important as the analysis of sexual differences. For her, 'a feminist approach that ignores the importance of ingroups difference also ignores the importance of various forms of political and social oppression, including sexual oppression, and how they relate to each other' (Elam, 1994: 31). The implication of this analysis being that, 'if feminism thinks that it has all the answers about women, if it never questions its own composition and exclusionary practices, it is destined to practise some of the worst forms of social injustice in the name of liberation' (Elam, 1994: 32). This insightful assessment of the role of social structures in defining women's experience of gender power hierarchies has important implications for the analysis of the legislation that is supposed to challenge them. More importantly, it dispels the myth that the category of woman can be understood either through the use of essentialising principles, or by ignoring those commonalities that have been used to define common values and norms.

Post-structuralist critiques of difference challenge the existence of a universal womanly experience. Instead, they focus on the deconstruction of those concepts sustaining gender power hierarchies: woman, equality and difference (Whitworth, 1994: 20–3). According to Joan Scott (1994: 366) it is possible to summarise post-structualist critiques of difference as follows:

> There is nothing self-evident or transcendent about difference, even if the fact of difference – sexual difference, for example – seems apparent to the naked eye. The questions always ought to be, what qualities or aspects are being compared? What is the nature of the comparison? ... When the opposition men/women is invoked, ..., it refers a specific issue back to the general principle. The differences within each group that might apply to this particular situation ... were excluded by definition in the antithesis between the groups.

The concept of difference itself becomes a 'contested site of meaning' (Elam, 1994: 33). As discussed previously, perhaps the greatest shortcoming of the difference paradigm is its acceptance of sexual differences as universal characteristics based on some kind of quintessential womanly experience. Overstressing women's difference, however, limits the overall applicability of this theoretical approach to the analysis of current policy developments. Although it is important to recognise women's needs as workers, mothers, carers, etc., it is equally important not to assume that biological difference will automatically result in different roles in the private sphere. An example of how sexual differences have been transposed into policy rhetoric is evident in the campaign for improved child-care. The basic assumption upon which this position is based is that, as women give birth to children, they are therefore primarily in charge of the day-to-day care arrangements. The association of this particular policy agenda with that of women's employment rights high-lights the persistence of traditional gender division of labour in the private. More importantly, it challenges the values upon which such hierarchies are based (Chodorow, 1978; Lovenduski and Randall, 1993; Scott, 1994).

The limitations of the difference discourse raise important questions about the concept of 'woman' as a category for theoretical and policy discourses. What arises from the analysis conducted thus far is that both equality and difference base their critique of society and social norms on two different concepts of 'woman'. Given the centrality of this concept/category to any analysis of the aims and scope of equal rights legislation, the next section will turn to a discussion of various interpretations of this concept, and the implications of each on policy strategy.

Post-structuralist feminism: challenging the concepts of woman and mother

The critique of difference as a universalising concept at the heart of feminism raises important questions about the quintessential meaning of womanhood, as a feminist principle and as a reality. Elizabeth Spelman's (1990: in Evans, 1995) claim that 'though all women are women, no woman is only a woman', thus highlights the essentially contested nature of womanhood. This section will discuss feminist critiques of this concept and their possible application to the analysis of employment policies. First of all, it will focus on the concept of universal woman, drawing attention to how the experience of motherhood has been used to define women's position in society. Then, it will provide an overview of post-structuralist critiques of this concept. This section will finally conclude with an assessment of the social construction of gender roles.

Universal woman

Over the last thirty years there has been much discussion between feminist scholars about the nature of being a woman; however, as the analysis outlined in the previous sections of this chapter points out, this is a question that has remained unresolved. Feminist discourses therefore turned to post-struc-turalist approaches in order to overcome the limitations that characterised the debates of the 1970s and 1980s (De Lauretis, 1994). The main aim of this approach was to present a critique of the very foundations of gender struc-tures and norms. As Wheelehan (1995) explains, post-structuralism sought to draw attention to 'a reliance [in feminist theory] of totalizing categories, such as the apparent binary nature of gender and the universality of the concept of *woman*'. Judith Grant (1993: 131) drives home this point arguing that,

> the truth of what Woman is, or the truth that Woman knows, both key questions in Anglo-American feminist theory, become oppressive notions in themselves for post-modern feminists. The problem becomes how to trace the historical development of the 'truth' of Woman in order to avoid it. The object is to investigate the mechanisms of power that have forged the female identity in order to resist identity itself.

Alternatively, as Elam (1994: 27) points out, 'we do not yet know what women *are*... We do not yet know what women *can do*'. What is particularly important about this approach is that it draws attention to the main dividing lines between feminist theories and policy-makers involved in the development of women's rights and family friendly policies. The combination of post-modernism and feminist politics therefore inspired a critique of the historical origins of power and gender relations that would ultimately break down the power structures that define binary oppositions such as masculine and feminine, man and woman.

Despite starting from two very different ontological positions, both equality and difference assume that women's experiences of womanhood and oppression are universal. There is no recognition of the impact of other social structures (such as class, race and ethnicity) on women's sense of self and experience of womanhood. Linda Birke (1986: 11) warns of the dangers implicit in such approaches, arguing that by ignoring the heterogeneity of women's experiences, feminists run the danger of portraying the concept of woman 'as a single entity'. By taking this position, feminists validate the biologically determinist argument that 'defends and legitimises the existing social arrangements' (Birke, 1986: 11).

The temptation to adopt a universal concept of woman is great, in as far as it simplifies feminist discourses and provides a focus for the women's movement (Grant, 1993: 19). However, this approach should come with a 'warning', as it is not only inaccurate, but it also undermines the radical potential of feminism. In many ways, the critique of the concept of universal woman mirrors that of the principle of equality. As difference feminism criticises the principle of equality for failing to recognise women's needs and merging men and women into a single entity, so post-structuralist deconstructions of the concept of woman highlight the dangers of constructing a feminist agenda based on the experience of one group of women. As Deborah Rhode (1992: 158) summarises:

> what gives feminism its unique perspective is its claim to speak for women's experience. But that same experience counsels attention to the differences in women's backgrounds, perceptions and priorities. There is no 'generic woman', nor any monolithic 'woman's point of view'.

As male norms cannot represent adequately women's needs, so too, it is impossible to expect that a single/universal category of woman can represent the diversity of women's experiences.

As Grant (1993) and Whitworth (1994) summarise, the deconstruction of 'woman' is one of the most important contributions of post-modern discourses to feminist debates. In order to understand better the power of this critique, I shall now turn to the discussion of the main tenets of post-structuralist feminism, as the primary advocates of this position.

Post-structural feminism and the social construction of gender

The question of the comparability of women's experience of oppression remains one of the main themes of feminist discourses/debates. For Ramazanoglu (1989: 20), 'while all schools of feminism are agreed that men very generally dominate women, the question of divisions between women is more controversial'. The post-structuralist approach to the analysis of gender roles and social structures has much to offer to the analysis presented here, as it challenges the very foundations of the contemporary gender order. More specifically, gender structures are no longer considered independent of the social framework within which they have developed, but they are seen as an important source of power. Power thus becomes an important element for the analysis of social relations. Feminist post-structuralism incorporates the analysis of social structures of oppression into a wider framework that seeks to deconstruct how these structures define the process of identity formation and the development of gender power hierarchies (Flax, 1990: 45–6).

As noted in the previous section, the central focus of this particular approach is the exploration of the diversity of experiences that come under the broad category of 'woman'. The deconstruction of the subject of 'woman' is located into a wider critique of society and social structures. In this context, gender is no longer constructed as a universal female experience, but is evaluated as a source of power and social hierarchies. Gender is perceived as the product of the same social structures that validate and perpetrate the division between the public and the private sphere. Challenging binary oppositions, such as public–private, man–woman, equality–difference, becomes one of the main aims of such critique. Only by accepting the fluidity of social norms, will scholars and policy-makers actively create the opportunity to challenge the very foundations of oppression in its diverse forms. As McDowell and Pringle (1992: 15) explain, 'the public and the private constitutes another of the key dichotomies that ... has been central to the development of Western political thought, to the definition of 'woman', to feminist theorising (and retheorising) and to feminist political actions'. In this context, the concept of woman is constantly being constructed against the background of social structures that are also responsible for defining an individual's position in society (Flax, 1997: 52–3; McDowell and Pringle, 1992: 15–17; Zalewski, 1993: 121–2).

Jane Flax (1997: 52–3) explains how current feminist discourses tend to overemphasise the distinction between nature and the social, which in turn 'have become conflated in our understanding of "woman"'. She identifies these binary oppositions as the main reason for the association of woman with nature and man with the political. It is in this framework that women become the other, and come to represent difference. Rather than looking at gender and gender roles as a universal experience, post-structuralist approaches seek to draw attention to the complex web of relationships that define gender power hierarchies and socio-cultural relations. This critique highlights the limits of any approach, feminist or otherwise, that tries to redefine gender and oppression as separate from the social, economic and political environment that generates and reproduces them.

For Barbara Marshall (1994: 108–9), this kind of critique of the concept of 'woman' is the result of post-structuralists' rejection of the 'the humanist subject whose essential core is repressed by society and who lies in wait of our peeling back of culture to find it'. This takes us back to the original claim that feminist post-structuralism rejects the notion of a quintessential womanly experience. As Marshall (1994: 108–9) further explains:

> the focus of analysis is shifted from the subject as a manifestation of her/his 'essence' to the 'subject in process' – never unitary, never complete. Rather than looking to universals such as reproductive capacities, our gaze is directed towards the realm of the symbolic – most significantly, to language – as implicated most centrally in the construction of 'men' and 'women'.

In the context of family-friendly policies, this paradigm offers some useful analytical tools. More specifically, it draws attention to the idiosyncrasies embedded within this new policy area, which concurrently challenges and reinforces gender power hierarchies. Maternity and parental leave policies in particular reflect essentialising tendencies that portray women and mothers as the primary carers. The legislation and the policy-making process thus become an integral part of the social processes that construct gender power hierarchies and the concept of 'woman' (Birke, 1986: 32, 49, 105).

Although biological differences may be a commonality between men and women, the values associated with these differences are the product of gender power hierarchies. In turn, it is the values associated with gender roles that also help to maintain the current gender order. Hare-Mustin and Marecek (1994: 52) have argued that the main tenets of this paradigm seek to uncover the processes by which representations of society have not come to reflect what is out there but instead are actively participating in its construction. And, to elaborate this point further, 'representations of reality are shared meanings that derive from shared language, history and culture' (Hare-Mustin and Marecek, 1994: 52). It is the accumulation of these shared meanings that gives power to traditional gender hierarchies and divisions of labour. The post-structuralist claim that 'woman' is not the product of biology or destiny, but the result of socially constructed gender hierarchies becomes a liberating force. If history, biology and woman are not universal truths but the product of social interactions, then women are not bound by a destiny that is beyond their control (Hare-Mustin and Marecek, 1994: 52).

Elam (1994: 33) unequivocally challenges the validity of theories that seek to merge difference and diversity in favour of a universal concept of 'woman'. In her own words, 'I am suspicious of the universal particular which the singular form "woman"' forces us to consider, and likewise I would not want to suggest that there is something that women have in common. ... My interest here is to explore the ways in which "woman" is a *permanently contested site of meaning*'. And one of the sites in which the concept of woman remains highly contested is in the use and application of language. As Elam (1994: 33) further explains, language is not gender neutral, but is complicit in the alienation of women's experience from the public sphere. Language is defined by the status quo, which at present is unfamiliar with women's experiences of sexual oppression and exclusion. It is through the gendering of language that women continue to be constructed as the Other (Elam, 1994: 33). The argument about language and the volatility of the concept of 'woman' questions the framework within which equal rights and family-friendly policies are ratified and implemented. These two points taken together are particularly important for the analysis presented in this book as they raise important questions about the relationship between the social construction of gender power hierarchies and the policy-making process. Most importantly, they draw attention to the links between the language of family-friendly and equal rights policies, and that of gender power hierarchies and social structures of oppression. Taking this analysis to its logical conclusion, it is possible to argue that in order to ascertain the usefulness of current policies aimed at reconciling work and family life, it is necessary to assess the assumptions embedded within the language used.

The recognition that there is no universal or quintessential woman, and that gender is constructed through social, political and economic interactions, provides some useful insights for the analysis of family-friendly policies. Whereas the equality and difference approaches accept traditional representations of womanhood (whether by embracing it or by denying its relevance to the policy-making process), post-structuralist deconstructions of 'woman' question the very ability of feminists and policy-makers to define and quantify women's roles and needs (Bacchi, 1990; Evans, 1995). Only through the analysis of the concept of 'woman' it is possible to deconstruct the assumptions underpinning current policy debates seeking to promote women's participation in the official labour market.

To conclude, the deconstruction of the subject of woman has added a new dimension to feminist analyses of social structures of oppression. However, this paradigm is not without its critics, who claim that it has deconstructed the concept of woman to the point of challenging the very foundations of feminist politics (Di Stefano, 1990: 75–6; Flax, 1997: 82;

Hartsock, 1990: 159). In spite of this, the contributions of this approach are still substantial. Firstly, the deconstruction of the concept of 'woman' remains an important political exercise because it questions the basis of gender power hierarchies, and challenges those assumptions of feminist politics that have their roots in the modernist project. Given the increasing diversity of European society and social relations, it is possible to argue that post-structuralist critiques of modernity and the concept of 'woman' provide feminism with the necessary tools to deal with the challenges of twenty-first-century society. Secondly, post-modern deconstructions of 'woman' are also a useful tool for 'metatheoretical analysis' (Flax, 1997: 50). By deconstructing the social and cultural values associated with gender, post-structuralist critiques allow feminists to challenge those binary oppositions that support the current gender order. Gender can thus be understood as a social relation that is culturally defined rather than biologically determined. In this context, the deconstruction of the concept of woman has important repercussions for our understanding of the role and function of the legislation in constructing gender structures. It is also this very challenge to traditional feminist enquiry that makes this paradigm one of the most appealing approaches to the analysis of gender power hierarchies in contemporary Europe.

Conclusions

To sum up, this chapter has outlined three possible approaches to the analysis of family-friendly policies. Having discussed the key features of each approach, its strengths and weaknesses, what emerges from the analysis presented in here is that socio-cultural assumptions about women's role in society are a defining feature of gender identities. The impact of social hierarchies, however, is not only limited to social relations in the private sphere, but permeates every aspect of economic and political life. As Hare-Mustin and Marecek (1994: 63) have argued, beliefs about men, women and their role in society, are founded upon gender power hierarchies that inform social knowledge and ultimately construct social dynamics.

In this context, social interactions and knowledge should not be seen as some kind of abstract concept, but as the driving force of contemporary debates in social policy. The focus of this chapter on substantive equality, the recognition of equality in difference, and persistent questioning of the meaning of woman, should be seen as a challenge to traditional gender hierarchies. The analysis presented in this book will seek to merge together the strengths of each approach, thus presenting an original contribution to feminist understanding of women's relationship to the policy-making process, and an alternative approach to policy analysis at large.

Three interrelated issues emerge as central to the analysis conducted in this book: 1. The principle of substantive equality; 2. The need for recognition of women's needs; 3. The social construction of women's role in society and in the social function of reproduction. Moreover, this chapter highlights how a holistic approach to women's rights must take on board the challenges raised by the analysis of each of these issues. A critique of traditional assumptions about women's role in the social function of reproduction is therefore central to this discussion and a comprehensive evaluation of the needs of the family for work–life balance.

The only definitive conclusion this chapter arrives at is that the concept of formal equality is a narrow interpretation of this principle, which ultimately undermines its radical potential. It is, however, an interpretation that has been widely accepted and endorsed. Unfortunately, this approach to equality and equal rights has ultimately failed to challenge the power of gender hierarchies in the public and the private sphere. As Pateman (1991: 222) explains,

> If women had been merely excluded from civil life, like slaves, or wives when coverture held sway, the character of the problem would have been self-evident. But women have been incorporated into a civil order in which their freedom is apparently guaranteed, a guarantee renewed with each telling of the story of the social contract in the language of the individual.

The all-encompassing language that has incorporated women within mainstream socio-economic structures endorses the male standard of work and worker. Although it presents itself as gender neutral, it actually reinforces the social hierarchies and divisions of labour upon which it is based. What the analysis presented in this chapter highlights is that, although it is unfair to discount the successes of first and second wave feminism in terms of women's social, political and economic rights, it is equally important to present a critique of the norms and values embedded within these rights.

In this context, post-structuralist deconstructions of the concept of woman and mother provide a useful tool for the analysis of current policy developments. At this point, it is useful to go back to Nancy Chodorow's analysis of mothering, which identified the social function of reproduction as a defining feature of women's social interactions. In her words, 'women's mothering as an organisation of parenting is embedded in and fundamental to the social organisation of gender' (Chodorow, 1978: 34). However, the experience of mothering, just like the experience of womanhood, is not and should not be represented as universal. At its most basic level, it is important to distinguish between the social and the biological function of mothering. Diana Gittins (1992: 71) explains that there are only two biological features of mothering: pregnancy and childbirth. As she goes on to argue, motherhood consists of a set of socially constructed values that are neither biologically determined nor historically and culturally universal. The analysis of the relationship between the social and biological function of mothering is very important to the discussion of family friendly policies as it draws attention to the assumptions at the heart of policy-making structures.

The recognition that social and biological mothering are distinct, and that women do not have a universal experience of motherhood, highlights how the values ascribed to this function, and reinforced by current legislation, reflect the kind of social structures and power hierarchies present in wider society. Carole Pateman's (1992: 20–1) analysis of motherhood as a social structure raises important questions that will underpin the analysis presented in the next chapters in this book: 'How is motherhood to be understood? Does motherhood refer only to the relationship between women and children; or does motherhood also refer to women's standing in the political order?'. Pateman's analysis highlights the complexity of social relations and networks that surround the social function of reproduction. The answer to each of the questions she poses will determine the values to be embedded in the legislation and the overall reach of family-friendly policies.

In other words, the analysis of the public–private dichotomy, the challenging of biological essentialism attached to the social function of reproduction, and the analysis of discourses around the principle of substantive equality draw attention to the variety of social and political forces that need to be considered when investigating a policy area that deals with some of the core values in Western socio-economic structures. This chapter sought to evaluate the quality of each approach's contribution to the struggle for women's rights and, in so doing, it brought to light some key issues and trends that need to be considered in the analysis of family-friendly policies. It therefore provides an analytical framework for the examination of current policy debates and legal developments in this particular field of social policy.

2

The development of women's rights in Europe: equal pay, equal treatment and constitutionalism

The progressive development of European integration has been a driving force in post-Second World War European politics. Gender politics have also been influenced by the power of this new actor. European institutions in particular have played an important role in the establishment of women's employment rights in Europe. The development of an extensive body of socio-economic rights under the umbrella of the European Community, highlights the positive role played by this organisation in the development of formal equality in Western Europe (Boch, 1993; Hoskyns, 1996; Kaplan, 1992).

The aim of this chapter is twofold. Firstly, it will trace the development of women's rights as a European policy competence. Secondly, it will discuss the scope and reach of European equality directives with reference to the impact of gender and gender roles on European institutions and policy-making. This discussion will, in turn, provide the context for a detailed discussion of current policy developments in this field, which will take place in the next chapter.

It is possible to identify four phases in the development of the European equality agenda. The structure of this chapter will follow the historical development of equal opportunities as a policy concern for the EU. Section one will discuss the inclusion and development of women's rights within the Treaty Establishing the European Economic Community (Treaty of Rome). The aim of this section is twofold. Firstly, it will examine why the principle of equal pay was incorporated in the Treaty; secondly, it will assess the overall aims of the legislation, focusing in particular on the question of formal and substantive equality. The analysis presented in this section will therefore revolve around three specific questions: What are the aims of European integration? How and why was equality introduced within the European framework? And what concept of equality is enshrined within the founding 'constitution' of the process of European integration? The second section will discuss the evolution of equal rights from equal pay to equal treatment. This section will focus on the various equal treatment directives, and will discuss the implications of this shift in policy for the promotion of substantive equality. Section three will finally complete this historical overview by discussing current developments in the areas of equal pay and equal treatment, presenting a brief overview of the European Commission's action programme (2000–2005), the Amendment of the Equal Treatment Directive and the Burden of Proof Directive.

At this point, it is worth noting that the overall framework for the introduction of women's rights within the founding treaties was twofold. On the one hand, it was the result of fears about economic dumping, which will be discussed in detail in the next section of this chapter; on the other hand, it was part of an embryonic social dimension. The aims of the process of European integration are set out in the Preamble to the Treaty, which establishes the foundations for an economic and social community as follows:

> determined to lay the foundations of an ever closer union among the peoples of Europe; resolved to ensure the economic and social progress of their countries by common action to eliminate the barriers which divide Europe; affirming as the essential objective of their efforts the constant improvements of the living and working conditions of their peoples.

The social aims of the newly-established Community are summarised in Articles 117 to 122 Treaty of Rome. Article 117 in particular reaffirms the need to integrate social and economic concerns:

> Member States agree upon the need to promote improved working conditions and an improved standard of living for workers, so as to make possible their harmonisation while the improvement is being maintained.
>
> They believe that such a development will ensure not only from the functioning of the common market, which will favour the harmonisation of social systems, but also from the procedures provided for in this Treaty and from the approximation of provisions laid down by law, regulation or administrative action.

More specifically, social integration focused predominantly on the rights of workers, and concerns over social policy were limited to those areas that were directly related to the development of the Common Market. As part of these social provisions, the principle of equal pay became entrenched as one of the founding principles of the EEC. Hervey and Shaw (1998: 76–7) argue, however, that at its inception the EEC did not regard such issues as important as economic concerns. For this reason, the social provisions of the Treaty of Rome were, and some would argue continue to be, subsidiary to economic affairs.

Establishing the legal foundations of the European equality agenda: equality as equal pay

This section will concentrate on the first phase (1957–1975) in the development of the European equality agenda, which was identified with the principle of equal pay. The aim of this section is to provide an overview of the historical foundations that led to the inclusion of equality between men and women in the project of European integration. Clearly, the focus on equal pay endorsed by the legal developments taking place in the first twenty years after the creation of the Common Market draws attention to the limits of the equality agenda endorsed by European institutions at that time. It was within this wider framework that the principle of equality made its way into the negotiations and ultimately was included in the Treaty of Rome. In this context, it is therefore important to consider the rationale for the introduction of this principle when discussing its overall aims, strengths and weaknesses. This section will focus on the three stages in the development of equal pay legislation at the European level: 1. The inclusion of Article 119 in the Treaty of Rome; 2. The Defrenne cases; 3. The ratification of the Equal Pay Directive in 1975.

Article 119 – establishing the foundations for the equality agenda
The foundations for the development of equal rights as a Community competence are to be found in Article 119 of the Treaty of Rome. A controversial issue in itself, the negotiations that led to its inclusion into the founding treaty draw attention to several issues that go to the heart of the argument presented here: 1. The role and position of women in the public sphere and the official labour market; 2. Policy-makers' assumptions about the relationship between social and legal structures; 3. Assumptions about the overall trajectory of the process of European integration. In order to understand current developments in this policy area, it is therefore necessary to assess the foundations from which it developed. Only through this analysis it will be possible to shed light on the biases and assumptions that construct the parameters for action with which current policies have to contend.

Much has been written about the negotiations that led to the inclusion of Article 119 in the final draft of the Treaty of Rome. As Warner (1984: 142–3) summarises, this development should not be seen as the result of the enlightened vision of the 'founding fathers', but as a way of ensuring fair trade in the newly established Community. For Gisela Kaplan (1992: 11) the ratification of the Treaty of Rome and the inclusion of Article 119 within the Treaty was an important step forward in the development of equality legislation. Indeed, the idea of a unified Europe has had serious consequences on the development of equal rights policies in the individual member states. As Kaplan (1992: 26) points out, the EU 'acted as a motive force and pioneer in legislation on parity, leaving a clear mark on national legislation'. Despite the positive outcomes that emerged from the process of European integration, this argument does not consider the economic scope of the legislation. Although it was an important milestone in the development of women's employment rights in Europe, it is important not to overestimate the scope of the legislation itself. The objectives of the social provisions included in the Treaty of Rome were solely devoted to improving the welfare conditions of workers. And the concern with equality was limited to women's employment rights (Bercusson and Dickens, 1996: 3; Guerrina, 2003a; Hoskyns, 1996: 45, 52–7; Macedo van Overbeek, 1995: 7; Rees, 1998: 51–2; Tiessalo, 1996).

Catherine Hoskyns (1996: 43) draws attention to the socio-economic hierarchies embedded within the Treaty, arguing that 'Article 119 raises questions, always central to EU development, about the relation of the economic and the social, and about whether it is possible to construct an economic market without a social content'. This background, she goes on to argue, established the framework for the inclusion of the principle of equal pay, which sought to harmonise practices and thus achieve fair competition in the new market. As she further points out,

> what is particularly striking about what we know of the debates and manoeuvres which produced Article 119 is the level of abstraction at which they took place. At no time are the interests of women considered even obliquely or the issues of social justice raised. (Hoskyns, 1996: 57)

This brief overview reaffirms the primacy of economic interests. More importantly, it highlights how the principle of equality was included in the founding Treaty more by accident than by intent (Duchen, 1992: 18; Hoskyns, 1996; McCrudden, 1993: 238).

Despite the shortcomings of a primarily economic approach to equality, Article 119 created the necessary preconditions for the establishment and development of basic standards for equal rights between women and men as a policy area in the member states. It specifically stated that:

> each Member State shall during the first stage ensure and subsequently maintain the application of the principle that men and women should receive equal pay for equal work.
> ... Equal pay without discrimination based on sex means:

> a. that pay for the same work at piece rates shall be calculated on the basis of the same unit of measurement; b. that pay for work at time rates shall be the same for the same job. (Article 119, Treaty of Rome, 1957)

More importantly, Article 119 introduced women as an *official category* in the structural framework of the newly established Community. For Gisela Kaplan (1992: 29) the incorporation of Article 119 in the Treaty of Rome, and the simple fact that women are finally represented in an official document is in itself a step forward towards the recognition of women's issues. The incorporation of women's rights within mainstream politics, she argues, will eventually lead to greater consideration of women's rights as part of the 'general societal, economic and political questions' (Kaplan, 1992: 29). Questions, however, have been raised as to the scope, reach and overall purpose of this article. Most criticisms have focused on three key areas: 1. The rationale for inclusion; 2. Implementation record of the member states; 3. The principle of equality it endorses and promotes.

A closer analysis of the principles enshrined in the Article reveals several biases and limitations that revolve around the division between formal and substantive equality. Firstly, Article 119 endorsed a very narrow definition of equality, whereby equality is tantamount to equal pay. Secondly, as the next section will show, member states were not committed to the operationalisation of this principle. This institutional failure would ultimately undermine the radical potential of this development. As Boudard (1986: 61) explains,

> equal pay for equal work is an obvious principle which is clear and simple. But such obviousness, clarity, simplicity must be more apparent than real since, to date, ..., they have not led to the full practical implementation of this principle in all the enterprises throughout the Member States.

Finally, as a number of cases brought to the ECJ throughout the 1980s show, Article 119 did not cover indirect discrimination. This gap in the principle established by the Treaty further highlights the general unwillingness on the side of European policy-markers to address the structural dimension of gender inequality, the overall economic impetus of the Treaty and the limitations of its social provisions (Barnard, 1996; Tillotson and Foster, 2003)

One conclusion emerges from this brief outline of the Treaty foundations: the focus on employment rights, and specifically equal pay, highlights the biases of the 'founding fathers' in favour of economic integration. Moreover, the implicit assumption that economic, social and political rights are separate also draws attention to the impact of gender power hierarchies in post-war European society. This interpretation of the role of economic policies ultimately created a policy-making framework that could persistently ignore the impact of structural inequalities upon women's participation in the official labour market. In other words, these biases reaffirm the centrality of the male standard in the employment market, and reinforce the public–private dichotomy.

Notwithstanding these serious criticisms, it is important to recognise the legacy of Article 119 for the development of women's rights in Europe. The actual inclusion of this article within the treaty foundations of the European Community is a meaningful development, particularly considering that at the time of the negotiations France was the only signatory state to have ratified equal pay legislation. Secondly, it included equality between men and women as an area of Community competence. This second point is particularly significant because it provided the justification for developments that took place starting in the 1970s. More specifically, by investing European institutions with the power to question national policies and practices, the obligations introduced by the Treaty of Rome established the foundations for the development of more wide-reaching legislation and equal rights policies. As Meehan (1992: 3) further explains, Article 119 provides a favourable framework for the European Court of Justice to judge upon the work of national governments, thus favouring the development and implementation of far-reaching legislation (Buckley & Anderson, 1988: 6; Boudard, 1986: 63; Hoskyns, 1996; Nielsen and Szyszczak, 1993: 109–13; Quintin, 1988: 71).

The Defrenne cases: implementation and the reality of inequality in Europe

The overarching lack of political commitment towards the principle of equal pay became apparent at the beginning of the 1970s, when the European Court of Justice was asked to rule on the case of Gabrielle Defrenne. It is in this context that the ECJ was to assert its role as an important actor/player in the development of the European equality agenda. As chapter 4 will discuss in greater detail, this is a role that this institution is not entirely at ease with, particularly when the cases in question challenge traditional power hierarchies. In the 1970s, however, when the Court was first asked to adjudicate on cases in the field of equality, its interpretation of European law was ground-breaking, particularly with regard to the principle of direct effect and the applicability of Article 119 to national legal systems. These cases are important for three reasons. First, this was the first time that the scope of Treaty's provisions in the area of equality was being tested. Secondly, they are testament to the Member States' failure to implement the Treaty obligations. Finally, they reassert the Court's position in the European legal order. The rulings of the Court were thus to define the approach of the Community in this particular policy area (Hoskyns, 1996: 68–75, 90–3, 111; Warner, 1984: 148–50).

In actual fact, the Defrenne case is made up of three distinct cases brought in front of the European Court of Justice. A flight attendant with the Belgian national airline Sabena, Gabrielle Defrenne's employment contract was terminated when she reached the age of 40, under a rule that did not apply to male members of the crew. More specifically, the Court was asked to consider three issues/questions: 1. Do different rules governing the termination of contract for men and women constitute discrimination under the terms of Article 119? Within this question, the Court also had to decide whether the principle of equal pay, as enshrined in Article 119, was directly applicable regardless of national regulations. 2. What is the scope of equal pay under the term of the Treaty of Rome? It was thus forced to consider whether the principle of equal pay encompasses equality of treatment. 3. Do social security benefits fall under the broad umbrella of the equal pay principle? In sum, what the Court was asked to arbitrate upon was the vertical and horizontal effect of European law. In this context, it is important to note that the Court's deliberations had an impact on the reach of the Treaty foundation both in terms of the direct effect of European law and the overall scope of the principle of equality (Lasok, 2001; Macedo van Overbeek, 1995: 11–17; Tillotson and Foster, 2003).

The decisions by the Court can be summarised as follows. In *Defrenne I*, which asked the Court to consider the link between pay, equality, and social security schemes, the ECJ found that Article 119 was not applicable. As Macedo van Overbeek (1995: 12) summarises, the ECJ ruled that 'a retirement pension established within the framework of a social security scheme laid down by legislation does not constitute consideration which the worker receives indirectly in respect of his employment from his employer within the meaning of the second paragraph of Article 119 of the EEC Treaty'. In *Defrenne II*, which asked the Court to consider the applicability of the principles at the very core of Article 119 (equal pay for equal work), the ECJ reiterated the economic and social ambitions of the Treaty. However, in this case the Court judged Article 119 to have direct effect in the case of direct discrimination, i.e. 'direct and overt discrimination which might be identified solely with the aid of the criteria based on equal work and equal pay referred to by the article in question' (Macedo van Overbeek, 1995: 13). The Court also went on to point out the mandatory nature of the principles enshrined within the Treaty, and the obligation on member states to comply with such provisions. It is in this context that this particular case draws attention to the poor implementation rate by member states. In the final case, *Defrenne III*, the Court was asked to consider the link between conditions of employment and the more general principle of equality of treatment beyond the scope of equal pay. In this case, as Macedo van Overbeek (1995: 15–16) summarises, 'in the opinion of the Court, it was impossible to extend the scope of Article 119 to elements of the employment relationship other than those expressly referred to therein as this could jeopardize the direct effect of the provision's own sphere'. Although the Court's ruling reiterated the importance of equality as a founding principle of the European Economic Community, it also found that the scope of Article 119 was limited to remuneration (Hoskyns, 1996: 68–75; Macedo van Overbeek, 1995: 11–16; Tillotson and Foster, 2003: 357–8).

The real achievement of this test case was to highlight the plight of working women in the Community. Ultimately, the Defrenne affair drew attention to a number of key areas in need of reform. As Hoskyns (1996: 75) explains, 'the *Defrenne* saga exposed a level of discrimination against women in employment which blew apart the self-serving platitudes of governments, routinely made at both national and European level during the sixties'. In this context, the judgement in the second *Defrenne* case was particularly important as it challenged the division between the private and public sectors of the labour market (Boch, 1993). However, the most important legacy of this case to the European equality agenda is to be found in the Court's interpretation of the role of Article 119. As Nielsen and Szyszcsak (1993: 112) illustrate, the

Court interpreted Article 119 as having a dual function: 'an economic function to avoid the distortion of competition and a social function to fulfil the
purposes of Article 117 EEC and the Preamble of the Treaty of Rome 1957'.
By linking social and economic issues, the Court established the binding
nature of Article 119 in both sectors of the labour market. The importance of
this link must not be underestimated, even though it is also important to note
that the ruling further crystallised the hierarchy of values enshrined within
the Treaty of Rome. In this context, it is possible to conclude that the social
function of Article 119 was included only in order to advance the
Community's economic objectives (Barnard, 1996: 327; Hoskyns, 1991: 26;
Hoskyns, 1992: 21; Macedo van Overbeek, 1995: 11–16; Prechal and Burrows,
1990; Rozes, 1986: 48; Warner, 1984: 148–50). Although in later years the
Court has become increasingly unwilling to rule broadly on social matters,
especially those revolving around established social structures such as the
family, these rulings represent a ground-breaking development in the evolution of women's (employment) rights in Europe.

The first signs of development in the area of women's rights: the Equal Pay Directive

This section looks at the first major policy development in the area of equality at the European level: the Equal Pay Directive (75/117/EEC). The debates
leading to the ratification of this particular policy signal a change in the role
of European institutions in promoting women's rights as an area of
Community competence, and are representative of complex institutional
dynamics.

The 1974 Social Action Programme represents the first attempt to expand
the scope of Article 119. More specifically, this programme sought to broaden
the focus of European social policies, the primary concern of which continued to be employment and economic matters (Hoskyns, 1996: 81; Warner,
1984: 147). Despite the limitations of this approach, through the Action
Programme the Council resolved to:

- undertake action for the purpose of achieving equality between men and
  women as regards access to employment and vocational training and
  advancement and as regards working conditions, including pay, taking
  into account the important role of management and labour in this field;
- ensure that the family responsibilities of all concerned may be reconciled
  with their job aspirations. (Council Resolution, 1974)

The ratification of the Equal Pay Directive was a direct result of the commitment established by this programme (Hoskyns, 1996: 85).

The stated objective of the Equal Pay Directive was to 'reinforce the basic
laws with standards aimed at facilitating the practical application of the principle of equality to enable all employees in the Community to be protected, as
there are still disparities between Member States, despite all efforts'

(Commission, 1997). In general terms, the aim of this policy was threefold. Firstly, it expanded the principle of equal pay for equal work to include work of equal value. Secondly, it sought to include indirect discrimination within the remit of the legislation. Finally, it endeavoured to tackle the issue of sexual segregation in the official labour market. Its main objective, however, was the expansion of the principle of equal pay for equal work to include work of equal value (Williams & Lamb, 1997: 7).

For Rozes (1986: 32) the actual ratification of this directive represents an implicit admission of the failure of the EEC and especially the member states to successfully implement the principles established by Article 119. As she further points out, the directive 'highlights the socio-economic difficulties which the actual application of the principle of equal pay and remuneration cause the national authorities ... and the public or private employers on whom this principle was incumbent' (Rozes, 1986: 32). Hoskyns (1996: 85) agrees with this assessment, adding that the development of the directive highlights the failure of the member states to implement at the national level the principles enshrined within the Treaty of Rome. Remuet Alexandrou *et al.* (1986: 2) draw attention to the 1961 Commission Recommendation and the subsequent Council Resolution, both of which highlight the lack of commitment by the member states' governments towards the full implementation of the regulations on equal pay.

Another important achievement of this directive was the inclusion of indirect discrimination within the overall scope of the principle of equal pay. As Williams and Lamb (1997: 7) explain: 'the Directive ... creates the obligation to apply the principle of equal pay for the same work at piece rates calculated on the basis of the same unit of measurement and equal pay for work at time rates for the same job'. The inclusion of the principle of equal pay for work of equal value substantially broadened the scope of the legislation by acknowledging the impact of structural inequalities on the organisation of the European labour market, and brought indirect discrimination into the picture. At a concrete level, the directive attempted to deal with the problem of wage differential between full-time and part-time workers, at least within the framework of collective agreements; it established institutional protection for employees seeking legal redress; and, it sought to promote women's awareness of the stated objectives (Byre, 1988: 22; Remuet Alexandrou, 1986: 8).

The introduction of the principle of indirect discrimination within the remit of the directive was an important step towards tackling inequalities of access to power and resources; a development that is all the more important when considering the pervasive nature of sexual segregation in the official labour market. Unfortunately, the overall reach of the directive in this particular area is curtailed by the fact that, as Byre (1988: 22) points out, it 'can only be effective in areas where both men and women are employed'. It thus fails to account for the impact of gender hierarchies in the public/political sphere.

The apparent gender neutrality of the policy ultimately undermines its radical potential. Moreover, as with Article 119, this policy fails to consider the link between public and private and thus focuses solely on the establishment of a framework for formal equality. For Hoskyns (1996: 93) this blindness is both the strength and the weakness of the principle of equal pay. Although this principle allows legislators to establish a framework for the development of women's employment rights, its focus on the public sphere and employment reinforces the division between paid and unpaid work. In this context, it is thus important to draw attention to a trend started with the ratification of Article 119, which favours formal equality at the expense of wider considerations about the role of the law in challenging gender power hierarchies. It is possible to draw a preliminary conclusion from the analysis presented so far: the introduction of equal pay as the founding principle of the European equality agenda has served to limit its radical and destabilising potential.

Unfortunately, the issue of equal pay was not resolved with the implementation of the 1975 Directive. It is worth noting that in the 1990s this issue returned to the top of the European equality agenda. Following the 1994 memorandum on equal pay, the European Commission (1996b) published a *Code of Practice on the Implementation of Equal Pay for Work of Equal Value.* The publication of these guidelines highlights the persistence of a wage differential between men and women in the European Union, and draws attention to the obstacles that prevent the full implementation of the principle of equality. One of the issues that received particular attention was the failure of the process of collective bargaining to advance the position of women's rights in employment. More worryingly, the report claims that collective bargaining has served to limit the implementation of the principle of equal pay through various forms of restricted categories that continue to differentiate the value of male and female labour (European Commission, 1996b: 7–8, 19–20; European Commission, 1997b: 7). What this analysis points to is the overarching failure of the Equal Pay Directive to challenge the root causes of inequality. Perhaps this is a shortcoming of the principle of equal pay in itself, which by its very nature focuses on a very narrow agenda. It was left to the equal treatment directives to address the impact of these practices on women's participation in the official labour market (Bercusson and Dickens, 1996: 6).

Equal treatment: broadening the scope of European legislation

A necessary development for the establishment of a comprehensive equality agenda is the recognition that equal access to employment is a necessary precondition for equality of pay and opportunities. The ratification of various equal treatment directives in the 1970s and 1980s is the second phase in the development of the European equality agenda. This section will focus on the

principle of equal treatment as espoused by European Community legislation. What is important to note for the analysis presented in this book is the
introduction of some limited form of legal protection for pregnant workers.

The ratification of a second equality directive was supposed to complete
the equal pay programme. Accordingly, Article 1 of the 1976 Equal Treatment
Directive states:

> The purpose of this Directive is to put into effect in the Member States the prin-
> ciple of equal treatment for men and women as regards to access to employment,
> including promotion, and to vocational training and as regards working condi-
> tions and, ..., social security. This principle is hereinafter referred to as 'the
> principle of equal treatment. (Art. 1(1), 76/207/EEC)

This article summarises what is perhaps the most important achievement of
this directive, which is the extension of the principle of equality beyond pay.
Although the scope of this legislation is still very narrow, for Warner (1984:
151) it represents the unofficial admission that equal pay is irrelevant or ineffective if not accompanied by the principle of equal access to the official
labour market.

Article 2 also displays increased awareness of the kind of structural
inequalities that prevent the full implementation of the principles enshrined
in Article 119 and the 1975 Equal Pay Directive. Article 2(1) and (3) state:

> (1) ..., the principle of equal treatment shall mean that there shall be no discrim-
> ination whatsoever on grounds of sex either directly or indirectly by reference in
> particular to marital or family status.
> (3) This Directive shall be without prejudice to provisions concerning the protec-
> tion of women, particularly as regards pregnancy and maternity.

Article 2(1), in particular, draws attention to the impact of gender power
hierarchies in European society and, more specifically, to women's participation in the official labour market; Article 2(3), on the other hand, strengthens
the previous point by institutionalising some form of protection for pregnant
workers.

Although this directive expands the principle of equality, it is important
not to overestimate its overall impact on the European labour market. As
Bercusson and Dickens (1996: 15–16) point out, there is a difference between
equality of treatment and equality of outcome. From this position, whereas
the first concept of equality of treatment focuses on formal equality, the
second seeks to tackle the impact of structural inequalities and focuses on the
principle of substantive equality. Although the 1976 Equal Treatment
Directive covers some forms of structural inequality, Ellis (1991: 137) argues
that the scope of the directive merely extends to an acknowledgement of such
forces, instead of promoting greater awareness of the impact of social and
gender structures upon women's employment and equality in the official
labour market. The nominal inclusion of pregnant workers is further
evidence of this trend.

The focus of European institutions on formal equality is evident in the absence of any consideration for the impact of sexual differences on the practice of equal treatment. Such bias is evident in the overarching failure of equal opportunities policies to deal with the primary causes of discrimination against pregnant workers. Despite having established a legal framework for the protection of pregnant workers, European policy-makers have failed to recognise that the promotion of the rights of pregnant workers is essential for the operationalisation of substantive equality. Prechal and Burrows' (1990: 108) assessment of the current situation summarises commonly held beliefs about sex based discrimination: 'a woman is not discriminated against on the grounds of sex, but on the grounds of her pregnancy'. What this position fails to acknowledge is that it is indeed impossible to differentiate between sex and pregnancy. Moreover, discrimination against women on the grounds of pregnancy occurs because of deeply rooted assumptions about the male breadwinner model and gender divisions of labour in the family. In this context, employers have been reluctant to employ women in their reproductive years because of their expectations about the link between the social and the biological function of reproduction. Women's role as primary carers is thus seen as diametrically opposed to their role as workers (Prechal and Burrows, 1990: 108; Valentini, 1997).

In this context, the Equal Treatment Directive introduced some limited protection for the health and safety of pregnant workers. However, as Prechal and Burrows' analysis summarises, in the process of developing this policy, European institutions failed to address the role of gender in defining the social function of mothering. The following comment by a Court official highlights the gender biases of European institutions and the European legal order:

> it is clear from the express reference to pregnancy and maternity that the Directive is intended to protect a woman's biological condition and the *special* relationship that exists between a woman and her child. (Case 222/84 [1986] cited in Ellis, 1991: 172)

In other words, this statement implies that protecting the health and safety of pregnant workers corresponds to protecting women's social function as primary carers, thus highlighting the all-encompassing nature of the current gender order. As Hoskyns (1996: 107) points out, this directive 'highlighted the imbalance which exists in the caring responsibilities of men and women, and the difficulties this poses for a policy based on equality', and calls for the establishment of an equality agenda that seeks to address the complexities of socio-economic trends in the late twentieth century (Prechal and Burrows, 1990: 110).

This analysis highlights the discrepancies entrenched within the European equality agenda. Despite having made an abstract commitment to the removal of structural barriers to women's equality, it did not seek to achieve wider social change. These contradictions not only reinforced the division between public and private, but they also crystallised the institutional bias in favour of formal rather than substantive equality. These issues and contradictions are elucidated by two 1984 cases in which the ECJ called for the *mitigation* of substantive inequalities within the workplace, but failed to rule in favour of paid leave for fathers. These rulings ultimately reinforced traditional assumptions about gender roles and gender divisions of labour in the public and the private sphere (Ellis, 1991: 173; Hoskyns, 1996: 107).

The three equal treatment directives that followed sought to expand the scope and reach of the principles of equal treatment and equal opportunities (Hoskyns, 1996: 109). The ratification of the 1979 Equal Treatment in Social Security Directive, in particular, was expected to complement and complete the work of the 1976 Directive (Commission, 1986: 37). Hoskyns (1996: 107) argues that this directive is significant because

> by entering into this field, even by trying to impose on it 'only' a rather crude notion of equality, the EC was moving into a sensitive arena, and one where intervention disturbed national policies of redistribution and social control, and challenged deep-seated assumption and traditions.

As she further explains, this directive officially acknowledges the relationship between social and economic matters in the area of women's rights (Hoskyns, 1996: 107).

The aims of the directive are outlined in Article 1, which states that:

> the purpose of this Directive is the progressive implementation in the field of social security and other elements of social protection ... of the principle of equal treatment for men and women in matters of social security. (Art. 1, 79/8/EEC).

The scope of the directive is instead defined by Article 3, which lists the schemes targeted by this policy as: 'sickness, invalidity, old age, accidents at work and occupational diseases, [and] unemployment' (Art. 3, 79/8/EEC). Although this policy has only limited applicability, Hoskyns (1996: 107) claims that this directive, more so than the 1976 Equal Treatment Directive, incorporates the principle of difference and different needs in the derogations to the overarching principle of equality. One of such derogations that is of particular interest to the analysis conducted here is reported in Article 4, which recognises the possible impact of pregnancy upon the implementation of the principle of equal treatment.

Hoskyns' analysis raises some interesting questions about the overall effectiveness of this policy. On the one hand, the introduction of a discussion or debate about equal treatment in the area of social security has wide-reaching repercussions for the establishment of gender sensitive and/or women-friendly employment and welfare structures. On the other hand, as Hoskyns highlights, the kind of 'special measures' introduced to target the different condition of men and women have not translated into a commitment toward substantive equality. Rather, as she points out, 'these special measures look like, and indeed can easily become, reinforcements for women's continuing domestic role' (Hoskyns, 1996: 112).

The next directive on Equal Treatment in Occupational Social Security Schemes (86/378/EEC) addressed some of the limitations of the 1979 Directive. The stated objective of this directive is 'to define the meaning of Article 119 of the EC Treaty, and the scope and ways of applying the principle of equal treatment for men and women in occupational social security schemes' (86/378/EEC). The implication of this directive is that 'pensions under private company schemes must be paid to men and women at the same age' (Williams and Lamb, 1997: 9). Since its ratification in 1986 and following various cases brought to the ECJ, this directive has been amended by Council Directive 96/97/EEC. The most important case which led to the new Directive was the *Barber* case, in which 'the ECJ ruled that benefits from supplementary pension schemes made available to the employees by the employer constitute an element of pay under Article 119 of the Treaty. Consequently, discrimination between men and women in such schemes is not permissible' (Williams and Lamb, 1997: 9).

The next directive on equal treatment implemented in 1986 further extended the scope of equality of treatment in social security by targeting Occupational Social Security Schemes for Self-Employed Occupations (86/613/EEC). Although this policy is a rather weak attempt to widen the scope of the legislation, the recognition that the areas in which women are more susceptible to discrimination are those furthest away from state control constitutes an attempt to bridge the public–private division present in the official labour market. More specifically, Ellis points out that this directive targets all those women who do not 'enjoy a clearly defined occupational status' (Ellis, 1991: 175).

This new piece of legislation is particularly important for the analysis conducted here because it reintroduces the question of pregnant workers in the official labour market. Ellis describes the legal framework of this directive as follows: it 'is based on both Article 100 and 235 of the EEC Treaty and its preamble makes special note of the fact that specific provisions are required to protect persons engaged in a self-employment capacity' (Ellis, 1991: 175–6). In many ways, however, this directive incorporates the weakness of the 1976 Directive. For instance, Ellis (1991: 177–8) argues that the directive establishes the political role of the EC in *protecting* women's rights, but it does not address the issue of financial protection during and after pregnancy for self-employed women.

In conclusion, this last directive is probably the weakest policy ratified by the EU for the protection of women's employment rights. While acknowledging the need to officially recognise the rights of self-employed female workers, it does not address the division between public and private, which continues to be incorporated in European and national legislation. The most important contribution of this directive is the attempt to target specific issues.

On the positive side, Ross and Schneider (1992: 14) point out that this phase in the development of the European equality agenda was successful in as far as it established the standard for equality in Europe. The principles enshrined in these laws, they argue, can be applied more generally than prescribed in the text of the laws. The analysis presented in this chapter, however, questions the validity of an approach that focuses on achieving a minimum standard for equality as opposed to promoting a comprehensive restructuring of employment structures and social interactions. As with the analysis of the previous directives, the scope of this policy reveals the bias of the process of European integration in favour of formal equality and unob-trusive measures for the achievement of equal opportunities (Ellis, 1991: 137; Kaplan, 1992: 27).

Consolidation of equal opportunities as a fundamental aim of European integration

The third phase in the development of a European equal opportunities strat-egy coincided with the signing of the Treaty of Maastricht. Particularly important in this context were three emerging trends. Firstly, the equality agenda was undergoing a process of amendment and consolidation. Secondly, international discourses on gender had started to shift towards the principle of mainstreaming. And finally, the principle of reconciliation between work and family life had become established as a new strategy for increasing women's participation in the official labour market. This section will focus on the first two trends, whereas the next chapter will discuss in detail the devel-opment and policy impact of the principle of reconciliation between work and family life.

The 1992 Treaty of Maastricht reaffirmed the centrality of the principle of equality in the process of European integration. Moreover, the result of the Amsterdam negotiations (1997) on the Charter for the Fundamental Rights of Workers signalled a move towards expanding social provisions. Although the actual establishment of a 'European Social Dimension' remains a contro-versial, and by and large unresolved matter, the ratification of the Treaty of Amsterdam marked the beginning of a new phase in the development of women's rights in Europe. More specifically, the introduction of gender *mainstreaming* was welcomed by policy-makers and feminists alike as a new tool for the achievement of substantive equality (Mazey, 2001). More recently the EU's commitment to the principle of equality was reiterated in the Charter of Fundamental Rights (2000). However, the virtual disappearance of the issue of equality from the programme of the two European Conventions held thus far, draws attention to how these matters have become increasingly removed from the more general European agenda. The silencing of women's concerns can be seen as a by-product of mainstreaming which, although it helped to include gender into policy areas traditionally closed to such analysis, also helped to perpetrate the myth that gender inequality is a thing of the past. This section will thus look at the latest policy developments that have sought to consolidate the position of women within the European labour market and will conclude with an assessment of the debates surrounding the principle of mainstreaming and the role of equality in a future European constitution.

Gender mainstreaming and the Treaty of Amsterdam

As mentioned previously, at the heart of the consolidation phase is the principle of gender mainstreaming. This concept gained currency amongst policy-makers and scholars following the Fourth UN Women's Conference and the adoption of the Beijing Platform for Action in 1995. It was formally introduced within the scope of the European treaties with the Amsterdam negotiations (Arribas and Carrasco, 2003: 24–5; True, 2003).

The first mention of mainstreaming in a European document came in 1996, with the publication of a European Commission Communication on *Incorporating Equal Opportunities for Men and Women into all Community Policies and Activities*. In this document, the Commission defined the principle of mainstreaming as follows:

> Gender mainstreaming involves not restricting efforts to promote equality to the implementation of specific measures to help women, but mobilizing all general policies and measures specifically for the purpose of achieving equality by actively and openly taking into account at the planning stage their possible effect on the respective situation of men and women (gender perspective). This means systematically examining measures and polices and taking into account such possible effects when defining and implementing them. (European Commission, 1996a)

For Arribas and Carrasco (2003: 24) mainstreaming 'is a strategy aimed at changing the working method with regard to gender equality policy'. Gender is no longer solely the concern of the equal opportunity agenda, but it is to become entrenched into all European activities. This approach is thus supposed to revolutionise the way in which equal opportunities are institutionalised by extending gender analysis to mainstream policies. In other words, mainstreaming is supposed to widen the reach of equal rights polices by tackling gender inequalities in areas that have traditionally been portrayed as gender neutral. In theory, this approach is supposed to expand policy-makers' and practitioners' understanding of gender power hierarchies and their impact on every aspect of policy. However, this strategy has come under increasing criticism on the grounds that such extensive introduction of gender into all areas of policy has not been accompanied by an increased understanding of gender power hierarchies. The intrinsic vagueness of this concept has been seen as instrumental in silencing women's needs and voices through the rhetoric of inclusion (Arribas and Carrasco, 2003: 24; Guerrina, 2003a; Mazey, 2001; Mazey, 2002; Pollack and Hafner-Burton, 2000; Rees, 1998; Shaw, 2002).

The Amsterdam revisions of the Treaty on the European Union introduced the principles of mainstreaming within the scope of the Treaties. More specifically, Article 3(2) and Article 13 articulate the general principles of equality, whereas Article 141 (formerly 119) is amended to include the revisions to the principle of equal pay brought about by forty years of European legislation and jurisprudence. It is in this context that Mazey (2002: 2) argues that,

> the Amsterdam Treaty established a broad human rights framework which commits the EU to combating various forms of discrimination. This development has highlighted the need for European women to think more systematically about the relationship between *gender* mainstreaming and the more inclusive strategy of *equality* mainstreaming.

Mazey's (2002) analysis draws attention to the opportunities that this development has engendered, whereas Shaw (2002) highlights the potential wide-reaching impact of this strategy in the struggle for the institutionalisation of substantive equality.

The question that remains to be answered is whether this strategy represents a way forward for the operationalisation of substantive equality in Europe. Mazey's (2002: 2) survey of mainstreaming in the European Union found that this approach has been most influential 'in those sectors with prior experience of dealing with equal opportunities issues'. This should not come as a surprise, as it is in the area of social policy that gender-sensitive analyses have found most support. The practice of mainstreaming, however, was supposed to have its greatest impact on those areas of policy action, i.e. high politics, at the national and international level that have been traditionally portrayed as detached from the politics of gender. In those areas, Mazey (2002: 2) found that 'mainstreaming has thus far made less headway'. The reason for this particular outcome is twofold. On the one hand, the perception of gender neutrality works counter to the practice of mainstreaming which assumes that gender defines all areas of policy and politics. On the other hand, policy-makers have become more versed in paying lip service to the rhetoric of gender, without actually substantially changing their practices and/or policy outcomes. In this context, mainstreaming has served to silence women's voices and thus reinforce the current gender order.

Amendment of the equality directives and consolidation of equal opportunities as an EU policy area

Three policy developments that took place during the 1990s are indicative of the general mood around the principle of equality in Europe. Each one of these directives highlights the important achievements in the area of equal rights and equal opportunities that have taken place in the last thirty years. At the same time, they also draw attention to the inequalities that are still present within the European labour market. This section will outline the aim of the Equal Treatment Framework Directive (2000/78/EC); the Amendment to the Equal Treatment Directive (2002/73/EC); the Burden of Proof Directive (97/80/EC); the Fifth Framework Programme (2001–05); and finally, the recently proposal for a Directive on Implementing the Principle of Equal Treatment in the access to and supply of goods and services (COM/2003/0657 Final).

As discussed in the first section of this chapter, in the context of a persistent gap in pay between men and women (Fagan and Burchell, 2002: 49; Rubery *et al.*, 1999) the Commission (1996c) adopted a *Code of practice on the implementation of equal pay for men and women for work of equal value*. The main aim of this policy is to strengthen the equality provisions at the European level and to ensure the implementation of the principle of equal pay for work of equal value at the national level. This initiative was supposed to encourage member states' government to expand national equal opportunities provisions. However, what the publication of this particular code highlights is the persistence of gender power hierarchies in the official labour market.

More radical was the Directive on the Burden of Proof in Equality Cases (97/80/EC). The aim of this policy was to share the burden of proof between plaintiff and defendant. Nielsen (2001: 4) summarises the overall thrust of this policy as follows:

> the Directive aims to ensure that the measures taken by the Member states to implement the principle of equal treatment are made more effective, in order to enable all persons who consider themselves wronged because the principle of equal treatment has not been applied to them to have their rights asserted by judicial process after possible recourse to other competent bodies.

In particular she claims that Article 4 of this policy outlines its overall scope:

> Member States shall take such measure as are necessary, in accordance with their national judicial systems, to ensure that, when persons who consider themselves wronged because the principle of equal treatment has not been applied to them establish, before a court or other competent authority, facts from which it may be presumed that there has been direct or indirect discrimination, it shall be for the respondent to prove that there has been no breach of the principle of equal treatment. (Art. 4 97/80/EC in Nielsen, 2001: 4)

What this directive implicitly sought to achieve is the establishment of a framework for equality in the workplace by making employers responsible for ensuring that equality of opportunities and treatment is achieved. This is a clear improvement on traditional approaches to equal opportunities, in as far as it seeks to ensure the full participation of employers in the process of creating a fairer workplace.

Despite the innovation of these provisions, Nielsen points out that this policy was ratified as a 'minimum directive', which means that it only establishes a basic framework for further development. As Nielsen (2001: 5) further highlights, 'it is open for the Member States to introduce rules of evidence which are more favourable to the plaintiffs'. The limitations of this policy become apparent when assessing its overall scope. The principles enshrined in this policy apply to equal pay, equal treatment, maternity rights and parental leave. They do not, however, extend to equal treatment in social security or equal treatment for the self-employed.

The question that needs to be raised is whether this is a radical development for the promotion of women's rights in Europe. There are some clear innovations embedded within this policy that highlight a change in policy discourse. First of all, by shifting the focus from the plaintiff to the respondant, this directive ensures that employers are actively involved in the removal of all formal barriers to the achievement of equality. Secondly, it introduced within the European legal framework a formal definition of indirect discrimination. Finally, it revitalised scholarly and policy-making debates about the role of equal opportunities in European social policies (Nielsen, 2001: 5).

The amendment of the Equal Treatment Directive (97/80/EC) and the ratification of a Directive for a Framework of Equal Treatment in Employment and Occupation (2000/78/EC) are perhaps the most extensive set of amendments to the original policies of the 1970s. With reference to the amendments to the Equal Treatment Directive, Arribas and Carrasco (2003: 23) draw attention to the context within which this policy was negotiated. The development of a wider body of legislation against various forms of discrimination proved to be a vital incentive to update and widen the scope of the equal treatment provisions. As they explain, 'the Equal Treatment Directive was finally amended last year [2002], in order to respond to developments achieved in the field of gender equality, and to the case law of the European Court of Justice' (Arribas and Carrasco, 2003: 23).

The main contributions of this policy revolve around the introduction of a formal definition of direct and indirect discrimination. Unfortunately, as the legal basis of this policy remains Article 141 (formerly Article 119), it continues to focus solely on employment and employment related matters. This clearly limits the overall scope of the amendments, which ultimately reassert a division between public and private, formal and substantive equality (Arribas and Carrasco, 2003: 23).

More significant in the way in which it widened the scope of protection against various forms of discrimination was the Council Directive Establishing a General Framework for Equal Treatment in Employment and Occupation (2000/78/EC). Unlike the policies on equal treatment between men and women, the Treaty foundation for this directive is Article 13 of the Treaty of Amsterdam. It was also greatly influenced by previous developments in the area of equality as established by the 1976 Equal Treatment Directive, the race equality directives, and the presentation of the Charter of Fundamental Rights (Arribas and Carrasco, 2003: 23). According to Arribas and Carrasco (2003: 23), this development is particularly important because it 'has also helped trigger the debate on gender equality which, at least in legislative terms, seemed to be on stand-by'.

The Preamble of the Directive starts out by prohibiting all types of discrimination, in whichever form. What follows is a definition of the terms of reference. Article 2(2) defines discrimination as follows:

(a) direct discrimination shall be taken to occur where one person is treated less favourably than another is, has been or would be treated in a comparable situation,...

(b) indirect discrimination shall be taken to occur where an apparently neutral provision, criterion or practice would put persons having a particular religion or belief, a particular age, or a particular sexual orientation at a particular disadvantage compared with other persons...

Whereas Article 2(3) defines harassment as follows:

harassment shall be deemed to be a form of discrimination... In this context, the concept of harassment may be defined in accordance with national laws and practice of the member states.

The directive also allows for positive action which seeks to 'prevent or compensate for disadvantages' (Article 7 (1)). Unfortunately, the overall scope of the policy is still limited to employment. This weakness, ultimately, highlights one of the main shortcomings of European legislation in the field of equal opportunities, which reinforces the principle of market citizen.

The Fifth Equality Programme (2001–05) represents what is perhaps the most significant widening in the overall scope of EU policies on gender equality. The programme outlines five objectives that must guide future policy development: 1. Equality in economic life; 2. Equal representation and participation; 3. Equality in social life; 4. Equality in civil life; 5. Changing gender roles and overcoming stereotypes. For Mazey (2002: 1–2) this represents the establishment of a positive action programme. For Arribas and Carrasco (2003: 25), on the other hand, this development is indicative that 'mainstreaming has thus become a central element in the Commission's new Framework Strategy'. It is important to note that, as in the case of its predecessors, this equality programme is an example of soft law. What this means is that it provides a framework for future developments, but it is by its very nature non-binding on the member states. It is not unusual for member states to agree to substantial proposals at this stage in the policy process. As history shows, however, it is significantly more difficult to translate such developments into concrete rights.

The latest development in the area of equal rights, the Commission's Proposal for a Council Directive Implementing the Principle of Equal

Treatment Between Men and Women in the Access to and Supply of Goods and Services (SEC (2003) 1213), reflects the equality framework set out by the Fifth Community Action Programme. The wider context for this proposal is the extension of the European social policy agenda. As part of this process, member states requested that the Commission put together a proposal to expand the reach of the European equality agenda beyond the field of employment. Given the progressive expansion of equal rights at the European level, it was felt that the time was ripe for a further widening of the scope of these rights. As the explanatory memorandum attached to the proposal illustrates:

> It is thus as a result of a moral and legal obligation, aimed at consolidating the concept and the reality of a Europe of citizens that the Commission presents its first proposal for a Directive aimed at establishing equal treatment between men and women in an area outside of the labour market. (Commission, 2003)

This statement implies a recognition of the failures of current policies and the need to establish a framework for the operationalisation of substantive equality. Potentially, this is a radical step in the development of the European equality agenda.

The Treaty foundation for this proposal is Article 13 of the TEC. As in the case of the Equal Treatment Framework Directive (2000/78/EC), it is worth noting the shift in legal basis, from Article 141 (Equal Pay) to Article 13 (Equality). Clearly, the latter provides a much wider reaching framework for the operationalisation of the principle of equality and mainstreaming within EU policies. The importance of this shift resides in a general recognition that despite the significant advances in the area of employment rights, gender inequality is still a defining feature of many areas of life (European Commission, 2003). Given this background, the key areas targeted by this proposal are: insurance, banking and financial services, housing, transport and trade. This proposal would ensure that sex is no longer considered a factor in defining an individual's access to goods and services, and the principle of equality is extended to the calculation of cost for accessing such services.

What is interesting to note about this proposal is the justification for expanding equal opportunities outside the remit of employment. Aside from being a Union objective, this proposal officially recognises the link between inequality and social exclusion (European Commission, 2003). This is a significant advance, particularly in the context of establishing substantive equality as a working principle of EU politics.

At the time of writing, the proposal was still going through the various institutions and committees. It is therefore too early to judge what its impact will be for the establishment of a comprehensive framework for equality between men and women in the EU. However, the negotiations on the European Constitution that took place throughout 2003 and 2004 are a good indication of the level of commitment towards the principles enshrined within these policies and equality at large.

Constitutionalism and the quest for equality

To conclude, it is interesting to outline some of the most recent developments in the process of European integration and their impact on furthering the European equality agenda. The work of the European Convention on the Future of the Union has recently received substantial attention, particularly as it allowed for the articulation within policy circles of a long-standing debate about constitutionalism in Europe. Two conventions have been convened thus far. The first sought to negotiate and codify an EU Charter of Fundamental Rights, whereas the second, which completed its work in the summer of 2003, presented the IGC 2003 with a draft constitution for the EU. Part of the reason why these developments have caught the imagination of scholars and policy-makers alike, is because the documents produced define the very foundation of European integration. When applying gender sensitive lenses to the analysis of these processes a few issues emerge that are worth noting.

The Charter of Fundamental Rights, as presented at the Nice Summit in 2000, includes a chapter on Equality. Shaw (2002: 3) argues that this chapter 'contains a veritable "potpourri" of rights, some of a traditional justiciable and constitutional type, some of a more aspirational nature'. More importantly, this chapter is not only concerned with gender, but it seeks to address wider questions of inequality (Shaw, 2002: 3). What is interesting to note for the analysis presented here are the following articles. Article 21 outlines generic provisions on non-discrimination. Article 23 deals directly with equality between men and women. And Article 33, entitled family and professional life, seeks to include into the charter some recognition of the importance of reconciliation between work and family life (Guerrina, 2003: 108–11). For Shaw (2002: 3) these are substantial developments in the European constitutional architecture. As she explains,

> the evidence points towards an equality principle which is deeply embedded in the EU's constitutional fabric, at least in formal terms. It also highlights the different ways the principle can operate within the constitutional order. ... This is fertile territory to argue that gender mainstreaming can be more than just a technique for policy-makers and can be instead the basis for a transformation of politics via the overall polity-generative capacity of constitutionalism.

Unfortunately, the principle of equality enshrined within the charter still favours formal rights as opposed to substantive equality. Moreover, it reasserts the link between equality and participation in the official labour market, thus failing to engage in any depth with gender power hierarchies (Guerrina, 2003: 110–1).

The recent negotiations on the European constitution highlight further discrepancies in the European approach towards equality. The launch of the European Convention on the Future of the Union was welcomed by many commentators as an opportunity to bring the Union closer to the people of Europe. The process was certainly portrayed as citizen-centred and transparent. However, it is debatable whether the convention achieved this aim. When evaluating this process and its end result, the Draft Constitutional Treaty, through gender sensitive lenses, it becomes even more apparent that the issue of equality has become a marginal issue in European negotiations.

Understandably, the main preoccupation of European political leaders at the time of the negotiations was the forthcoming round of enlargement. That said, the introduction of a wider debate about European constitutionalism could have been a valuable opportunity to address the shortcomings of national and European governance, particularly in the area of equality between men and women. Notable in this context is the under-representation of women in the actual convention. As Hoskyns points out (2003: 2), 'of the 105 full members of the Convention only 17 are women (approximately 15%)'. The European Women's Lobby (EWL) also criticised the structure of the convention on similar grounds, highlighting the continued failures of European democratic structures to include women into political process (EWL, 2002). For Hoskyns (2003) the absence of women from the proceedings has more concrete repercussions on the topics perceived to be of interest by this body. More specifically, she argues that the absence of women from the process also helped to marginalise the issue of social policy and resulted in 'the general downgrading of the social in the initial conception of the Treaty' (Hoskyns, 2003: 2).

Two preliminary conclusions emerge from this brief discussion of current debates about constitutionalism in Europe. Firstly, European political leaders have not taken on board feminist criticisms of democracy, governance and participation advanced in the last thirty years. This trend is evident in the under-representation of women in the structure of the convention and the general thrust of the debates taking place at the European level. Secondly, despite the rhetoric about the value and importance of mainstreaming, gender power hierarchies still pervade the political arena; so much so that gender has become tantamount with social policy, an area of policy action traditionally associated with women and the feminine.

A closer examination of the Draft Constitutional Treaty highlights the impact of gender power hierarchies on the negotiations and the political agenda of the Union. The principles of equality and non-discrimination make a few appearances in the draft treaty, some of which are of constitutional importance, and others which reiterate long-standing commitments to equality of opportunities. Firstly, Article 2, entitled 'Union's values', states:

> The Union is founded on the values of respect for human dignity, liberty, democracy, equality, the rule of law and respect for human rights. These values are

common to the member states in a society of pluralism, tolerance, justice, solidarity and non-discrimination.

The European Women's Lobby considers this a significant improvement on the Amsterdam provisions. More specifically, 'mentioning equality in the first sentence of this Article gives it a stronger legal basis than if it were in the second sentence' (EWL, 2003). As the EWL further explains, the inclusion of the principle of equality amongst the values at the heart of the Union makes a clear commitment to this principle.

Article 3(3), entitled 'Union's Objectives', reiterates the principles established in Article 2, and makes an active commitment to the following principles,

> It shall combat social exclusion and discrimination, and shall promote social justice and protection, equality between women and men, solidarity between generations and protection of children's rights.

At a first glance these two articles include equality between men and women and non-discrimination as key principles of the process of European integration. A more careful analysis, however, highlights the shortcomings of this approach. It is also worth mentioning that despite the Union's official position on gender equality, earlier drafts of the Treaty did not include this principle within these two articles, or as one of the values underpinning the process of European integration (Hoskyns, 2003: 2–3). The belated inclusion of gender into the articles outlining the values of the Union highlights the lack of political commitment towards the implementation of this principle.

In the first place, the principles enshrined in Article 13 of the Treaty of Amsterdam have been transferred to Part III (Policies and Functioning of the Union) of the Draft Treaty. More specifically, Article III-2 and Article III-3 restate the Union's commitment to the elimination of inequalities. In particular Article III-3 states:

> In defining and implementing the policies and activities referred to in this Part, the Union shall aim to combat discrimination based on sex, racial or ethnic origin, religion or belief, disability, age or sexual orientation.

Although this article reiterates the commitment of the EU and its institutions to the elimination of discrimination and inequalities, by changing its position in the Treaty the Convention downgraded its importance as a basic principle of European integration. Whereas in the Treaty of Amsterdam Article 13 was included in the section on the Principles of the Union, Articles III-2 and III-3 refer specifically to EU policies.

Arguably, some of the criticisms raised by this analysis of the Constitutional Treaty have been addressed by the inclusion of the Charter of Fundamental Rights into the treaty. Unfortunately, given the difficulties encountered during the original negotiations for the charter, the text was inserted without any amendments. What this means is that the shortcomings of the charter outlined above have been included and will become part any future development in this area.

This analysis ultimately draws attention to the limitations of current debates about constitutionalism in Europe. The focus on 'high politics' has occurred at the expense of those policy areas traditionally more 'women friendly'. Certainly, the failure of the Convention to include equality as a key value and objective of the Union in earlier drafts of the treaty highlights the continuity of gender power hierarchies at the national and European level. It also draws attention to the gap between political rhetoric and political action in the field of equality between men and women. Finally, this analysis points to the failure of gender mainstreaming to engender a political context that actually seeks to challenge structural inequalities and pursue gender democracy.

What is interesting to note with reference to this particular phase in the development of European equality policies is a three dimensional shift in overall strategy and practice. Firstly, there is an attempt to refine pre-existing legislation in the area of equality and employment; secondly, there has been a change in rhetoric, which is identifiable with the principle of mainstreaming; finally, there has been a marked shift in focus toward soft policies. This last point will become particularly evident in the next chapter and refers to a more recent shift in the area of employment policy that can be traced back to the development of the European Employment Strategy (Mazey, 2002: 2).

Conclusions

This chapter has outlined the main developments in the area of equal rights and equal opportunities since the signing of the Treaty of Rome. As the evidence presented here highlights, the last fifty years have been marked by the progressive widening of the aims of the European equality agenda. Starting from a rather narrow interpretation of equality as equal pay for equal work, European law now recognises the political and economic importance of the principle and practice of equality.

Despite the improvements discussed in this chapter, there are several issues that ultimately undermine the overall impact of these policies. Firstly, the focus of the European equality agenda remains strictly within the realm of employment policy. In this context, the introduction of mainstreaming as a Community objective has mostly symbolic value. Much remains to be done in order to implement the full scope of this principle. Secondly, equality, as embedded within the European equality agenda, is first and foremost formal equality. This bias emerges from the essentially economic nature of the project of European integration. Regardless of why or how such bias has come to be incorporated within the European *acquis*, what is important to note is that it still works to limit the overall scope and reach of the equality agenda.

Finally, current debates about constitutionalism and fundamental rights highlight a certain degree of disinterest in this policy area. For many critics, this is the result of mainstreaming.

To conclude, substantial improvements in the condition of working women in Europe have been matched by the absence of a gender dimension in current debates about the future of the Union. These concerns have also been made more urgent by the introduction of soft policies in the area of employment, such as the Open Method of Coordination and the European Employment Strategy (Rubery *et al.*, 2003). The next chapter will explore in greater detail these critiques by taking a detailed look at the establishment of the principle of reconciliation between work and family life as an aim of EU employment and gender policies.

3

Reconciliation between work and family life: a concrete move towards establishing substantive equality as a working principle for the Union?

The analysis presented in this chapter builds on the discussion outlined in chapters 1 and 2, and must be contextualised within current discourses about the relationship between public policies and gender power hierarchies. Clearly, the concept of reconciliation between work and family life is central to the advancement of substantive equality. Representative of a move towards greater recognition of the link between public and private, this principle is embedded with the potential to challenge the social values and structures that perpetrate gender inequalities. The inclusion of this principle within the EU equality agenda can be seen as a positive step in the evolution of women's rights. However, as the analysis of the actual policies ratified under this broad umbrella will highlight, they are not immune from hierarchical economic and political relations and, as such, they contribute to maintaining gender structures.

The analysis of policies targeting reconciliation between work and family life has to be informed by various issues currently providing the backdrop against which current employment structures have started to emerge. The main issues under consideration are: the power of gender divisions of labour; the persistence of a dichotomy between public and private, with the consequential division between paid and care work; and finally, current employment trends, which have seen a move towards flexible, non-traditional employment patterns.

The shift in focus towards reconciliation of work and family life can be seen as phase four in the evolution of women's rights in the EU. This shift has been marked by a variety of policy statements and the ratification of five key policies: the 1992 Pregnant Worker Directive (92/85/EC); the 1996 Parental Leave Directive (96/34/EC); the 1992 Child-Care Recommendations (92/241/EC); the 1993 Working-Time Directive (93/104/EC); and, the 1997

Part-Time Worker Directive (97/81/EC). Despite the formal and legally binding nature of these policies (apart from the Childcare Recommendations), McGlynn (2001: 242) claims that in the case of reconciliation 'the EU's approach is one dominated by rhetoric and symbolism at the expense of action'. What this discussion points to, is the need to assess the values enshrined within these policies and how such normative statements shape their ultimate outcomes.

The European social dimension as a platform for work–life balance

The wider framework within which debates about family-friendly polices took place during the 1990s was greatly influenced by two key events: the signing of the Treaty of Maastricht and the annexation of the Charter for the Fundamental Social Rights of Workers to the Treaty through the Agreement on Social Policy. What these debates draw attention to is the increasing importance attached to the development of a European social dimension. As equal opportunities had been the main area of policy action in the field of social policy, and as this is the umbrella under which family-friendly policies will develop, it is necessary to outline how these initiatives came to be included within the overall scope of European integration.

The Social Charter established that equal treatment for men and women was to be assured and developed as follows:

> action should be intensified to ensure the implementation of the principle of equality between men and women as regards particular access to employment, remuneration, working conditions, social protection, education, vocational training and career development.
>
> Measures should also be developed enabling men and women to reconcile their occupational and family obligations. (Commission, 1990: 17)

This is a commitment that is reiterated by the Agreement on Social Policy (Article 2, annexed to Protocol 14 on Social Policy). These developments are very important for the analysis of family-friendly policies as they officially acknowledge that equality of opportunities cannot be achieved through legal rights alone. This shift implies a substantial rethinking about the impact of gender divisions of labour on social and employment structures. Increasing calls by the Commission for policies that would allow men and women to reconcile their roles in the public and private sphere can be seen as a turning point in political rhetoric about equality and equal opportunities (McGlynn, 2001; Pillinger, 1991).

This change in political discourse seemingly implies that European institutions are trying to redefine social structures through the development of programmes that seek to bring balance to the division between public and private work. The 1994 European Commission White Paper on Social Policy is exemplary of this trend. In this context the Commission has stated that 'progress towards new ways of perceiving family responsibilities may slowly relieve the burden on women and allow men to play a more fulfilling role in society' (European Commission, 1994: 43). This position is further supported in the same document by the following proclamation:

> greater solidarity between men and women is needed if men are to take a greater responsibility for the caring role in our societies and if flexibility in employment is not to lead to new pressures on women to return to the ranks of non-salaried population or be obliged to accept paid work at home in isolation from the community. (European Commission, 1994: 43)

These statements are significant on various levels. On the positive side it is important to recognise the significance of such a shift in discourse. Firstly, it opens the way for a more proactive pursuit of equality in the official labour market. Secondly, it marks a shift towards a formal acknowledgement of the role of both parents in the social function of reproduction. Although this approach still focuses upon formal rights of women as workers, the Commission finally acknowledges that the achievement of substantive equality is dependent upon social restructuring. This quote also highlights some important issues that surround the development and ratification of equal rights policies. For instance, the explicit call to 'greater solidarity', is not reflected in the text of the law which focuses on women's role as primary carers. On the negative side, McGlynn (2001) has drawn attention to the gap between rhetoric and reality that has accompanied this shift in discourse.

One of the issues arising from this analysis is the continued prevalence of economic concerns. For Hoskyns (1991: 29) 'when the 1992 Programme and the Single European Act were proposed, fought over and adopted in the mid-1980s, it is hardly surprising that the issue of women's rights was not mentioned, nor gender specific effects of these developments considered'. On the few occasions in which equal opportunities entered the debate, the issue was approached from a specifically economic standpoint. This bias, in turn, jeopardised discussions about widening the scope of European legislation towards substantive equality. A clear example of these attitudes is the position of the Commission in the White Paper on social policy:

> the contribution which women can make to the revitalising of the economy is one of the reasons why the issue of equality should be seen as a key element to be taken into account in all relevant mainstream policies. European efforts should be redoubled to develop actions and policies which reinforce women's rights and maximise their potential contributions. (European Commission, 1994: 41)

It is with reference to such economic considerations that family-friendly policies have become important in discussions about the future of European integration. Recognition of the substantive changes that have been taking place in the European labour market forced policy-makers to discuss how to make employment practices more inclusive for women. Such considerations, however, only tangentially touched upon those issues that ultimately limit the scope of the European equality agenda. Although this shift in the policy agenda is a positive move towards the introduction of a comprehensive framework for equal opportunities, it can hardly be defined as a significant contribution to the establishment of substantive equality as a working principle. It is therefore possible to conclude that the European policy framework thus continues to ignore the impact of gender power hierarchies on employment practices, ultimately reinforcing the division between women's public and private responsibilities. These are considerations that become all the more apparent through the analysis of specific family-friendly policies.

The Pregnant Worker Directive: between health and safety and equality

Helen Collins' (1994) discussion of the assumptions underlying the ratification of the 1992 directive highlights the constraints within which the aims of this policy were developed. As she explains, the introduction of the 1992 Pregnant Worker Directive

> followed concerns over the falling European population and shortages of skilled workers. The Commission felt that it had proposed the minimum requirements that were necessary to protect the health of pregnant women and their foetuses, without reducing women's employment opportunities. (Collins, 1994: 5)

In this context, women's role in the reproductive process becomes the focus of legislative attention as a matter of concern for the relative gains of the state and the European economy. Two considerations emerge from this analysis: firstly, economic concerns took precedence over the emancipatory objectives of this policy area. Secondly, normative assertions on gender, power and work became implicitly embedded in the overall aims of this policy. For these reasons, the analysis of maternity provisions is particularly useful to understand the influence of traditional assumptions about gender roles and the overarching influence of gender power hierarchies in contemporary European society. This section will seek to establish the extent to which assumptions about gender and the gender order have become entrenched within the policy objectives of this legislation. As part of this analysis, it is important to assess the cost and value of mothering to the European economy.

The 1992 Pregnant Worker Directive (92/85/EEC) became the centre of attention for any discussion about the overall scope of EU family-friendly policies in the early 1990s. The idea of developing a policy aimed at protecting working mothers emerged within the framework of the Third Action Programme on Equal Opportunities (1991–95), and was subsequently developed by Medium Term Programme (1995–97), which broadened the scope of the principle of reconciliation between work and family life. The focus of political rhetoric was on enabling women to reconcile career and family life, as well as providing an extended interpretation and application of the principle of equal treatment. The limitations of the political context within which maternity rights entered the European policy arena are wide ranging, however the policies that emerged from this framework provided the basis for some influential developments in European social legislation (Council Resolution, 1991; Ellis, 1991: 223; McGlynn, 2001: 252–4).

These introductory remarks are very important because they establish the context within which maternity rights entered the European equality agenda. The preamble of the directive outlines the rationale for maternity rights as follows:

> Whereas pregnant workers, workers who have recently given birth or who are breastfeeding must be considered a specific risk group in many respects, and measures must be taken with regard to their safety. (Preamble, 92/85/EEC)

The first statement is particularly important because it draws attention to the special position of pregnant workers in the official labour market. The directive then goes on to state,

> Whereas the protection of the safety and health of pregnant workers, workers who have recently given birth or workers who are breast feeding should not treat women in the labour market unfavourably nor work to the detriment of Directives concerning equal treatment for men and women. (Preamble, 92/85/EEC)

This statement draws attention to the fact that pregnancy is a condition which differentiates the needs of male and female workers. Having recognised this, it also establishes two principles: 1. This "condition" must not justify discrimination against the female labour force; 2. The legislation must protect the health and safety of pregnant workers and workers who have recently given birth. The focus on the health and safety of pregnant workers is particularly important as it highlights the assumptions about work, pregnancy and mothering that pervade the policy-making framework and the official labour market. From this position pregnant workers, and by default all working mothers, are to be protected because of their special position in the social and biological function of reproduction. The rights of women to fair treatment thus become linked to their position in the gender order as opposed to being a precondition for justice and equality in the official labour market (McGlynn, 2001).

In more general terms, the overall aims of the Pregnant Worker Directive can be summarised as follows: it outlines the basic health and safety requirement for the protection of pregnant workers; it sets out the basic regulations on prohibited work, night work, maternity leave, time off for ante-natal care, and protection against dismissal; and finally, it reinforces the link between equal opportunities and employment rights. The purpose of the directive is outlined by Article 1(1) which defines the scope as follows 'to implement measures to encourage improvements in the safety and health at work of pregnant workers and workers who have recently given birth or who are breast-feeding'. Particularly important was the inclusion of a minimum leave period (fourteen weeks) and the recognition that employment structures must be flexible enough to accommodate women's special needs during pregnancy and immediately after giving birth (Articles 4, 6, 7–12). Based on Article 118(a) of the Treaty of Rome, and therefore focusing on health and safety concerns, the directive fails to provide European women with a social framework that would widen the scope and reach of European equal opportunities policies. Despite asserting that maternity pay and leave are not to be considered on a par with sick leave, the actual allowance is based upon the model of sick pay, consequently reaffirming male norms (Collins, 1994; Ellis, 1991: 207–8; McGlynn, 2001: 256–7).

The institutional dynamics that surrounded the debate on maternity rights are particularly telling about the socio-political context within which this policy developed. Generally speaking, the Commission, the Parliament and the ECJ have shown an active commitment to the cause of women's employment rights. More specifically, they have been fighting for the elimination of indirect discrimination and the institutionalisation of equal opportunities. On the other hand, the Council of Ministers continued to act as the restraining force. Composed of the representatives of the member states' governments, it has proved to be an uncompromising obstacle that prevents the institutionalisation of substantive equality by limiting the scope and reach of various proposals when they came up for approval and ratification (Anon., 1992: 3; Ellis, 1991: 223–5).

The complex set of negotiations that took place around this directive highlights the intricate dynamics, and contrasting interests, that characterise European policy-making. Whereas the European Parliament and the European Commission supported the implementation of sixteen to eighteen weeks paid maternity leave, negotiations in the Council of Ministers reached an impasse over the issue of equal pay. After prolonged debate, and following the Italian government's veto, the Council accepted a previously agreed common position that limited the overall scope of this policy. Notwithstanding earlier objections by the EP concerning the equalisation of maternity pay with sick pay, lack of interest in the Council for such issues forced both the EP and the Commission to agree upon the limited statutory rights now enshrined in the Directive (Anon., 1992).

Moreover, persistent opposition by the Italian and UK governments forced the European Commission to reconsider its strategy. Originally proposed as an equality directive, this policy was finally ratified under Article 118(a) (health and safety). The reason for this shift in Treaty basis is due to decision-making mechanisms within the Council. Whereas, at the time of the negotiations, equality provisions (Article 119) had to be agreed upon unanimously, health and safety measures fell under the Qualified Majority Voting rule. The change in Treaty basis thus allowed the Commission to bypass Italian and British objections to this policy. For Hoskyns (1996: 157) this shows the creativity and entrepreneurship of the Commission, which in this way succeeded in addressing two interrelated issues: firstly, it contributed to the establishment of a minimum standard for workers' rights, and secondly, it 'suggested a new degree of integration between equal opportunities and mainstream social policy development' (Hoskyns, 1996: 157). However, because it is based upon Article 118(a) of the Treaty of Rome wider issues of integration of social and economic factors influencing women's employment remain excluded from the scope of the directive, ultimately limiting the reach of this policy.

Although the adoption of the final text of the directive represents a victory of pragmatism over the principle of substantive equality, and a compromise in favour of economic rather than social integration, the 1992 Pregnant Worker Directive still represents the first major step towards the establishment of wide-reaching legislation for the reconciliation between work and family life in Europe. Despite its weaknesses, this policy provides a minimum standard of *protection* for working mothers in the EU, thus improving the legal standing of women in the member states where maternity legislation is weak or altogether absent as in the case of the UK (Anon., 1992: 2–3; Hoskyns, 1996: 157).

The ratification of this directive was therefore a groundbreaking development that 'brought considerable improvements in the rights of pregnant women in many member states of the EU' (McGlynn, 2001: 256). This is perhaps more telling about the overall level of provisions for working mothers available in EU member states than the actual innovations included in the directive. Unsurprisingly, this policy was not welcomed by all member states' governments. The opposition to the principles enshrined in the original draft sheds light on the overall climate within which the directive was negotiated and then ratified. The position of the UK and Italian governments are exemplary of the predominantly employer centred interests that were driving the negotiations. It is in this context that Meehan and Collins (1996: 232) argue that European policies embody a 'fiction of sex equality', rather than a concrete commitment to women's rights and substantive equality. The implicit gender bias entrenched within this policy reinforces gender divisions of labour rather than challenging power hierarchies and the current gender order. As Meehan and Collins (1996: 232) explain, an example of this bias is 'the thoughtless adoption of concepts such as "breadwinner", which while eliminating direct discrimination, may reinforce indirect discrimination'. Despite the rhetoric surrounding the implementation of the Social Agreement and the various social action and equal opportunities programmes (Commission, 1981; Commission, 1991, Council, 1995), the focus of governmental opposition exposes the economic bias embedded within the European equality agenda. Although it can be argued that most European policies have an inherently economic focus, in the case of equal rights and reconciliation between work and family life, this tendency ultimately commodifies equality, thus limiting its overall scope (Anon., 1992: 3–4; McGlynn, 2001: 256–7; Meehan and Collins, 1996: 223–36).

There are many issues that arise from the analysis presented in this section. Despite the efforts to incorporate women workers as equal member of the labour force, and the artificial use gender neutral language in the directive, the actual text implicitly reinforces women's role as carers and the male standard of worker. The main problem in the development of maternity legislation revolves around the definition of worker that transpires from the text. As discussed extensively throughout this book, traditionally policy-makers and employers have conceptualised the typical worker to be male, consequently focusing health and safety legislation around the notion of disabling illnesses. If the EU is committed to promoting women's rights, pregnancy needs to be re-conceptualised to promote substantive equality in the public and the private sphere. As Hoskyns (1996: 229–30) explains, although European law introduced the notion of *special* needs, it failed to provide a satisfactory legal structure for the reconciliation between work and family life. This change, however, cannot occur at the expense of reinforcing traditional assumptions about mothers and mothering. The focus of this policy on protecting the "special relationship" between mother and child ultimately undermines the radical potential of family-friendly policies. In this context, by conflating the biological needs of working mothers/pregnant workers with the economic needs of society for women to fulfil the function of care, the Pregnant Worker Directive ultimately reinforces the male breadwinner model (Hoskyns, 1996: 229–30; McGlynn, 2001: 256–7).

To sum up, one of the most important shortcomings of this directive lies in the lack of recognition for the impact of gender power hierarchies on social and economic relations in the official labour market. The assumption that the public sphere and the official labour market are, or indeed can ever be, gender neutral not only undermines the principle of equal opportunities, but also prevents the institutionalisation of substantive equality. The Council's reluctance to ratify stronger and more effective social provisions is expected to increase the levels of indirect discrimination (Meehan and Collins, 1996: 232). The end result of this approach is an increase in the domestication of women for whom it is not economically viable to return to their original position in the official labour market. McGlynn (2001: 257) takes this point further arguing that 'a directive which details considerable rights and entitlements for women upon the birth of a child, but does not address men as fathers, is almost certainly likely to reproduce traditional approaches to pregnancy and parenting'. In a similar fashion, Townsheld-Smith (1989) explains:

The ideology of domesticity is that paid work must not interfere with child-rearing. Employers assume that all women will conform to this stereotype which is regarded as freely chosen. Furthermore, employers assume that potential employees who are unable to conform to the traditional model of a five-day working week for an entire working life are inadequate and unlikely to be successful employees. For many women this is true, as employers have seen no need to adapt their practices to account for women's career break. Low pay reinforces the stereotype by making it relatively less costly for women than men to remain at home. (Quoted in Ellis, 1991: 207)

Given these critical accounts, it is possible to conclude that the question of gender roles and gender divisions of labour is what the Pregnant Worker Directive fails to address.

Despite the significant shortcomings outlined above, what starts to emerge from this discussion is a shift in the overall thrust of the legislation. Increasing attention is being given to the development policies that would enable women to *reconcile* professional and family life, thus highlighting the increasing importance of women's participation in the official labour market (see for instance the 1994 Commission White Paper). Clearly, this change is a welcome improvement over gender-blind social policies, even though it fails to challenge the assumption that women are the primary carers.

The importance of the 1992 Directive should not be understated as it established a minimum threshold of health and safety standards for the physical protection of working mothers. However, the emphasis on the physical safety element of maternity legislation was achieved at the expense of greater attention to the social impact of maternity upon employment in the official labour market and women's position in society at large. The consequence of this oversight is the reproduction of social structures that equate motherhood to maternity, ultimately reinforcing women's role as primary carers (Guerrina, 2001; McGlynn, 2001). What this analysis confirms is the continued prevalence of formal over substantive equality, an issue that becomes all the more apparent through the analysis of the Parental Leave Directive.

The Childcare Recommendations

The Childcare Recommendations are the second pillar of European family friendly policies. It is generally accepted that the provision of good quality and affordable childcare is important because it goes to the very core of the gender division of care work. In this context, it is particularly interesting to note the EU's attempt to deal with the socio-economic structures that influence women's decisions to enter or return to the official labour market following the birth of a child.

The main aim of the Childcare Recommendations (92/241/EC) is to encourage member states to develop a comprehensive set of measures to allow women to reconcile work and family life. The preamble of the recommendations summarises the main objectives of this policy as follows:

> Whereas the reconciliation of occupational, family and upbringing responsibilities arising from the care of children has to be viewed in a wide perspective which also takes into account the particular interests and needs of children at different age levels, where it is important, in order to achieve this, to encourage an overall policy aimed at enabling such reconciliation to occur. (Preamble, 92/241/EC)

This statement is particularly interesting because it represents a clear sign that European policy-makers have started to acknowledge the impact of gender divisions of labour on labour market trends. The issue of childcare thus entered the policy-making agenda on the grounds that women's participation in the European labour market was key to the long term success of the European economy (McGlynn, 2001: 256).

The recommendations set out the principles for the establishment of good practice in the area of childcare. More specifically, they seek to tackle four key issues as set out in Article 2: 1. Provision of services; 2. Special leave for working parents; 3. Work organisation; 4. Equitable distribution of care work. This change in discourse represents a significant widening of the European equality agenda. Given the wide range of issues addressed by this policy, it is unfortunate that the recommendations are not legally binding on the member states. As such, they represent a statement of intent and seek to define future policy action, but are not bestowed the power of other EU policies. Despite these important shortcomings, for McGlynn (2001: 256) 'its adoption did represent a symbolic achievement'. If nothing else, this development highlights the establishment of a new policy agenda that seeks to encourage women's participation in the official labour market, and a more comprehensive engagement with the socio-economic structures that characterise public–private divisions and gender hierarchies (McGlynn, 2001: 256).

A more in-depth analysis of the recommendations, however, brings to light a different agenda, which is altogether more in line with the overall economic thrust of the Union. As McGlynn (2001: 256) explains,

> although the Recommendation is highly significant in terms of the development of EU policy, the Commission and Council's preoccupation appears to be with women's access to labour markets, hence the necessity of childcare services, despite the references to men's caring roles. Reconciliation is promoted as part of the 'removal of obstacles' to access to the labour market.

In this context, it is worth noting that the adoption of the recommendations coincided with the establishment of a new economic agenda in the 1990s, which focused primarily on flexibility and competitiveness. Women's labour became essential to the long term success of the Single Market. The introduction of family-friendly policies cannot be seen as the answer to feminist calls for a progressive move towards substantive equality, but as fulfilling the requirements of the business community for an increase in flexible labour, normally provided by working mothers. This is a compelling argument, which becomes all the more evident in the context of the analysis of working time regulations such as the Working Time Directive and the Part-Time Work Directive.

To sum up, although these recommendations have been welcomed as a positive step towards the development of a comprehensive childcare strategy, their status as a soft-law highlights the lack of a concrete commitment by member states to this policy area. Moreover, despite the degree of consensus between member states about the need to provide affordable childcare in order to encourage women with children to participate in the official labour market, the adoption of the recommendations did not engender substantial change in national policies. One area that could be have been addressed, but as it happens, was ignored by the recommendations, was the establishment of a network for the transfer of good practice, a strategy that is now becoming increasingly more mainstreamed thanks to the European Employment Strategy (Guerrina, 2003b).

The Parental Leave Directive

The Parental Leave Directive (96/34/EC) is the third pillar of European policies for the reconciliation between work and family life. As it will be discussed in the next section of this chapter, the Working Time Directive and the Part-Time Work Directive are also important developments in this field, but they were not developed with the specific aim of helping working parents to reconcile the responsibility of work and care (Williams and Lamb, 1997: 10). The debate and controversy surrounding the ratification of this directive revolves around the influence of traditional gender divisions of labour in contemporary European society. As Jane Pillinger (1991: 6) points out, 'at the heart of parental leave is the acknowledgement that parents have a responsibility for the care of children. Equally important is that employers need to recognise that parental duties do not stop when work begins'. The introduction of this directive therefore marks the beginning of a more substantial challenge to the artificial division of economic and social interests embedded within the European equality agenda. In this context, the Parental Leave Directive is the main policy seeking to challenge traditional gender roles and foster the participation of men/fathers in the function of care.

Although this directive represents the latest development in the establishment of a comprehensive policy framework for the reconciliation between work and family life, it is worth noting that the original proposal predates either the Childcare Recommendations or the Pregnant Worker Directive. As Hoskyns (1996: 143) points out, the concept of parental leave was originally introduced in the first Community Programme for the Promotion of Equal

Opportunities for Women as part of new programmes pursuant to equal treatment (1981). More specifically, Action 7 of this Programme focused on two issues: 1. Gender divisions of labour in the practice of care; 2. Reduction of working time (Hoskyns, 1996: 143–4). As part of this re-evaluation of working conditions, Action 7 calls for the development of a directive on Parental Leave:

> The sharing of family responsibilities is a precondition of the achievement of equal treatment for men and women. Community action should lend support to the change of attitude on this question ... The extension of family and parental leave is one aspect of a new distribution of time between work and other activities. In this context the reorganisation of working time should avoid reinforcing traditional family roles and instead to be used to make an important contribution in the achievement of equal opportunities. (Commission, 1981: 8)

The inclusion of these objectives within this programme highlights a certain degree of awareness of the impact of gender divisions of labour upon women's employment practices.

Substantial discussions and negotiations on the issue of parental leave began in 1983 following the tabling of the first proposal by the Commission for the development of a directive tackling this issue (Commission Proposal, 1983). A second amended proposal came only one year later (COM (84) 631 Final). Whereas the preamble and the aims remained the same, by the time the second proposal was presented/tabled, the scope of this policy had been narrowed down. Despite Hoskyns' (1996: 163) claim that at this stage the changes were only minimal, the introduction of such changes highlights the diluting process this directive has been subject to over the course of the years.

The aim of the original proposal was to 'encourage the involvement of fathers' by virtue of 'a three-month *non-transferrable* entitlement to leave' (Hoskyns, 1996: 146). Article 1 of the 1983 proposal specifically described parental leave as follows:

> *Parental leave* shall mean entitlement to leave of a given duration to wage-earners, fathers, mothers, ..., consequential upon the birth of a child, during the period following the termination of maternity leave, or to workers, ..., on the adoption of a child during the period following its reception in the adoptive parents' household, during which period of leave the beneficiary takes responsibility for the actual care of the child. (Article 1, Commission Proposal for a Council Directive on Parental Leave and Leave for Family Reasons)

For Hoskyns (1996: 147) this approach was the downfall of the proposal, which 'was seen as too prescriptive and too controlling for the deregulatory eighties, and it was shelved in June 1986'.

The next attempt at a Directive on Parental Leave came in the wake of the *Hofmann* case of 1984. The position of the ECJ in this case diverged from previous practice, which had seen it become of the of the main advocates of women's rights. Up until then, the ECJ had succeeded in widening the scope and reach of European legislation through case law. For Hoskyns (1996: 134–5), however, the Court's judgement in this case highlights a more fundamental issue: 'the judges, while willing by this stage to take audacious rulings concerning women in employment, were still wary about issues which involved motherhood, or the role of fathers in childcare'. The position of the Court highlights the presence of conflicting interests within the Community. Although by this stage, the Commission was willing to introduce substantive measures to readdress gender divisions of labour, other European institutions were more hesitant to institutionalise social changes that would readdress structural inequalities. Another example of this resistance was the persistent refusal of the UK government to ratify this policy on the grounds that it would involve high costs for employers (Hoskyns, 1996: 134–5, 147; Pringle, 1998: 139).

Following various calls for the implementation of the Commission's proposal and the redefinition of women's role in the private sphere, in 1995 the Commission once again commenced the proceedings to ratify the Parental Leave Directive; this time, however, it was to push for this policy under the auspices of the Agreement on Social Policy. As in the case of the Pregnant Worker Directive, it is possible to see the creativity and entrepreneurship of the Commission, which endorsed this approach in order to overcome member states' objections, and particularly the possibility of a British veto. Unfortunately, this approach also had the adverse effect of limiting the reach of the directive to the signatory states. Moreover, as Pringle (1998: 140) points out, 'the measure did not go as far as some parties would have wished' (Conroy Jackson, 1990: 28, 30–1; European Parliamentary Labour Party; Hertogs, 1990: 36–7; Pochet et al., 1996: 163–8).

Negotiations on the Parental Leave Directive took place under the auspices of the Social Protocol. This process, introduced by the Treaty of Maastricht, is based on the principles of collective agreements and social dialogue. As such, it is highly dependent upon the wishes and concerns of 'the three major cross-sectoral interest federations (ETUC, CEEP and UNICE)' – that is, the European Trade Union Confederation, the European Centre of Enterprises with Public Participation and Enterprises of General Economic Interest and the Union of Industrial and Employers Confederations of Europe – (Falkner, 1997). The achievement of some kind of agreement over this policy was an innovation on several counts. Firstly, it was the first directive ratified using the Social Protocol; a development that has important implications for the development of a social Europe. Secondly, the directive was in itself a significant step forward in the creation of a family-friendly workplace. Unfortunately, the very nature of the negotiation process and the actors involved reinforced the economic interests of the process of European integration. This bias highlights the continued focus of the European equality agenda on employment and employment-related matters. It could be argued that the Commission's loss of agenda-setting power in this process influenced the ultimate outcome of the negotiation, which focused predominantly on the public sphere. Moreover, the UK's opt-out of the Protocol and Agreement on Social Policy served to marginalise the overall impact of this policy (Falkner, 1998; Hardy and Adnett, 2002: 162).

The preamble of the Framework Agreement on parental leave adopted by the social partners assumes that it will encourage changes in attitudes towards women as workers in the official labour market and women as carers in the private. The official aims of this policy are threefold. Firstly, it seeks to develop a framework for the reconciliation of professional and domestic responsibilities; secondly, it endeavours to redefine gender division of labour in the practice of caring by encouraging greater male participation in domestic responsibilities; thirdly, it establishes a minimum set of rights for working parents (Falkner, 1998: 119–23).

More specifically, the directive defines a number of rights for working parents. First, it provides a minimum three month non-transferrable parental leave to be used in the first eight years of life of a child. It also increases the statutory rights of working mothers by ensuring that parental leave can be added to maternity leave and allows working parents to structure the period of leave according to their individual and family needs. Finally, it ensures that working parents taking leave under these provisions have a right to reinstatement. Two issues are particularly important with reference to this directive: the non-transferable nature of the leave entitlements; and the right to return. The first point is particularly significant because it fulfils the policy's aim to expand the right to reconciliation between work and family life to working parents/fathers (Caracciolo, 2001: 334–5; Hardy and Adnett, 2002: 162).

For the European Commission (1997b: 63) the ratification of this directive concluded the long-standing debate on this issue, and established a minimum grounds for the protection of workers seeking to undertake parental leave. As the Commission (1997b: 63) explained, thanks to this development 'parental leave can be organised on a family or individual basis', thus ensuring a more balanced division of care work in the private sphere. Unfortunately, parental leave provisions in many member states are curtailed by measures that require working mothers to waive their right to maternity leave. The Commission maintains a positive vision of this policy's role in challenging traditional gender hierarchies, despite acknowledging that in a large number of member states these rights are limited by social attitudes and economic structures (European Commission, 1997b: 64; Hoskyns, 1996: 144–7).

Despite the innovations introduced by this policy, there are several gaps in the provisions outlined above which ultimately undermine the radical potential of the principle itself. Although the directive establishes an individual right to parental leave, it does not provide for payment during the period of leave. This omission has important implications for the overall reach of the provisions. Despite the rhetoric included in the directive, which seeks to reddress the imbalance in the division of care work in the family, the exclusion of pay fails to address one of the key factors contributing to gender power hierarchies: the gender pay gap. This division is further compounded by the temporary interruption of payments to social security and other benefits. This analysis of omissions and oversights in the Parental Leave Directive has led analysts to argue that these provisions are, in reality, aimed at women and at securing greater participation of women in the official labour market (Caracciolo, 2001: 334–5; Hardy and Adnett, 2002).

Two issues emerge from the analysis presented here. As Caracciolo (2002: 335) explains, '*prima facie*, this measure represents a valuable step towards the creation of a family-friendly workplace. A closer look, however, reveals that it is not flawless and is based on the idea that mothers still have the main responsibility for child-care'. It is possible to conclude that, despite the rhetoric surrounding the development of this policy and the gender-neutral language used throughout, in reality the directive fails to challenge gender divisions of care work. Moreover, the inability of the social partners to agree upon a universal right to parental leave, further undermines the radical potential and practical effectiveness of the provisions (Caracciolo, 2001: 335; Hardy and Adnett, 2002: 162–3).

Allocation of working time

In order to create a family-friendly workplace, it is necessary to move towards a more flexible allocation of working time for parents. In the context of current discussions about flexible employment structures, however, it is necessary to distinguish between the interpretation of this concept by employers and the business community on the one hand and that of working parents on the other. The development of policies targeting the allocation of working time is the fourth and final pillar of this policy area. Two directives are the core of this pillar: the Working Time Directive and the Part-Time Worker Directive.

The drive to increase flexibility in the European labour market reached an all-time high following the Treaty of Amsterdam. Faced with high unemployment rates, an ageing population, and declining birth rates, the member states agreed to find new strategies to ensure the long-term growth of the European economy. The employment chapter included in the Treaty thus sought to combat unemployment and ensure the competitiveness of the European market. In this context, the strategy that came to be regarded as the most plausible, and least costly, was to restructure the labour market in favour of flexible employment patterns. The concept of flexibility endorsed by European governments and the various economic interests operating within the single market focused on rendering the European labour force more mobile and interchangeable. A flexible employment market was to encourage a wider proportion of the population to enter and remain active in the labour market. Flexibility, however, became tantamount to job insecurity, part-time work, fixed term contracts, and the deregulation of employment structures (Deakin and Reed, 2000; European Foundation for the Improvement of Living and Working Conditions, 2002: 2–4;).

Flexibility and restructuring of the official labour market are also concepts often cited in the context of establishing a family-friendly work-place. In this case, however the emphasis is on challenging the traditional patterns of work that separate public duties from private responsibilities, rather than flexibility *per se*. Reconciliation between work and family life implicitly recognises that the focus of employment policies must shift from the needs of employers to those of employees. It challenges the long-hour culture and the assumption that only the full-time worker model can ensure competitiveness and commitment. This approach thus seeks to extend employment security to atypical workers. Such an objective, however, does not necessarily coincide with the aims of market-driven flexibility (Deakin and Reed, 2000).

Both approaches have proved to be very influential. The business case for increased labour market flexibility and family-friendly discourses seem to have found an unlikely ally in each other. This 'coalition' of sorts, however, has important implications for the kind of gender power hierarchies that are now becoming embedded within the labour market. Whereas the shift towards flexible employment and atypical working patterns has encouraged a greater amount of women with responsibilities of care in the family to (re-) enter the labour market, it has also served to crystallise gender power hierarchies. The introduction of flexibility has not challenged the male-breadwinner model, but has increased the pressure on women to participate in the official labour market. Gender divisions of labour in the private have remained by and large unaltered, whilst employment security has been undermined (Bailyn *et al.*, 2001: 12–3; Rubery *et al.*, 1999).

Two EU policies have sought to establish a framework of employment rights for atypical workers. In the first instance the Working Time Directive (93/104/EC) sought to establish 'minimum safety and health requirements for the organisation of working time, minimum periods of daily rest, weekly rest and annual leave, breaks and maximum weekly time, certain aspects of night work, shift work and patterns of work' (EFILWC, 2002: 2). The overall thrust of this policy is to ensure that employment structures allow for work–life balance. As a matter of fact, the main aim of this policy is to chal-lenge the long-hours work culture that, over the last two decades, has become entrenched within the European labour market. Clearly, this issue is also central to the development of a family-friendly workplace; however, it does not in itself presume a more substantive challenge to the gender bias present within the labour market (Fagan and Burchell, 2002; Guerrina, 2003b).

The principles enshrined within this policy are very important for the establishment of a greater commitment to substantive equality, particularly as it implicitly recognises the impact of the long-hours culture on the private lives of European workers. As Fagan and Burchell (2002: 57) explain, this policy is 'designed to promote the quality of working life through setting upper limits on the volume of working hours'. As various surveys have shown, the demands of the labour market for long hours are diametrically opposed to the demands of the family; and it is widely accepted that the opposition between public responsibility and private duties is responsible for the sharp decrease in European birth rates. These trends have important consequences for the long-term success of the European economy and have consequently come to the forefront of the employment agenda. Given this assessment, it is possible to conclude that despite the achievements of this policy in highlighting the impact of employment practices on the lives of European workers, the underlying economic agenda ultimately brings into question the motives of member states' governments for embarking upon such a project. More specifically, this underlying agenda undermines overall effectiveness of these provisions in the quest for substantive equality (Fagan and Burchell, 2002; Guerrina, 2003a; Hantrais, 2000: 72–3).

The Part-Time Worker Directive (97/81/EC) seeks to deal specifically with the issue of atypical work. Like the Parental Leave Directive, the negotiations for this policy took place under the auspices of the Social Agreement. The original proposal sought to deal with various forms of atypical work such as temporary or occasional employment; however, the final framework agreement only covered part-time work. The aim of the original Commission's proposal was to minimise the use of atypical work patterns and the impact of this type of employment contract on workers. The negotiations were wrought with disagreement between the social partners, who advocated different forms of flexibility. Whereas the representatives of labour sought to minimise the impact of atypical work on the rights of workers, the representatives of trade and industry sought to establish a framework which would allow them to pursue an increasingly deregulatory agenda. For employers, the negotiations on part-time and atypical work symbolised a move towards increased flexibility of the European labour market (Deakin and Reed, 2000; EFILWC, 2002; Falkner, 1998).

The final draft of the agreement 'established a general framework for the elimination of discrimination against part-time workers and for the development of opportunities for part-time working' (EFILWC, 2002: 3). For Deakin and Reed, the tensions and conflicting interests that marred the negotiations are evident in the final draft of the directive:

> on the one hand, Member States and the social partner are required to observe the principle of equal (or at least proportionate) treatment between part-time and full-time workers. ... On the other hand, the Directive speaks to a deregulatory agenda when it calls on Member States and the social partners to identify and review potential obstacles to part-time work and, where possible, to elimi-

nate them, subject only to the principle of non-discrimination between part-time and full-time workers. (Deakin and Reed, 2000: 75)

This assessment further outlines some of the dangers of relying on the regulations of atypical work to achieve substantive equality. Although it is important to challenge the assumption that only traditional forms of employment are worthy of protection, the framework that has become established within the EU for the protection of part-time, atypical workers as well as traditional workers, falls short of the ideal of substantive equality.

This directive thus fails to address the more substantial concerns surrounding atypical employment, namely the increasing gender segregation of the employment market. Although part-time work can help working mothers to re-enter the labour market, it does not challenge the male-breadwinner model that supports gender divisions of labour in the private. In this context, the position of the European Union and its member states continues to be one of paternalist protection for working women (Guerrina, 2003; Webster, 2000).

Given the discrepancies between rhetoric and reality that have started to emerge in the analysis presented here, this chapter will conclude with a discussion of the questions and puzzles arising from the development of a European policy on work–life balance. In particular, I will highlight some of the inconsistencies arising from the stated aims and objectives of the various policies and the overall framework within which such developments have been ratified and implemented.

Legislative questions and puzzles

This chapter has evaluated how family-friendly policies have become established as a key strategy for achieving the goals of the European equality agenda. What has emerged from the analysis presented in this chapter is that, despite the fact that the principles of work–life balance and flexibility have become common currency amongst policy-makers and employers alike, they have been used to support conflicting agendas. One the one hand, the equality agenda has sought to provide the context for the development of a women-friendly workplace; on the other, employers and the business community have keen to deregulate the employment market. These conflicting agendas have important repercussions on the overall achievements of the policies under discussion. Since the ratification of the Treaty of Maastricht, member states' governments have been keen to devolve decision-making in the area of employment and social policy to the Social Partners. The economic focus of policies for the reconciliation between work and family life draws attention to the bias inherent in the policy-making process.

Although the stated aim of the various Community programmes on equal opportunities has been to develop a 'women-friendly' labour market,

European institutions have not paid much attention to the impact of gender upon the context within which these policies have been developed. For instance concepts such as woman, mother, father, and family have been incorporated within the official texts as universals without any reflection on the values embedded within them. What becomes clear from the analysis presented here is that little consideration has been given to the divisions between formal and substantive equality. The main European policy actors have been incapable of addressing the relationship between the public and the private sphere in a way that challenges traditional gender power hierarchies.

What emerges from this analysis also are contrasting interpretations of the role of the European Union in social, economic and political affairs. If, as it is starting to transpire, the underlying aims of EU policies and equal rights legislation is to maintain a *stable and traditional* family as the basic building structure of the Union (Aldinger-Tziovas, 1984), then substantive equality will remain a secondary objective to equal pay. To be effective, new policy developments need to take on board the wide-ranging changes that marked the transition between the twentieth- and twenty-first-century social politics in Europe. Equal rights legislation, and work–life balance as an inherent feature of this policy area, must therefore reflect changes in women's expectations and participation in the official labour market. One issue that immediately emerges from the analysis presented in this chapter, and particularly with reference to parental leave and working time allocation, is the obstinate lack of reference to women's double burden. The policies have been widely criticised because, far from establishing a framework for substantive equality, they reinforce the male-breadwinner model and put extra pressure on women to participate in the official labour market on top of fulfilling the caring role in the family. In this context, these policies should be seen as women-friendly rather than family-friendly. The ultimate outcome of such perspective is the overarching failure of the principle of reconciliation between work and family life to challenge gender power hierarchies and divisions of labour in the private (Collins, 1994: 31; Hoskyns, 1994: 227).

Since the early 1980s, various Community action programmes have sought to redefine both women's role in the official labour market and gendered divisions of labour in the private sphere. The focus of European provisions on women's rights has undoubtedly been widening. However, the European labour market remains predominantly structured around male norms of work and worker, which ultimately is the biggest obstacle to the achievement of substantive equality (Pillinger, 1991: 8). As Hoskyns (1994: 234) explains,

> an examination of the structures of the EC, including those specifically dealing with the development of policy on women's rights, reveals deeply entrenched patriarchy. This is not just due to the small number of women present at the top, but rests much more centrally on the acceptance right through the institutions of a wide variety of gendered assumptions.

It is such gender power hierarchies that have become embedded within the European equality agenda and restrict the scope of family-friendly policies. In terms of the analysis presented in this book, it is these structures that are to be blamed for the lack of substantive equality within European policies.

To conclude, it is important to acknowledge that the EU might have provided a set of standards for the *protection* of working women, particularly in terms of maternity legislation. Unfortunately, the failure of European policies to address structural concerns surrounding women's employment patterns limits their overall scope to the public sphere. Women continue to be the focus of the equality agenda, even when the rhetoric seeks to encourage men to take on a greater share of the responsibilities of care. As Collins (1994: 322) explains,

> granting parents equal shares in parental leave, for example, means little choice for a couple with big differences in earning and career potential. Until men can take an equal share in the work of child-care and home life without financial or employment prejudice to either partner, they will not do it and women will be scorned for expecting them to.

In the same way, maternity legislation is based on stereotypical assumptions about the relationship between the social and the biological function of mothering. By failing to address the impact of gender structures on the policy-making process, the legislation reinforces the *status quo*. By contrast, in order to achieve substantive equality, it is necessary that European institutions and member states' governments recognise that the gender neutrality of employment policies and the economic agenda of the single market is not so neutral after all. Rather, it is important to draw attention to the social, political and economic framework within which the principle of reconciliation developed. This is not to say that policies for the reconciliation of work and family life cannot help to challenge gender power hierarchies. However, in order to achieve this objective, it has to be clear to policy-makers and employers alike that this is indeed one of the ultimate objectives of family-friendly policies and that flexibility cannot solely focus on the needs of the market. This approach ultimately entails a long-term perspective that recognises the implications of maintaining traditional gender hierarchies for the European economy.

Aware that 'attitudes and values which support and constrain female roles and the perception of those roles by both women and men have been changing in recent years', and that 'Europe is a large and complex cultural area and generalisations which refer to the whole continent are hazardous' (Buckley and Anderson, 1988: 14), it is nevertheless important to conduct an in-depth analysis of the representations that have instigated the debate about reconciliation between work and family life in the EU. With consideration of the differences between the member states, and the difficulties present in talking about European values, the next three chapters will focus on the impact of these policies on the rulings of the ECJ, and the European equality agenda on the development of women's rights and the incorporation of work–life balance within the socio-economic and legal framework of selected member states.

4

The European Court of Justice: ruling on gender

When considering the role of the European Court of Justice (ECJ) in promoting women's rights, it is essential to understand the impact of gender power hierarchies on the overall structure, function and nature of European and international law. In many ways, the EU is a microcosm of European social and political relations. It thus follows that European legal and political structures reflect gender dynamics at the national level. These issues have already been partially dealt with in the previous two chapters. For the time being, suffice to say that despite the rhetoric of the European equality agenda, gender relations within European institutions have been far from exemplary. As Shaw (1999: 15) points out, 'right up to the present time, most of the institutions of the European Union have had a very poor record in relation to the participation and employment of women'. The ECJ has been no exception.

Yet, over the last thirty years, the ECJ has been one of the main players in the field of equal rights. As discussed in chapter 2, the Court was instrumental in ensuring the application of the principle of equal pay in the 1970s. Since then, it has developed an extensive body of case law in the field of equality and equal rights. Its role as advocate for women's rights, however, is neither straightforward nor uncontroversial. This chapter will explore the assumptions about gender structures, mothering and the relationship between the public and the private sphere that emerge from the Court's interpretation of the European equality agenda.

The Court has seen a dramatic increase in the amount of cases seeking a clarification of the aims and scope of the principles enshrined within the Treaties and the equality directives. As Wobbe (2003: 98) explains, 'the interaction between the Court of Justice, the national courts, and individual litigants has increased ... The Court of Justice and national courts have engaged in dialogue regarding the meaning of EC gender equality in employment sources'. This dialogue is important for four main reasons: firstly, it has significant repercussions on the scope of the policies in question; secondly, it highlights the persistence of gender inequalities in the public sphere; thirdly, it emphasises the lines of conflict between the social/equality agenda and the business/economic agenda; finally, it raises important questions about the role of the Courts for the implementation of a wider equality agenda.

For Hoskyns (1996: 159) it is possible to distinguish between two types of equality rulings, one focusing on employment, the other on social security. The sheer number of cases brought forward under the employment umbrella as well as the Court's willingness to forcefully implement the principle of formal equality has meant that the rulings in the field of employment have had much greater reach than those in the field of social security. Unfortunately, this development has had negative implications for the insti-tutionalisation of the principle of substantive equality, as the area of social security, by its very nature, is more likely to challenge the binary opposition of public and private. This division between social security and employment is particularly interesting for the analysis presented here, as it highlights the difficulty enshrined within the implementation of a wider equality agenda within a socio-economic framework that favours male norms of employment and participation.

This chapter is divided into three sections. Section one will explore current debates about the role of the Court in promoting women's rights. As part of this discussion, it will also trace a brief history of the trends in the Court's judgement in the area of equality. Section two will assess current debates about the position of the traditional family in the judgements of the ECJ. This section will seek to uncover some of the idiosyncrasies that charac-terise the position of the Court vis-à-vis the public–private dichotomy, gender roles and gender divisions of labour. Section three will assess some of the most significant cases in the area of reconciliation between work and family life. Through the analysis of these cases, this section will bring to light some of the current trends, assumptions and biases that inform the Court's judgements in this particular policy area. In the conclusion of the chapter, I will use the analysis of the selected cases to highlight the effectiveness of the family-friendly agenda and its impact on the establishment of substantive equality as a working principle and the role of the ECJ as an advocate of women's rights.

The role of the Court in promoting womens's rights

Historically, the ECJ has played a crucial role in protecting women's rights. So much so that Hoskyns (1996: 158) claims that aside from the *Defrenne* judge-ments, between 1980 and 1992 'policy development was underpinned and given a continuing importance by a series of rulings from the European Court of Justice relating to the interpretation and enforcement of Article 119 and the three Directives adopted in the seventies'. Although an important player in the area of equal rights, the Court has sought various opportunities to advance its own agenda as part of the process of European integration. For some commentators, equal rights represents an area in which the Court has been able to assert and expand its power.

Judicial politics at the European level are a multi-faceted affair. Judicial activism on the side of national and European judges is an important element in this process, which is essentially remote from the European public (Tesoka, 1999: 17–18). The interaction of various interests determines the politics of such activism and can be seen in a rather inconsistent approach to the issue of equality. As Hoskyns (1996: 159) explains 'the ECJ's now numerous rulings on equal treatment are a mixed bag from the point of view of improving the situation of women, even given the wide range of views that exist on what that might involve'. There are several reasons that can explain these trends, but two have emerged from the current literature as the most plausible explanations: 1. The achievement of equality is one of the main objectives of the Court; 2. The Court used equality rulings in order to promote its own self-serving agenda (Hoskyns, 1996: 159; Shaw, 1999; Tesoka, 1999).

As briefly outlined above, employment is the area in which the Court has been most successful in protecting women's rights. Aside from the *Defrenne* cases, which were discussed in chapter 2, there are a number of other cases that have defined the wider framework for the establishment of equality in the EU. For Hoskyns (1996: 159), in some of those cases, the ECJ has been nothing less than radical in its interpretation of the principles enshrined within European documents. For instance, the Court's position in the case of part-time and pregnant workers has increased the recognition and the importance of women's issues within European policy-making arenas. Tesoka (1999: 18) supports this position, claiming that 'Community legal developments on gender issues have successfully challenged the imagination of players in the field and provided a real window of opportunity for judicial action in the field'. This willingness can be explained by linking the Court's agenda to European integration at large. It is also the case that equality in employment, or formal equality, is by and large an unquestionable and unquestioned principle.

Charpentier's (1998: 4) assessment of the Court's position in the case of positive discrimination leads him to conclude that the judges are aware of the tension implicit with dealing with the social and economic aims of European integration. He goes as far as to claim that the Court has sought to maintain a balance between these objectives. It is the role of the ECJ as an independent body with the interests of the Community at heart that has allowed it to play an important role as an advocate of women's rights. As he explains, 'the ECJ has played a major role in the mutation of national legal systems in the past 20 years, and has greatly contributed to the construction of a common legal patrimony, particularly in the field of gender equality' (Charpentier, 1998: 4). Although the role of the ECJ in establishing a comprehensive framework for the protection of formal equality is undisputed, its record in promoting substantive equality is somewhat less unblemished. As the analysis of section three will show, the Court is indeed aware of the complexities of socio-political and economic interactions at the European level, unfortunately, such awareness seems significantly more limited in the area of gender relations. In many ways, the Court has been unwilling to recognise the overwhelming power of gender structures because 'gender can have a disruptive power, challenging the conceptual bases driving two parallel agendas of a legal *and* political Court, such as "reason", "constitution" and "integration"' (Shaw, 1999: 1).

The Court's interpretation of the overarching objectives of European integration and its role within this process has important implications for the establishment of substantive equality as a working principle. This is all the more true when considering the relationship between national and European judicial structures. As a matter of fact, the vast majority of equality cases in which the Court is asked to adjudicate fall under the category of preliminary rulings. In this context, the Court's power is limited in a variety of ways. Firstly, in the case of preliminary rulings, the Court provides an opinion on the interpretation of European law, it 'does not actually decide the case' (Shaw, 1999: 10). Secondly, by the very nature of this procedure, the Court is dependent upon national courts referring a question to the European level. Finally, the scope of the ruling is limited to the actual questions posed to the Court. This means that the ECJ does not have the same power and/or authority as other institutions in constructing a framework for the operationalisation of equality (Shaw, 1999: 10).

Given the operational constraints the Court is faced with, it is worth noting that its work in the area of equality has been substantial and wide reaching. So much so that it is possible to divide the bulk of the ECJ's work in the area of equality into four broad categories: 1. Equal Pay; 2. Equal Treatment; 3. Social Security and Pensions; 4. Family-friendly policies. Section three of this chapter will discuss in detail the Court's position in the area of family-friendly polices. This section will discuss the first three categories, as they provide the backdrop against which the Court has developed its position on equality and work–life balance.

As discussed extensively in chapter 2, equal pay is the oldest equality provision introduced at the European level. Given the long-standing history of equal pay, it may come as a surprise that it is still one of the key areas of work for the Court. However, the permanence of a pay gap between men and women in the European labour market has ensured 'that issues of equal pay remain a constant preoccupation in case law before the Court of Justice' (Shaw, 1999: 11). The scope of such rulings, however, is limited by overarching constraints of the principle itself. They thus play an important role in strengthening the position of formal equality, but have only limited influence in terms of promoting substantive equality.

There is also a large body of case law in the area of equal treatment, even though the most interesting cases deal with the principle of affirmative/positive action. These rulings are particularly important because they test the Court's understanding of gender and highlight the mono-dimensional approach of the Court to the advancement of equality. Three cases are of particular interest: *Delauche* (1987); *Kalanke* (1995); and *Marshall* (1993).

The *Delauche v Commission* case sought to establish the legality of affirmative action programmes in the context of promoting equality of treatment (Charpentier, 1998: 4). The Court ultimately dismissed the case, but for Charpentier the approach of the Court signals the establishment of some worrying trends. As he explains,

> the ECJ's endorsement of a pure utilitarian perspective in order to assess the legality of preferential promotion focused exclusively on social utility. This in turn allowed the judges to avoid the most troublesome problem of assessing whether the pursuit of social utility frustrated Ms Delauche's individual right to equal opportunity. (Charpentier, 1998: 4)

As he further explains, this approach ultimately reinforces the bias in favour of formal equality at the expense of substantive equality.

The problems of this particular interpretation of the equality agenda became obvious in the *Kalanke* case. In this particular case the claimant argued that national provisions for affirmative action, that gave priority to the appointment of female officers in the case of two candidates (one male and one female) being equally qualified, was in direct contravention with the principle of equal treatment as established under European law. The Court supported the claim, stating that 'the purpose of directive 76/207/EC is to achieve equal opportunities between men and women, and not to guarantee to women equality of results' (Charpentier, 1998: 2). This particular interpretation of the principles enshrined with the equality directives, particularly the Equal Treatment Directive, highlights the overarching bias of the Court in favour of a concept of equality that creates only minimal disturbance of current socio-economic structures. Moreover, it challenged the possibility of developing affirmative action at the national and subnational level, further limiting the scope of the European equality agenda. The only positive outcome of this case was to bring the issue of equality back on the European agenda. This process ultimately resulted in a reworking of Article 119/141 to ensure the convergence of the aims of affirmative action and equality of treatment (Charpentier, 1998: 2–3; Shaw, 1999).

The opinion of the Advocate General in this case is particularly telling of the overarching nature of gender power hierarchies and how they play themselves out within the Court. As Charpentier (1998: 7) summarises:

> while analyzing the discrimination of women in the workplace, AG Tesauro mentions 'disadvantages' or 'disequilibriums' that would not be the product of separable or clearly definable acts of the employers, but the mere reflection inside

the organization of 'external' discrimination which has been occurring in the private sphere and the educational system. Since private life is reputed not to be covered by the equal treatment directive, it results that EC law shall not govern the domain of allocation that encompasses the social good targeted by the relevant domain of account ... Accordingly, this results in no apparent linear and direct link between the employer's behaviour (lack of evidence concerning a violation of equality law) and the situation of women in the organization.

The division between public roles and private duties is important for the analysis presented here. It highlights the persistence of binary oppositions that prevent the establishment of the necessary analytical and policy framework for the promotion of substantive equality. More specifically, although the Court apparently protects equality, it fails to acknowledge the complexity of gender relations and their impact on the ultimate achievement of the aims of the principle itself.

In contrast to *Kalanke*, in the case of *Marshall* the ECJ found that affirmative action and equality of treatment are complementary, in as far as they seek to achieve the same objectives. As Charpentier (1998: 1) explains, in this case the Court did judge there to be a conflict between these two principles, but interpreted their objectives as 'discoursive replies to the same dilemma'. What is particularly interesting about this case is the difference between the opinion of the Advocate General and the actual ruling of the Court. Although the Advocate General's opinion encouraged the Court to uphold the findings of *Kalanke*, the Court found that if the candidates were given due consideration and the individual merits of each case were considered thoroughly, then affirmative action was not in violation of the equal treatment principle. Key to the Court's ruling was the focus on individual merit and achievement (Charpentier, 1998).

For Charpentier, *Marshall* represents a turning point in the Court's understanding of the link between justice and equality. As he further explains,

> the decision of the Court ... joins together rhetoric as a *creative process* helping the judges to admit a more substantive and complex conception of equality, and rhetoric as a *wilful discursive operation* to warrant affirmative action while keeping antidiscrimination as the mediating principle that controls the meaning and content of the equal treatment directive. (Charpentier, 1998: 3)

Unfortunately, the scope of this ruling is limited by two issues. Firstly, the opinion of the Advocate General highlights an implicit institutional resistance to the establishment of justice as the driving principle behind equality; secondly, affirmative action is only permitted under certain/special circumstances, thus only marginally challenging the opinion of the Advocate General in the *Kalanke* case that distinguishes between principle and practice, and principle and outcome.

In terms of family-friendly policies it is possible to distinguish between rights of pregnant workers, parental leave and rights of part-time workers.

The issues emerging from recent rulings in the area of maternity rights and parental leave will be discussed later in this chapter; for now, it is important to note the impact of the case of *Bilka* (1986), on the establishment of an institutional framework that is sensitive to the needs of working mothers. In *Bilka*, the Court found that part-time workers are covered by the Equal Treatment Directive, and discrimination against part-time workers, who are mainly women, is tantamount to indirect discrimination. For Hoskyns (1996: 159) this case is a watershed in the establishment of a women friendly workplace. As she explains, 'in this it has had some success, despite the fact that the Council of Ministers has consistently failed to legislate in a similar direction. The significance of these rulings is that they begin to give a higher status in law to part-time work and the women who do it' (Hoskyns, 1996: 159).

The analysis presented here of the role of the ECJ in promoting and protecting women's rights allows us to draw some preliminary conclusions. The Court seems to be reacting to labour market trends which are seeking a flexibility-driven diversification of the workforce. As part of this shift in employment practices, the Court has started to recognise women's role and contributions to the European economy. The enforcement of substantive equality through case law, particularly through equal pay cases, is testament to the Court's commitment to equality of opportunities. For Hoskyns (1996: 159–60), judicial politics in this area is also starting to accept a wider notion of equality based on Bacchi's principle of 'same difference'. Unfortunately, this brief analysis also points out another trend, which is characterised by a staunch refusal to accept the link between public and private, as well as between equality and justice. Persistent focus on equality of opportunities highlights an institutional bias in favour of the economic aims of European integration, at the expense of greater recognition that social and economic trends are linked and mutually reinforcing. This analysis also starts to bring to light some of the issues that ultimately limit the overall impact of EU law in the area of work–life balance: substantive equality is secondary to economic outcomes and the family is portrayed as distinct and separate from economic structures (Hoskyns, 1996: 160).

The ECJ on family relations – some general considerations

As discussed in the previous section, the ECJ has been an important advocate for the full implementation of the 1976 Directive. Ellis argues that, strong in its role of guardian of equal rights legislation, the Court firmly proved that it would be 'most unlikely to permit exception to the Equal Treatment Directive other than those which are expressly mentioned in the instrument' (Ellis, 1991: 162). One of the exceptions upheld, however, was with regards to pregnancy. Although the ECJ has been a radical force in the Community, it has found the issues of motherhood and maternity difficult to deal with. In ruling about motherhood and maternity the ECJ has thus chosen a more conservative course of action. As stated by a Court official on the issue of maternity and paternity leave, European law 'is not designed to settle questions concerned with the organisation of the family, or to alter the division of responsibility between parents' (in Ellis, 1991: 162). The rationale behind the decision was thus justified as follows:

> a measure such as maternity leave granted to a woman on expiry of the statutory protective period falls within the scope of Article 2(3) of Directive 76/207, inasmuch as it seeks to protect a woman in connection with the effects of pregnancy and motherhood. That being so, such leave may legitimately be reserved to the mother to the exclusion of any other person, in view of the fact that it is the mother who may find herself subject to undesirable pressures to return to work. (In Ellis, 1991: 162)

The question that needs to be addressed here is what do working women need protecting from? Or in other words, what kind of social hierarchies is the ECJ protecting by taking such a stance? What this ruling does not account for is the gendered division of labour and the impact it has on the implementation of the underlying principles of the directive.

Further analysis of the last two statements by the Advocate General highlights a conceptual distinction between pregnancy and motherhood. The Court introduced the concept of motherhood to emphasise the difference between the need for post-partum protection of the health and safety of the worker, and the need to protect the development of the special relationship between a mother and a child. Ellis therefore argues that Article 2(3) of the Equal Treatment Directive could and might be interpreted as a means of legitimising 'other forms of preferential treatment for mothers which are based on outdated notions of parental role-playing within the family' (Ellis, 1991: 162). Taking this analysis further, it appears that the ECJ's ideology of mothering reinforces the same gendered power hierarchies that are entrenched within the concepts of 'woman', 'mother' and 'mothering'. In other words, a mechanism is instituted that strengthens traditional gender roles by means of the application and implementation of the directives (McGlynn, 2001b).

What is starting to become clear from the analysis of European case law is the prevalence of traditional conceptualisations of the family within the Court. These assumptions permeate the Court's understanding of family relations and their impact on the employment practices of men and women. The Court's understanding of gender relations is particularly evident in its rulings in cases in which maternity and pregnancy are at issue. As it will be discussed in detail in the next section of this chapter, over the last ten years the Court has been building up a body of case law against the dismissal of pregnant workers, or workers who have recently given birth. This is perhaps the most significant contribution of the Court to the establishment of comprehensive maternity rights in Europe. However, there is a cost attached to this endorsement: the scope of maternity rights has been constrained in line with the Court's understanding of (formal) equality.

For Caracciolo di Torrella (2000: 185–6) the work of the Court in the area of maternity rights can be divided into two categories: 1. Clarification of the meaning and principles of equal treatment; 2. Expansion of protection for pregnant workers and workers who have recently given birth. It is through a combination of these two processes that the Court came to recognise that discrimination on the grounds of pregnancy is tantamount to direct discrimination. As will become increasingly clear through the analysis of selected cases, the focus of the Court in this particular area is on the relationship between mother and child. In this context, the Court's focus on the protection of pregnant workers has been at the expense of any greater understanding of the role of gender in limiting women's access to equal rights. In doing so, the Court is able to ignore or deny the influence of gender on the judicial process.

McGlynn (2001b: 326) supports this analysis and argues that the Court has actively interpreted European social provisions to construct a concept of family that is in line with traditional values and hierarchies. In this context, she explains that 'the ideology of the "family" privileged by the European Court is that of the traditional "nuclear" family' (McGlynn, 2001b: 326). In *Marshall*, the opinion of the Attorney General includes a limited awareness of the interactions between socio-economic structures and gender power hierarchies. Such awareness, however does not acknowledge the link between women's roles in the family and the reproductive process on the one hand, and the marginalisation of women in the official labour market on the other; to the point that, as Charpentier (1998: 8) explains, 'it takes equality as a simple distributive condition following which, if both female and male candidates have equivalent qualifications, then they are equal'. This understanding of social and economic relations is very superficial, in as far as it fails to acknowledge the overarching nature of sexual relations of domination. Such an approach is also evident in the analysis of the Court's ruling in matters of social security. Its reluctance to 'establish the economic value of unpaid work or caring' (Hoskyns, 1996: 160) highlights the Court's assumptions about employment, gender and power. In taking this standpoint, the Court commits two mistakes: firstly, it reinforces the binary opposition of public and private; secondly, it portrays women as a homogenous group. As a result, the Court fails to challenge traditional power structures and gender hierarchies (Charpentier, 1998: 9; Hoskyns, 1996: 160).

In terms of mothering and women's roles as carers, the Court's biases were evident in two early cases: *Commission* v *Italy*, and *Hofmann* v *Ersatzkasse*. The 1983 case *Commission* v *Italy* will be discussed in much greater detail in the next chapter which will look at the impact of the EU policies on Italian gender politics. For now, suffice to say that the reason for the Commission's action was a discrepancy in Italian maternity law which, in case of adoption, gave women, but not men, access to leave. The argument presented by the Italian government in support of its policies was that such provisions were included to ensure that adopted children had the best possible start with their new family. In this context, the government felt that the conditions for entry into a family of natural and adopted children should be as similar as possible. What this meant was that the mother should be present to help the child to make the transition into his/her new family. As McGlynn (2001b: 331) explains, the position of the Italian government highlights the permanence of gender divisions of labour and gendered assumptions about women and mothering. As such, the 'decisive role of the mother (not the father) is emphasized, together with the implication that without this the emotional development of the child be harmed' (McGlynn, 2001b: 331–2).

The Court accepted this explanation, and thus the assumptions upon which it was based. For McGlynn (2001b: 332) 'underpinning this judgement is the belief that different treatment on account of motherhood (and not biological differences regarding the capacity to give birth) does not constitute unlawful discrimination'. It is clear that in the opinion of the Court, mothering warrants protection because it fulfils an essential social function. Unfortunately, the disassociation of women's rights and equality from the protection of women's mothering reinforces gender divisions of labour and power hierarchies in the public and the private. It is in this context that it is possible to ascertain the continued power of the male breadwinner model as the founding principle of European welfare systems (McGlynn, 2001b: 332).

Similarly, in the case of *Hofmann* (184/83), under German maternity provisions only women were entitled to an additional eight weeks' leave following childbirth. Once again, the rationale for such choice is to be found in the government's normative judgement about the importance of the male breadwinner model (McGlynn, 2001b: 332–3). The position of the Court in this particular case reinforces the findings of the analysis conducted above.

The Court's biases in the area of mothering are evident at every stage of the process. The Attorney General's initial opinion drew attention to the impact of gender divisions of labour and the double burden in order to justify the choice of the German government to provide extended leave only to women. As McGlynn (2001b: 333) explains, 'this is an argument which goes further than "protecting" women who are pregnant …: it preserves an ideology of motherhood that entails the performance of, and responsibility for, particular tasks within the home'. The Court went even further; when presented with the opportunity to challenge the public–private dichotomy and gender power hierarchies, it found refuge in such binary oppositions. Claiming that it was not the role of the Court to engage in some form of 'social engineering', it argued that 'EU law was not designed to settle questions relating to the "organisation of the family" or to "alter the division of responsibility between parents"' (McGlynn, 2001b: 333). It is interesting to note that the Court's judgement was based on four conflicting assumptions:

1. The Court, and the law that it interprets, are objective entities detached from society at large; 2. In maintaining the *status quo* the Court is not shaping society and social relations; 3. Public and private are separate and independent; 4. Pregnancy and mothering (particularly understood in terms of the mother–child relationship) are 'special' conditions that need to be protected (Hoskyns, 1996: 26, 160–1; McGlynn, 2001b: 335).

Some interesting trends emerge from the analysis of these two cases. Firstly, they provide some interesting insights into the ECJ interpretation of the role of women within the labour structures as well as within the family and society at large. Secondly, they highlight how the European equality agenda, as embedded in the equality directives, allows for the physical protection of the pregnant worker but fails to acknowledge the impact of gender in shaping the social practice of mothering. More worryingly, it would appear that the protection of the health and safety of pregnant workers has become equated with the protection of the social function of mothering and women's role as carers. In both cases, the Court called for the *mitigation* of substantive inequalities within the workplace, but failed to rule in favour of paid leave for the father. What this position highlights is a bias of the European judiciary in favour of formal equality at the expense of substantive equality, as well as chronic gender blindness. In seeking to maintain the public–private dichotomy, the Court ultimately reinforced gender power hierarchies (Ellis, 1991: 173; McGlynn, 2001b: 332–3; Prechal and Burrows, 1990: 110).

Even in the case of affirmative action, the Court's rulings seek to protect the social function of mothering. This bias arises from the overall thrust of the legislation, which focuses on the *protection* rather than the *promotion* of women's rights. Charpentier (1998: 12) explains that in taking such an approach 'their effects are ambivalent since they tend to maintain a perception of women as the less reliable part of the workforce, and reinforce their alleged prior commitment to the family'. Three assumptions are fundamental to this approach: 1. The male worker represents the norm for the employment market; 2. Women are the weaker sex/gender, and thus are in need of protecting; 3. The male-breadwinner model remains the standard for the organisation of interactions between the public and the private sphere. McGlynn (2001b) concurs with this assessment and argues that the Court's bias in favour of protecting women's role in the social function of reproduction highlights its implicitly gendered and paternalistic approach. In this context, far from challenging gender divisions of labour and power hierarchies, the Court becomes a key actor in maintaining them (Shaw, 1999: 23).

The ECJ's interpretation of gender roles – contradictions and representations

This section will consider how the dynamics outlined above are being played out through the analysis of selected cases. Three types of rulings will be considered, covering the broad framework of family-friendly policies: maternity rights, parental leave and access to childcare. By far the most extensive body of case law that has emerged over the last few years revolves around the implementation of the principles enshrined in the Pregnant Worker Directive, and thus focuses on maternity rights and the operationalisation of equality of treatment for pregnant workers. Although the legal foundations of these cases is the application of equal treatment, so vast is the body of case law in the area of pregnancy that it is possible to distinguish between three types of judgments: 1. Non-appointment or dismissal of pregnant workers; 2. Unfair dismissal relating to extended pregnancy-related illness and pregnancy; 3. Working conditions and equal treatment.

Maternity rights and equal treatment for pregnant workers
In the case of non-appointment of pregnant workers two cases articulated the position of the Court in this field: *Dekker* (1990) and *Webb* (1994). These cases are particularly important because they provide the background against which more recent cases, including *Mahlburg* (2000) and *Brandt-Nielsen* (2001), have been considered.

In *Dekker* v *VJV Centrum* (177/88, 1990), the complainant pursued a case against VJV because, despite being considered to be the most qualified and suitable candidate for the job in question, she was not appointed to the post on the grounds that the employer's insurance would not cover the economic expense of maternity leave (Caracciolo di Torrella, 2000: 186). Initiated before the ratification of the Pregnant Worker Directive, the background for this case was Article 2(1) and 3(1) of the Equal Treatment Directive.

In its judgement, the Court sent out some important signals that were to provide the foundations for the protection and promotion of women's rights as workers thereafter: 1. Pregnancy is not an illness; 2. Financial cost is not fair ground for dismissal or non-appointment. As Hoskyns (1996: 159) explains

> the ECJ in *Dekker* cut through a great deal of legal controversy and confusion by ruling that, because only women become pregnant, any kind of detriment in the work situation relating to pregnancy constitutes direct discrimination for which no justification can be argued. As a result, the pregnant woman as worker has gained both protection and greater legitimacy.

The repercussions of this case were enormous, in as far as it recognised the need to establish a body of law directly targeting the position of pregnant workers in the official labour market. It is thus unsurprising that, in terms of time frame, this case was followed by the ratification of the Pregnant Worker Directive, which was supposed to provide a clear set of guidelines for the protection of the heath and safety of pregnant workers and workers who have recently given birth (Hoskyns, 1996: 159; Wheat, 1998: 4).

McGlynn (1996: 238) and Caracciolo di Torrella (2000) claim that this case can be seen as a positive step in widening the scope of the European equality agenda. For both of them, the Court's focus on women, as bearers of rights, represents a significant change in emphasis. More significantly, this case establishes the foundations for the acknowledgement of difference as a means of protecting women's rights. The Court's interpretation of the principles enshrined in the Equal Treatment Directive is innovative and 'should also be regarded as an attempt to escape the limits of sex equality law' (Caracciolo di Torrella, 2000: 187). However, should the ECJ's position in this case be considered a positive move towards substantive equality? The only way to ascertain the answer to this question is by looking at the application of this ruling in later decisions by the Court.

The most notable case of dismissal on the grounds of pregnancy is the case of *Webb* v *EMO* (Case 32/93, 1994). In 1987, having announced to her employer that she was pregnant, Ms Webb received a letter informing her that despite having been appointed with permanent contract, the company would terminate her contract due to her pregnancy. The action that ensued highlights the prejudices of the employment market and legal structures against pregnant workers. As McGlynn (1996: 234) explains, 'it took the UK Courts eight years to recognise that the dismissal of Carole Webb because she was pregnant was discrimination on the grounds of sex'. The problem with this particular case emerged from a narrow interpretation of the principle of equality as sameness. In this context, pregnancy becomes a difficult concept/event to reconcile either with the needs of the market or those of formal equality (McGlynn, 1996: 234-7).

Faced with the conflicting requirements of employers and equal treatment, the House of Lords posed the following questions to the ECJ: does the 1976 Equal Treatment Directive cover dismissal on the grounds of sex or pregnancy if the following conditions apply. 1. The employee was appointed to cover the maternity leave of another employee; 2. The employer needs the said employee to be in post during the time of her maternity leave; 3. The employer would not have employed a pregnant worker, if her condition had been known at the time of appointment; 4. The employer would have applied the same treatment (i.e. dismissal) if it had hired a male employee for the same job and he was unable to fulfil the contractual requirements (C-32/93, paragraph 15). For McGlynn (1996: 237) the way in which these questions were posed to the ECJ represents a clear attempt by the Lords to find a loophole which would allow for the dismissal of pregnant workers.

Using the Court's judgements in the cases of *Dekker* and *Hertz*, and the Equal Treatment Directive (Articles 2 and 5) as the legal foundations for its decisions, the Court ruled that the dismissal of an employee on the grounds of pregnancy is indeed tantamount to discrimination. Discrimination is deemed to have occurred even though the said employee was initially appointed to cover another employee's maternity leave. For Wheat (1998: 5) this judgement 'had unequivocally rejected the view that pregnancy is a pathological condition'. This ruling pushed forward the equality agenda in two key areas. On the one hand it categorically rules that dismissal on the grounds of pregnancy amounts to direct discrimination, thus supporting the findings in *Dekker*; on the other, it recognises that pregnancy is a 'condition' in its own right, not comparable to disabling illnesses. According to McGlynn (1996: 241), 'at the end of the *Webb* litigation, and with the implementation of the Pregnant Worker Directive, it would appear that pregnant women are protected from pregnancy dismissals on two alternative grounds: unfair dismissal and sex discrimination'. Unfortunately, the Court allowed for a caveat to the application of these principles: the worker has to be in possession of a permanent/indefinite contract (McGlynn, 1996: 239). This case is important because it draws attention to the institutional obstacles that limit the scope of substantive equality at the national and European level. Moreover, current trends towards deregulation and flexibility, as dictated by the needs of employers, highlight some of the limits of maternity rights and family-friendly policies.

More recently, another case that has proved instrumental for the establishment of equality of treatment for pregnant workers is *Mahlburg* v *Mecklenburg-Vorpommern* (C-207/98, 2000). In this case the complainant was denied a permanent contract on the grounds of health and safety protection. Initially appointed on a fixed-term contract, once Ms Mahlburg notified her employer of her pregnancy, she was moved to alternative duties. According to her employer the legal grounds for refusing her appointment to a permanent contract was Article 2(3) of the Equal Treatment Directive which allows for a derogation of the equal treatment principle in case of maternity leave and/or pregnancy (Shaw, 1999: 12–13).

The Court was presented with the following question: is failure to appoint a qualified applicant to a permanent post due to her pregnancy tantamount to discrimination if at the time of appointment she is not able to fulfil her duties due to health and safety restrictions? (C-179/88, paragraph 18). The case was considered within the scope of Article 2(1) and 5(1) of the 1976 Equal Treatment Directive. Given the findings in *Dekker*, the Court upheld the complaint by Ms Mahlburg, arguing that discrimination against pregnant workers is a violation of the principle of equal treatment. There is, however, a caveat to this ruling: the principle applies only to workers in possession of indefinite/permanent contracts. Once again, financial arguments are insufficient justification for discrimination again pregnant workers (Shaw, 1999).

The case of *Brandt-Nielsen* v *Tele Danmark* (C-109/00, 2000) clarifies the position of the Court on such matters and highlights what may be a new, worrying trend that is becoming established within the European labour market. In this case the complainant was dismissed for failing to inform the employer of her pregnancy at the time of recruitment. The employer's position was supported by the Danish court, as Ms Brandt-Nielsen had been appointed on a fixed-term/temporary contract. The ECJ was thus faced with three questions: 1. Does a fixed-term contract, by its very nature limit the scope of protection against the dismissal of pregnant workers?; 2. Is it the duty of the pregnant worker to inform the employer of her condition at the time of recruitment?; 3. Is it acceptable to refuse to appoint a pregnant woman, if 'her pregnancy meant that the worker was unable to work for a significant portion of her period of employment'? (C-109/00, Paragraph 18).

Tele Danmark sought a favourable ruling on the grounds that, in this particular case, it would have incurred a significant loss by hiring this worker, who, due to the pregnancy, would have in fact been absent for a large part of the duration of the contract. For the employer, the issue at stake in this case was good faith, in as far as the employee knew at the time of recruitment that she would be 'unable to work for a substantial part of the contract' (Anon., 2001). Moreover, Tele Danmark argued that *Webb* recognises the impact of such a situation on employers and allows for dismissal of pregnant workers in case of fixed term contract.

The Attorney General Colomer disputed such a restrictive interpretation of the Court's position in *Webb* arguing that,

> this is an erroneous interpretation of the case-law, one which is overly faithful to the exact words used by the Court … It is true that the Court has made such declarations in the past. However, when making them, it restricted itself to taking the factual context of each c ase into consideration without prejudging whether the solution would have to be different where the contract was for a fixed, rather than an indefinite, term. (A.G. Opinion, paragraph 27)

In his opinion to the Court, the Attorney General contextualised the findings in *Webb*. This statement thus overturns the interpretation in *Webb* and sends a clear signal that the institutional view over the protection of pregnant workers has changed. The question that remains to be addressed is whether such change implies a move towards the promotion of substantive equality or is it a mere response to the provisions enshrined within the Pregnant Worker Directive, which had not been ratified at the time of *Webb*. Besides, by this point, the Court had clarified in the cases of *Dekker* and *Mahlburg* that financial loss is not a valid excuse for the dismissal and/or non-appointment of pregnant workers (Anon., 2001; C-109/00 paragraph 28)

In deciding upon this case, the Court referred back to Articles 3(1) and 5(1) of the Equal Treatment Directive and, the preamble and Article 10(1) of the Pregnant Worker Directive. Taken together, these provisions prohibit discrimination of any kind on the grounds of sex, including pregnancy. Given the equality directives and case law, the Court came to the following conclusions: 1. Pregnant workers have no obligation to inform the employers of their condition as the time of recruitment and/or appointment, for if such a provision was to exist, then it would 'render ineffective the protection of pregnant workers established by Article 10 of Directive 92/85' (C-109/00, paragraph 24). 2. Protection against dismissal as *per* Article 10 of the Pregnant

Worker Directive cannot be transcended, 'save in exceptional cases not connected with their condition where the employer justifies the dismissal in writing' (C-109/00, paragraph 27). 3. The protection of pregnant workers must, by its very nature, take priority over employers' needs and contractual agreements. Such a provision is essential to the proper implementation of the principles enshrined within the Equal Treatment Directive (C-109/00, paragraph 29). 4. The length of contract is irrelevant to the application of the principle of equal treatment. This is all the more relevant, as fixed term/temporary contracts can lead to a more permanent position (C-109/00, paragraph 32–33).

The discussion of these cases allows us to draw some preliminary conclusions. Each one of the cases outlined above provides a positive interpretation of the responsibilities of employers vis-à-vis the employment contract. The establishment of a solid foundation for the protection of pregnant workers in European law is particularly important at this particular juncture, as it is possible to envisage that these types of situations, particularly with regards to part-time and temporary contracts, will become increasingly more common in the future. The drive for increased flexibility in the European labour market could potentially undermine the position of women workers even further. Through these cases the Court has succeeded in clarifying the position of the European equality directives and has sent a clear signal vis-à-vis the extent of protection enshrined in European law.

In the context of the Court's position vis-à-vis the dismissal of pregnant workers it is also interesting to note its standpoint on the issue of pregnancy-related illness. Dismissal due to extended illness, normally pregnancy-related illness, raises some significant questions about the nature of maternity leave and the position of women on leave.

The case that has received the greatest amount of attention is that of *Hertz* v *Aldi Marked* (C179/88, 1990). In this case, the Court was faced with two questions: 1. Does pregnancy-related illness fall within the scope of the Equal Treatment Directive? 2. Are women on leave due to pregnancy-related illness protected indefinitely, or what are the temporal limits to the protection of pregnant workers who fall ill during the pregnancy? (Wheat, 1998: 3).

The argument presented to the Court was that it would be economically unfair to bind employers to pay for absences caused by pregnancy-related illness, particularly if such extended leave would lead to the dismissal of a male worker. Although the Equal Treatment Directive sought to protect women from discrimination arising from pregnancy, it did 'not envisage the case of an illness attributable to pregnancy or confinement' (Wheat, 1998: 3). Given this background, it was the view of the Court that pregnancy related illness should not be differentiated from any other type of disabling illness. The repercussions of this decision are very profound, and could be construed as an attempt by the Court to ensure market competitiveness. As Wynn (1999: 435) further explains, ever since the twin decisions of *Dekker* and *Hertz* the European Court of Justice has struggled to find an acceptable balance between the equality principle and the demands of a male oriented labour market. *Hertz* tipped the balance in favour of the latter by ruling that dismissal for absence after maternity leave was not discriminatory even where the illness originated in pregnancy.

This decision ultimately limits the scope of maternity rights and the protection available to pregnant workers (McGlynn, 1996: 238).

In *Brown* v *Rentokill* (C-394/96, 1998) the distinction between maternity rights/leave and rights of pregnant workers becomes even more acute. The case was referred to the ECJ by the Lords who posed the following question: can a pregnant worker who is absent for longer than the sick leave entitlement be rightfully dismissed as *per* employment contract? Implicit within this question are the following queries: can pregnancy-related illness be included in the normal period of sick leave to which a worker is entitled? Or, is sick leave due to pregnancy-related illness to be treated as a special case? (Wynn, 1999: 436–7).

In this case the Court ruled that 'protection against sex discrimination under Directive 76/207/EEC extended to all illnesses attributable to pregnancy which arose during the time of pregnancy. The Court also decided that the contractual term made no difference to the outcome' (Wynn, 1999: 436). In so doing, the Court recognised the 'special' and temporally limited nature of pregnancy-related illness. There is, however, a caveat to this principle. Protection against dismissal for extended leave due to pregnancy-related illness is only limited to the duration of the pregnancy and maternity leave. Unfortunately, the establishment of such a time limit allows for differential provisions across the Single Market, as the duration of maternity leave is determined by national regulations (Wynn, 1999: 437, 440).

The establishment of a time limit reinforced the Court's findings advanced in *Hertz* whereby protection against dismissal is tolerable only in as far as it does not compromise the long-term economic competitiveness of the firm/employer. As Wynn (1999: 438) further explains, this case is important because it 'clarified many of the questions relating to the legal protection afforded to women dismissed for pregnancy associated sickness'. It ensured that dismissal is prohibited for the duration of the pregnancy period and the related maternity leave, and thus clarified some of the ambiguities that emerged from the application of the Equal Treatment and Pregnant Worker Directives. However, it also established a new principle whereby the rights of women during pregnancy are distinct from those during the leave period (Wynn, 1999: 438–41).

Unfortunately, the case also reinforced assumptions that project male norms as standard for employment in the official labour market. It was assumed that absence due to pregnancy-related illness following maternity leave is to be considered on a par with disabling illnesses. The establishment of a temporal limit to such protection was deemed to allow for sufficient latitude to account for the 'special' nature of this particular illness (Wynn, 1999: 439). Wynn (1999: 441) concludes that the implications of this ruling are fourfold: firstly, it ignores the impact of gender segregation in the official labour market; secondly, it reinforces normative assumptions about work based upon the male standard; thirdly, it justifies discrimination against pregnant workers or workers who have recently given birth, albeit within limits; finally, it assumes that the 'costs' of motherhood end after confinement, thus reinforcing the public–private dichotomy.

The findings of *Brown* and *Hertz* were confirmed by the Court's judgement in *Larsson* (C-4000/95) and *Boyle* (C-411/96, 1998). On these occasions the Court ruled that discrimination on the grounds of extended absence due to pregnancy is justifiable inspecial circumstances, as in the case of *Larsson*. It also decreed that maternity leave is a block of time that is especially reserved to women and thus requires special protection. The analysis of dismissal for pregnancy-related illness thus leads us to the following conclusions: the protectionist nature of maternity rights and equal treatment provisions limit the scope of the European equality agenda and reinforce the paternalistic approach of the contemporary legal structures. Finally, it reasserts the hierarchy of values already presented with the market whereby justice is subservient to economic competitiveness (Wheat, 1998; Wynn, 1999: 444).

Working conditions and substantive rights for pregnant workers are another set of sensitive issues that the Court has to deal with in establishing the scope of maternity protection and equal treatment. Three cases seem to be particularly important in this context: *Habermann-Beltermann* (1994), *Thibault* (1998), and *Melgar* (2001). Here I will focus on the *Melgar* case because it highlights the links between equality, protection and promotion of women's rights. It also parallels some of the earlier discussions on unfair dismissal and draws attention to the predicament of a large number of women current employed on a part-time or temporary basis.

In the case of *Melgar* (C-438/99), the complainant was hired on a part-time basis for a limited period of time. The employer terminated the employment contract following Ms Melgar's announcement of her pregnancy. The questions posed before the Court were as follows: 1. Does the Pregnant Worker Directive, Article 10 in particular, have direct effect? (C-438/99, paragraph 20.1). 2. Does Article 10 of the Pregnant Worker Directive apply to workers in possession of a fixed-term contract? If so, is non-renewal of that contract due to pregnancy to be considered a violation of the principles of these provisions? (C-438, paragraphs 20.3 and 43).

In his preliminary opinion the Attorney General established that if the principles enshrined within European provisions are 'sufficiently clear, precise and unconditional, they are capable of producing direct effects' (paragraph 29). The Court reiterated this point drawing attention to the member states' responsibilities to implement and enforce European policies, in this case the principles established by the Pregnant Worker Directive (C-438/99, paragraph 20.2). Moreover, the case of *Brown* clearly highlights the special provisions that have to be upheld in order to protect the health and safety of pregnant worker and/or workers who have recently given birth (C-438/99, paragraph 38).

This case is important for two main reasons. Firstly, the Court reaffirmed the obligation on member states to uphold and enforce the obligations and principles of the European equality agenda. More specifically, 'the Court points out, first, that the provision in question imposes on the Member States, in particular in their capacity of employers, precise obligations which do not leave them any discretion in implementing them' (Anon., 2001). Secondly, although non-renewal of a contract does not equate to dismissal, it can, under certain circumstances, be deemed as failure to appoint and thus be regarded as direct discrimination (Anon., 2001)

The analysis of the cases outlined above starts to bring to light some interesting trends. In the first instance, it is possible to establish the permanence of discrimination against pregnant workers. Employers' economic gains seem to overtake any concern and consideration for justice and substantive equality. Secondly, although the Court has paid some lip service to the establishment of substantive rights, as in the case of *Thibault*, its rulings have crystallised the bias in favour of formal equality. In this context, it is possible to ascertain a certain degree of paternalism in the Court's interpretation of its role as 'protector' of women's rights. To conclude, it is now starting to become clear that the Court has succeeded in establishing a wide-reaching framework for the protection of formal rights, but has failed to challenge deeply-rooted assumptions about gender, gender roles and women's position in the official labour market.

Parental leave

In terms of parental leave two cases, *EUAPME* (1998) and *Lewen (1999)*, are particularly interesting for the analysis presented here. Both cases draw attention to the assumptions about gender and economic gains that pervade economic relations and judicial politics at the European level. In *EUAPME* v *Council of the European Union* (T-135/96) the complainant sought to challenge the very principles underpinning the parental leave directive. 'The European Association of Craft and Small and Medium-sized Enterprises (EUAPME) had brought the case, seeking principally the annulment of the June 1996 EU Directive on parental leave (96/34/EC), or secondarily the annulment of the Directive's applicability to small and medium-sized enterprises (SMEs)' (EFILWC, 1998). EUAPME claimed that during the negotiations that led to the ratification of the directive, the social partner failed to consult them.

On this occasion the Court dismissed the case, finding that EUAPME did not meet the legal requirements for being 'concerned' by the directive, and could thus not bring a case relating to it' (EFILWC, 1998). Although the case ultimately did not challenge the principle underpinning the Parental Leave Directive, it highlights the continued concern of employers with short-term economic gains rather than justice and substantive equality.

More important for the application of the principles of parental leave is *Lewen* v *Lothar Denda* (C-333/97). The background to this case highlights the impact maternity leave and leave for family reasons continue to have on women's pay and careers opportunities. The details of the case are as follows: following maternity leave and whilst on parental leave the plaintiff requested a Christmas bonus given to other employees. The legal foundations for the case are Article 119 (now 141), Article 11(2)(b) Pregnant Worker Directive, and Clause 2(6) Parental Leave Directive.

The questions posed before the Court raise some interesting issues about the link between pay and leave. First, the Court was asked to consider whether a bonus paid as recognition of work performed during the year and as incentive to ensure loyalty is to be considered within the scope of the principle of equal pay (Article 119). In second place, the Court was asked to deliberate on whether excluding women on parental leave from the award of a bonus, as such payment is to foster the relationship between employer and employee, is a violation of the principles enshrined within the Parental Leave and Pregnant Worker Directives. If the Court was to find that this provision was, in fact, a violation of such principles, can the employer then deduct an amount that is proportional to the period of leave, such as parental leave or compulsory maternity leave? (C-333/97, paragraph 16).

In this particular case the Court found that the award of a Christmas bonus, either for work performed during the year or as an additional incentive, is to be considered as pay. More specifically, in response to the first question the Court replied that 'for the purposes of Article 119, the reason for which an employer pays a benefit is of little importance provided that the benefit is granted in connection with employment' (C-333/97, paragraph 19). However, such bonus is not to be considered as part of the payments to be received during maternity leave as provided by the Pregnant Worker Directive or the Parental Leave Directive (C-333/97, paragraph 22). In response to the second question, the Court considered whether the practice constituted direct or indirect discrimination. On this particular issue the Court found that, given the gender division of labour in the family, women are more likely to be absent from the official labour market for a set period of time. The Court recognised the 'special' nature of maternity leave, but differentiated it from parental leave whereby the latter is to be considered as a temporary suspension of the contract of employment (C-333/97, paragraphs 33–4, 37, 41).

McGlynn (2001: 268) claims that the findings of the Court in this case send out conflicting signals. On the one hand, it recognises the special nature of maternity and its associated leave; on the other hand, it excludes some of the acquired benefits (as in this case the Christmas bonus) from the provi-

sions of the Parental Leave Directive, as this statement of the Court highlights:

> to exclude women who are on parenting leave at the time when the bonus is paid
> from the sphere of those potentially entitled to a special Christmas bonus does
> not take into account the fact that the employment relationships of those women
> still exist despite the suspension of their mutual obligations as a result of the
> parenting leave and accordingly that a mother on parenting leave continues to
> be loyal to the business. A threatened refusal of bonus payments may, moreover,
> contribute to dissuading women who have recently given birth from
> claiming their right to parenting leave in the interests of the child. (C-333/97,
> paragraph 15)

For McGlynn (2001) the Court's rationale in enforcing such rights was to
protect the special relationship between mother and child, rather then
promote substantive equality and widen the scope of family-friendly policies.
In this context, the norms upon which the Court's judgement are based reinforce gender divisions of labour. As she explains, 'this reinforces the
assumption that such childcare commitments are the primary responsibility
of women and it is only women whose employment rights require protection'
(McGlynn, 2001: 268). Unfortunately, this is a trend that we have already seen
in previous cases on the dismissal of pregnant workers and which will be reinforced by cases seeking to clarify the link between equal treatment and access
to childcare.

Access to childcare

The analysis of the ECJ's opinion in cases regarding access to childcare are
very interesting in view of the fact that the issue is covered by a Council
Recommendation and as such, it does not posses the same weight and power
bestowed to other policies discussed in this and the previous chapter.
However, as the case discussed in the previous section highlights, access to
childcare and assumptions about who is primarily responsible for discharging
this responsibility are important factors in the analysis of gender power hierarchies in the European labour market.

The first case worth mentioning in this context is *Gruber* v *Silhouette
International Schmied GmbH & Co* (C-249/97, 1999), where the link between
access and affordability of childcare and women's access to the official labour
market is particularly evident. This case is specifically about the link between
pay and access to childcare facilities. The issue at stake here was whether lack
of childcare services was an acceptable explanation as to why an employee
may reasonably be unable to continue with the employment contract.
Although the details of the case were about access to a higher rate of final
payment, the question at hand draws attention to the continued bias in favour
of male norms and employment patterns. In this case the Court found against
the complainant, ruling that the inability to access childcare does not consti-

tute a 'serious' enough reason for the termination of contract. In taking this standpoint, the Court chose to disregard what is perhaps the single greatest factor in limiting women's access to employment: inability to reconcile care work and the demands of the official labour market. In so doing, it ignored gender power hierarchies, it reinforced the division between public and private, and limited the scope of work–life balance in principle and in practice (Shaw, 1999: 12).

In the case of *Lommers* v *Minister van Landbouw, Natuurbeheer en Visseij* (C-476/99, 2002) the Court's ideology of mothering became very clear. The background was the restriction of access to childcare facilities only to women, in this case employees of the Dutch Ministry of Agriculture. Male employees were granted access to the nursery only in case of emergency, such as in the case of a single father who was responsible for discharging the primary responsibility of care. The position of the Ministry was supported by the Dutch Equality Commission, which welcomed this practice as an important part of allowing women to reconcile work and family life (C-476/99, paragraph 16). The Court was asked to consider whether such provisions were permissible under the Equal Treatment Directive.

The argument presented by Mr Lommers sought to challenge social assumptions about gender division of labour. Whereas the position of the Ministry was based on the claim that

> the priority given to women was the result of the Ministry's determination to tackle inequalities existing between male and female officials, as regards both the number of women working at the Ministry and their representation across the grades. The creation of subsidised nursery places is precisely the kind of measure needed to help to eliminate this *de facto* inequality. (C-476/99, paragraph 21)

The issues at stake in this case are very important because they are a direct challenge to gender power hierarchies and divisions of labour underlying the development of family-friendly policies. Mr Lommers' inability to access subsidised childcare, on an equal footing to female officials of the Ministry, highlights the inherently gendered nature of family-friendly policies. As contended in chapters 2 and 4, despite the gender-neutral language of these policies, they are, in fact, predominantly aimed at women, the implicit assumption being that it is women who are in charge of childcare, and who thus must be helped to reconcile public roles and private responsibilities. What this approach fails to tackle is deeply-rooted assumptions about gender divisions of labour that ultimately maintain (and in many cases reinforce) gender power hierarchies.

In its final decision the Court reiterated the statements of the Dutch equal opportunity commission, highlighting the fact that lack of affordable childcare is well recognised as the main reason why women are forced out of the official labour market. The measures adopted by the Ministry of Agriculture were supposed to provide women with the necessary infrastructure to continue working after pregnancy, and whilst fulfilling their responsibilities as mothers. In so doing these measures were portrayed as actively challenging structural inequalities and were viewed as a way of implementing substantive equality. In the context of this opinion, the Court recognised scholarly work in this field, which suggests that a gender-sensitive approach to policy would ultimately achieve an outcome that is much further-reaching if it seeks to challenge traditional divisions of labour (C-476/99, paragraphs 36–8, 42). In order to justify its ruling in support of the defendant, the Court explained that

> in the case now under consideration, account must be taken of the fact that, given the insufficiency of supply mentioned above, the number of nursery places available under the measure at issue is itself limited and that there are waiting lists for female officials working at the Ministry of Agriculture, so that they themselves have no guarantee of being able to obtain a place. (C-476/99, paragraph 43)

Moreover, as the Ministry's childcare policy was not seen to exclude men, in as far as male employee fulfilling the primary function of care could be considered on a par with a female employee with children, then the Court found that this policy was not in violation of the principles enshrined within the Equal Treatment Directive (C-476/99, paragraph 45).

It is interesting to note the Court's rationale/justifications for such a decision. In view of women's under-representation within the Ministry of Agriculture, the Court commended the implementation of such a scheme that sought to overcome structural impediments to women's pursuit of full-time employment. Moreover, given the limited nature of the resources available, the Court found that the Ministry was justified in targeting women as a special group. The exception, which allows for male employees fulfilling the primary function of care to have access to the same kind of provisions, ensures equality of treatment within this particular employment setting (C-476/99, paragraph 50). The Court recognises the limits of this approach in as far as it focuses on a single employer. However, it works on the principle that each employer is responsible for the implementation of equal opportunities in its enterprise (C-476/99, paragraph 49).

What becomes evident from this analysis is that the Court's position on equality and gender allocation of working time has served to maintain the division between formal and substantive equality in the Court's opinions. This is particularly apparent in the *Lommers* case, which constricted the scope of family-friendly policies by portraying them as women policies. Although it is clear that each employer has a duty towards its employees alone, what is not clear is why the application of equal opportunities should be limited to women. What starts to emerge is that the Court's position is the result of the protectionist nature of equal opportunities and maternity rights at the European level. Despite a semblance of substantive equality, the Court's narrow interpretation of the scope of reconciliation between work and family life ultimately serves to limit the reach of substantive equality.

Finally, the Court's interpretation of the scope of the Childcare Recommendations and the Equal Treatment Directive draws attention to prevalent assumptions about gender divisions of labour. The stated purpose of the Childcare Recommendations, the Equal Treatment Directive and Parental Leave Directive is to encourage a more equitable division of care in the family. Then, the application of these principles must ensure that men as well as women have access to those structures that would allow them to reconcile such responsibilities. This particular interpretation of the European equality agenda highlights that despite the gender neutrality of the language used in such policies, they are targeted predominantly at women, who continue to fulfil, and are perceived as primarily responsible for, care duties within the family.

Conclusions

Some interesting and important contradictions arise from the analysis of the Court's interpretation of the principles enshrined within the European equality directive, and more widely the overall aims of the European equality agenda. As discussed in the introduction of this chapter and more extensively in chapter 2, the European Court of Justice has been an important ally of women's rights. Its rulings have ensured the implementation of the principles established by the Treaties and the European equality directives. In the case of maternity rights, Caracciolo di Torrella (2000: 186–7) claims that the opinion the ECJ's judgement in the cases of *Hertz* (1990), *Habermann* (1994), *Webb* (1994), *Gillespie* (1996) and *Dekker* (1990) established a framework for the development of a comprehensive policy on maternity and pregnancy in Europe. Unfortunately, as has been argued in this chapter, the Court's judgements are also the product of the current gender order and, as such, they fail to challenge the very foundations of gender power hierarchies. What starts to transpire from the analysis presented above is that the ECJ struggles to reconcile the conflicting demands of substantive equality and business interests.

Given the current drive to increase the flexibility of the labour market, the limits of *Webb* (1994) and *Brown* (1998) have important repercussion for the position of working mothers. The caveat introduced in *Webb*, which distinguishes between fixed-term and permanent employment, does not acknowledge the increase use of atypical work. Moreover, it fails to recognise gender segregation in the official labour market, whereby women are more likely to be hired on a temporary, part-time basis than men. In this context, it severely limits the protection provided for under the Equal Treatment Directive. The implementation of the Pregnant Worker Directive increases the protection available to women, both in terms of health and safety and unfair dismissal. In so doing it helped to clarify the position of the Court.

Nonetheless, the number of cases that continue to be referred to the Court on this particular issue are a clear signal as to the significant shortcomings in the application of the principles enshrined within this policy (McGlynn, 1996).

It is clear from the analysis presented in this chapter that the Court's rulings do not occur in a vacuum, but are influenced by a variety of social, political and economic concerns. As such, Hoskyns (1996: 160) claims that the rulings in the field of social security highlight the impact of gender structures on the Court's understanding of the European social and economic order. The Court's inconsistent approach to cases dealing with questions relating to working conditions as opposed to those on social security matters, is the result of a misunderstanding about the relationship between public roles and private duties. This approach has important repercussions on the Court's understanding of gender dynamics and power hierarchies. In this process, substantive equality falls victim to internal politics, judges' personal bias and the interests of the Union as a whole. The ultimate outcome of these dynamics is restriction in scope and reach of European law and jurisprudence.

The Court's position on the relationship between mother and child is exemplary of the kind of gender order that is being protected by this institution. The Court's assumptions about the special nature of the mother–child relationship are evident in various cases outlined in this chapter. *Hoffman, Habermann-Berltermann, Webb, Brown* and *Thebault* are particularly good examples of how the Court regards maternity leave as essential to foster the 'special' bond between mother and child. The Court seems to differentiate between maternity and parental leave, and in so doing conflates mothering and pregnancy into a single concept or process. Women's role as primary carers is reasserted, as is the traditional male-breadwinner model. In so doing, the Court articulates an ideology of mothering and the family which is static and based on traditional gender divisions of labour. The position of the Court on family-friendly and maternity policies highlights the implicitly gendered nature of this policy area and the type of power hierarchies that women must contend with in the public and the private sphere (McGlynn, 2001b: 336, 339).

Implicit within the Court's judgments are also a number of normative statements about the economic order. As the analysis of *Webb* highlights, the ECJ buys into accepted norms of 'common sense' economics whereby the business case can be used to justify discrimination. The increasing amount of cases being brought forward on the grounds of unfair dismissal highlights the difficulty in changing the political and business culture which perceives pregnancy and maternity as an additional cost associated with women's employment. These attitudes are based on the assumption that women will continue to fulfil the primary function of care. However, this is a very short-sighted measure that fails to take into consideration the long-term implications of forcing upon women a dichotomisation of mothering and employment. As the next chapter will highlight, this binary opposition has an impact on fertility rates and marginalises valuable economic resources (such as highly-skilled female workers).

So, what does the analysis of the Court tell us about the equality directives? Three principles are central to the Court's rulings: pay, treatment and leave. In as far as the implementation of the principle of equal treatment is concerned, the Court has favoured a narrow understanding of its overall scope. This is particularly evident in the Court's position on affirmative action. As Charpentier (1998: 69–70) explains, by

> adopting antidiscrimination as the prescriptive rule required that male and female workers be granted the same rights and opportunities. Consequently, the postulate of equality is confined to a simple framework where the principle of equal treatment takes on male worker as a norm, and is applied to all female workers ... Under this simple framework of equality, as opposed to Walzer's *complex equality*, we shall see that there is no space for preferential treatment.

The division between formal and substantive equality that was originally introduced in the equality directives, has been subsequently crystallised by the Court's judgements.

The principles enshrined in the Pregnant Worker Directive challenge the interpretation of equality favoured by the Court (i.e. sameness) and, as discussed previously, they provide an opportunity for the Court to articulate its specific position/ideology of mothering and the family. For Wynn (1999: 442) the Pregnant Worker Directive seeks to establish the parameters whereby equality and difference can coexist. The focus on the special nature of the relationship between mother and child, and the unique position of mothering within equality legislation has created a number of idiosyncrasies. As Wynn (1999: 442) further explains 'the Court has repeatedly used instrumental reasons as the basis for protection of pregnancy and maternity, with the consequence that paternal ideologies have emphasised women's vulnerability rather than their rights to be treated equally as workers'. Two issues emerge from the Court's interpretation of scope of maternity legislation: 1. It reinforces the public–private dichotomy by portraying women on maternity leave as temporarily excluded from the labour market; 2. It supports gender power hierarchies in the family by reasserting the centrality of the male-breadwinner model (McGlynn, 2001b: 327; Wynn, 1999: 442)

The position taken by the Court and the idiosyncrasies entrenched within its rulings are a direct result of the disassociation of maternity rights from equality. The opportunistic strategy embarked upon during the negotiations for this policy, whereby it was ratified as a health and safety measure as opposed to an equality measure, allows for a division in the implementation of the principles enshrined in the directive itself. Moreover, it highlights the problems enshrined in protective legislation, which reaffirms gender power hierarchies.

The considerations outlined above reaffirm the case presented in this book, which claims that the European equality agenda promotes only a limited understanding of the principle and practice of equality. The focus of the policies on formal equality has been transposed by the implementation of these policies and the Court's understanding of the function of mothering in contemporary European society. As Charpentier (1998: 11) outlines, 'the antidiscrimination criteria reduces the principle of equality as established by the Equal Treatment Directive to a purely formal requirement, insisting that like cases be treated alike'. Unfortunately, as he further explains, the limitations of this principle become blatantly obvious when attempts are made to apply it to those areas of policy which are defined by difference. The outcome of this approach has been the reaffirmation of male standards in the official labour market and gender divisions of labour in the family, and women's marginal position in the public sphere.

It should now be clear that the Court's rulings have limited the scope of family-friendly policies as a tool for the establishment and the promotion of substantive equality. Moreover, the inability of member states' governments to agree upon a comprehensive framework for the reconciliation between work and family life has the ultimate outcome of limiting the scope of the policies that have been ratified. On top of that, it has also served to reassert gender power hierarchies associated with the social function of reproduction.

Given the analysis presented here, it is possible to conclude that over the course of the years, the ECJ has been both friend and foe. In evaluating the role of the Court in promoting women's rights, Hoskyns (1996: 158) has drawn attention to the *ad hoc* nature of the developments that have taken place under the guardianship of this institution. It is worth remembering that despite the façade of impartiality, the ECJ is also a political animal. It is in this context that Shaw (1999: 23–4, 29) has drawn attention to how the Court's activism in this particular policy area has been by and large self serving, rather than indicative of a commitment to the feminist goals of substantive equality and justice. The body of case law on equal treatment for pregnant workers is now bringing to light a bias in favour of formal equality. The failure of the Court to reconcile the needs of employers with those of women is testament to such bias. Given this background, McGlynn (1996: 242) argues that, 'the advances so far gained in the relation to pregnancy dismissals do not represent a cultural shift in attitudes towards accommodating pregnant women and women with children into the workplace'.

Caracciolo di Torrella (2000: 191) disputes these evaluations, arguing that the Court has succeeded in clarifying the principles of the equality directives within the limits of its powers and role within the process of European integration. Within those constraints, the Court has been able to protect the position of working women and mothers. There are, however, a number of shortcomings with this particular interpretation. Starting with reference to the cases of *Hoffman, Commission* v *Italy,* and *Commission* v *France,* the Court seems reluctant to challenge traditional family structures. The Court's apparently neutral position vis-à-vis this social institution denotes its lack of understanding of how gender interacts with social structures. As McGlynn (2001b: 334) explains, 'in not intervening, the court, and thereby EU law, legitimates the status quo. The court sanctioned a policy which helped ensure that women are, and should remain, primarily responsible for child care' (McGlynn, 2001b: 333). Recent judgement by the Court (see for instance those cases dealing with childcare) highlight a more careful approach in articulating how gender power structures should operate.

The analysis of current case law targeting the reconciliation between work and family life supports McGlynn's (2001b: 330) assessment that the role of the Court in this area is defined by three interrelated principles: 1. Paternalist protection of working mothers; 2. Ideology of motherhood based on the assumed special relationship between mother and child; 3. Women being the weaker sex, and in need of protection. It is interesting to note that these are the same principles that underpin the male-breadwinner model and that perpetrate gender power hierarchies.

Couple this with a number of judgements that limit the scope of maternity rights for workers on fixed-term contracts, and what starts to emerge is a Court that actively reasserts traditional gender power hierarchies. The perceived gender neutrality of these policies ultimately masks the assumptions of European policy-makers about the gender order, and highlights the limitations of current EU policies for the reconciliation between work and family life. To conclude, what emerges from this analysis is a general tendency to conflate pregnancy/maternity with motherhood, thus bringing together the social and the biological function of reproduction. The implication of these trends, as discussed in chapter 1, is that in doing so it reinforces normative assumptions about mothering as well as traditional gender power hierarchies (McGlynn, 2001b).

5

The family-friendly discourse in Italy: mothering, the family and the nation

According to various categorisations of European welfare states, the Italian social and political system is heavily dependent on the traditional family to provide financial and emotional support for its members. In particular, the focus on the family as provider of care draws attention to the many dimensions involved in the study of gender dynamics, and the application of reconciliation between work and family life as a principle and a policy outcome. Firstly, it highlights the impact of the European equality agenda on the national sphere. Secondly, it brings to light the process of cultural mediation to which labour market reforms are subject. And finally, it allows us to engage with the idiosyncrasies embedded within any policy that seeks to challenge traditional gender divisions of labour without addressing the underlying issues that maintain social hierarchies of power (Bimbi, 1993; Duncan, 1995; Duncan, 1996; Esping-Andersen, 1990: 27; Pringle, 1998: 7–8).

This chapter will explore the impact of the European equality agenda and family-friendly policies on the development of women's employment rights in Italy. Given the importance of family structures to the economic and political survival of the state, section one will look at the centrality of the traditional family as the main provider of the care, and the impact of the fascist era on the crystallisation of gender roles in the country. This section will outline the social and historical background that provided the backdrop for the development of women's rights in the post-war era. Section two will look at the development of family-friendly policies, starting with the establishment of maternity rights in the 1970s. Finally, section three will endeavour to assess the impact of European policies on the national framework for the reconciliation of work and family life. This section will also seek to establish the patterns of change and continuity in the affirmation of gender roles and gender divisions of labour in the country.

The family and women's employment in Italy: general consideration

Any analysis seeking to establish the role and position of women in contemporary Italian society must include a brief overview of the historical legacy of the fascist regime on social dynamics. The overall impact of the fascist regime on the construction of social and gender structures in the country has been widely documented. Accounts of the position of women within the regime have had to contend with the complex set of power dynamics that defined social and political relations in the 1920s. However, there is one dimension of the gender order during this period that is considered the linchpin of the regime's policy towards women: the confinement of the *gentil sesso* to the private sphere. Women's social and political role was defined in terms of their function as child-bearers. Slogans such as, 'make babies, make a lot of babies, large numbers mean power' (Weber, 1981: 184), summarise the gender ideology of the regime. As a matter of fact, from 1923 onwards, the regime actively worked to exclude women from the public sphere and the labour market. More specifically, the regime instituted a social framework that was built upon representations of women as carers and cared for. Motherhood and women's role in the social function of reproduction was invested with a whole new set of values, and the traditional family became the carrier of such norms. In this social order, women became important to the state as guardians of traditional family values and the gender order (Angelilli, 1991: 23; Di Lello, in Pace *et al.* 1991: 53–4; Kaplan, 1992: 234–6; Terranova, 1991: 37; Weber, 1981: 184).

The gender ideology of the regime reflected the power hierarchies present within the family. Mussolini's aim was to make the family and the private sphere a tool in the hands of the state. In this context, the regime politicised women in order to reinforce its grip over the country. The relationship between women and the state was played out in two mutually reinforcing dimensions. On the one hand, women were the carers of the family and the nation. One the other, they were to be cared for, thus allowing the 'male' state to assume a paternalistic position vis-à-vis the nation. By fulfilling this dual function, women were to ensure the survival of the traditional family and the gender order. This relationship, however, was based upon the domination of women's bodies, identity and sexuality. The regime tried to expand its reach on Italian society by pursuing various policies aimed at establishing a new type of social involvement which would 'recast older notions of maternity and fatherhood, femaleness and masculinity' (De Grazia, 1992: 2). This type of propaganda greatly influenced the popular imagination, and linked men's and women's worth to the social function of reproduction. The representations of gender roles upon which this social order was based derived their power and endurance from the apparent normality and acceptability of gender divisions of labour. Finally, the support of the Catholic Church further cemented the position of gender power hierarchies in this new social and political order (De Grazia, 1992: 1–2; Weber, 1981 184–5).

Fascist policies and propaganda were so successful in eliminating women from the public sphere that it was not until the end of the Second World War, and the defeat of fascism, that women again became the subject of political debate and public policy. Article 3 of the 1948 Constitution introduced the general principle of equality, whereas Article 37 established the parameters for the implementation of equality between men and women in the field of employment. The principle of sexual equality also appears in Article 29 and Article 31, which focus on marital relations and family structures. Despite the importance of the political changes that took place surrounding these reforms, it is important to cast a critical eye over how gender structures became incorporated in the new Republic. In particular, Article 37 (in Cappiello *et al.*, 1984: 8–9) states that,

> The working woman has the same right and, for equal work, the same remuneration due to a man. Working conditions should allow her to fulfil her essential family function and ensure adequate protection to the mother and child.

Articles 29 and 31 reinforce the assumptions introduced here by privileging the traditional family and women's role in the social function of reproduction. In this context, the new constitution thus establishes a gender order for the Italian state (Bimbi, 1993:147–8; Del Boca, 1988: 131; De Luca, 1994: 461; Governatori, 1992; 170; Remiddi, 1993: 10; Saraceno, 1978: 199).

What emerges from this brief historical overview is the importance of the traditional family and gender power hierarchies to the Italian social and political psyche. Moreover, it is worth noting that the fascist legacy provided the foundations upon which post-war Italian society was built, and highlights the continued role of the family as the main arena in which gender dynamics are being played out.

Motherhood, maternity and the concept of the family remained the main focus of political debates on women's rights long after the fall of the fascist regime. Although the 1950s and 1960s marked an increase in female participation in the labour market, gender divisions of labour remained a defining characteristic of government policy and employment practice. Most women entering the labour market were employed in typically feminine jobs, and the government upheld traditional views and representations of women. The social repercussions of this market segregation were further compounded by the absence of social services that would allow women to fulfill the function of care. These socio-economic trends ultimately reinforced traditional gender power hierarchies in the private sphere (Bimbi, 1993:148–52; Del Boca, 1988: 127–8).

By the late 1970s, Saraceno (1978: 49) drew attention to the continuity in social practices and divisions of labour. She claimed that despite the significant changes that had taken place in the public sphere, women's role in society was still defined primarily in terms of their position as wives and mothers. Since then, several studies on household work patterns have sought to describe the permanence of gender divisions of labour in the private sphere, and its detrimental effect on women's employment in the official labour market. The conclusions of these studies point to the fact that the legislation 'may not substantially change women's condition if there are many social and economic factors working against it' (Del Boca, 1988: 121). The overwhelming dependence of Italian welfare structures upon women's care work in the private sphere impacts directly upon women's access to and employment in the official labour market. A direct consequence of these social patterns is that women's employment is often perceived as charac-terised by absenteeism, 'non-availability for over-time' and 'lack of timetable mobility' (Weber, 1981: 192). What this points to is that despite the achieve-ments of women in education and employment, social change is occurring at a much slower rate (Bimbi, 1993: 152–7; Del Boca, 1988: 121; Reinicke, 1994: 21; Valentini, 1997: 56–63; Valentini, 1997: 85–96).

Despite the criticisms outlined above, in the last five decades Italian women have obtained legal recognition of their rights as workers. And, some of the main developments in women's rights have been in the area of mater-nity and pregnancy protection. Unfortunately, conservative interpretations of the law by employers and policy-makers alike, have led some feminists and legal analysts to describe maternity legislation as an obstacle to women's liberation and empowerment. As Romito (1993: 587) explains, the construc-tion of motherhood and maternity legislation are the by-product of social structures that are based upon the gendered division of labour, which will be incorporated in the legislation itself. As a matter of fact, women's employ-ment is still commonly perceived as secondary to that of their husband or main family breadwinner. And, the ease with which maternity legislation is used and abused portrays a society in which the concept of woman as *focolare domestico* is deeply rooted in the national consciousness (Bimbi, 1993; Del Boca *et al.*, 2000; Valentini, 1997: 93, 99–100).

Perhaps the most significant changes in the position of women in Italian society have taken place within the last decade. The most obvious signs of such change are the sharp decline in birth rates, the continued rise in women's participation in the official labour market and the 'democratization of family life' (Sacchetto, 2003: 8). Despite these developments, it is impor-tant to draw attention to the complexity of interactions between gender hierarchies and family structures that is still being played out within the domestic sphere. The decline in birth rates is a prime example of such dynam-ics. This demographic trend can be interpreted in the context of national economic trends and family policies, as well as a reaction to narrowly defined gender structures. More specifically, the decline in birth rates may just as well be the result of a clash between social norms and employment practices. Despite the marked change in women's aspirations that has taken place in the last thirty years, for young Italian women it remains difficult to reconcile the choice of motherhood with the inflexible patterns and structures of the labour market (Bonzini Andiñach, 2002; Del Boca *et al.*, 2003; Sacchetto, 2003; Valentini 1997).

Maternity rights and family-friendly policies

This section will discuss how successive Italian governments have sought to address the tension between employment and care. One of the issues that will emerge from the analysis presented here is the *protective* nature of maternity policies. This bias is particularly important in the context of this case study, as it highlights the persistence of a paternalist state and an institutional resistance to widening the principle of equality to include family structures.

It is interesting to note that the first major piece of equal rights legislation ratified by the newly established Italian Republic is the 1950 Law for the Physical and Economic Protection of Working Mothers (Legge No. 860). In many ways, this policy was radical for its time as it sought to regulate the employment relationship with regards to pregnant workers. More specifically, this law targeted three key areas of the employment relationship. Firstly, it protected women from unlawful dismissal on the grounds of pregnancy (Article 3); secondly, it outlined basic health and safety requirements for the protection of pregnant workers (Articles 4 and 5); finally, it allowed for special arrangements for women who were breast-feeding (Articles 9 and 10). Despite these important innovations, this policy was laden with normative judgements about the role and position of working mothers and women in general. In this context, women were portrayed as a group in need of protection and pregnancy was classed on a par with disabling illnesses. Although this law was innovative for its time, it was not until 1971 that 'motherhood became an object of [serious] legislative attention' (Weber, 1981: 131).

A direct development of the 1950 regulations targeting working mothers, the stated aims of the 1971 Protection of Working Mothers Law (Legge No. 1204) was to provide a framework for the protection of all women employed in the official labour market. In terms of health and safety, it established the terms of maternity leave (compulsory and voluntary), employment protection/right to return which lasts for one year (Articles 2 and 4), and limited the use of female labour for heavy-duty work (Article 3). Concerning the economic treatment of pregnant workers and workers who had recently given birth, the law established a daily allowance equal to 80 per cent of the normal salary to cover the whole period of compulsory maternity leave. Article 15 specifically states that,

> the allowance ... is to be assigned with the same criteria provided for the distribution of mandatory insurance of illness within the proper sickness insurance body within which the workers insured and are not subordinated to specific required insurance contributions (*anzianità assicurativa*).

This law also entitles women to two break periods during the working day for breast-feeding. These breaks are to be considered as an integral part of the working day. Finally, this entitlement lasts for the whole of the child's first year of life (Article 10).

Welcomed by many as some of the most progressive maternity provisions in Europe, the 1971 law was invested with a great deal of hope for the establishment of an egalitarian labour market in the country (Primicerio, 1976: 725). For Ada Grecchi (1996: 71) these provisions remain some of the most developed and progressive regulations for the protection of maternity rights in the European Union. However, a closer analysis of the text of the law brings to light a set of biases that reinforce gender power hierarchies and the public–private dichotomy.

One of the main problems with this policy is the implicit assumption that maternity and pregnancy can be equated to a disabling illness. This interpretation of maternity absence discloses an institutional bias towards male patterns of work. Women's work in the private sphere is ignored and the concept of leave assumes that work only takes place in the public domain. As Patrizia Romito (1993: 586) explains,

> obviously, doctors ignored the domestic responsibilities of their pregnant patients' lives. But the realities are obviously ignored in social policies too. Measures such as early maternity leave and sick leave in pregnancy, specifically intended for female employees, are actually based on the experience that the male worker has of being at home.

Another problem with this policy arises from the limited reach of the legislation and the extensive nature of the underground economy in Italy. In the first instance, there are several fields of the official labour market that are not covered by the legislation, such as domestic work and the agricultural sector. Secondly, given the extensive use of women's employment in the underground economy, this policy fails to protect the most vulnerable sections of the labour force. More worryingly, employers often cite the costs associated with these provisions to excuse direct and indirect discrimination. As Romito (1993: 592) further points out, 'in some cases, employers may decide that employing women is too complicated or expensive: therefore, the existence of the law turns out to be an obstacle to women's access to the regulated labour market'. These attitudes consequently exacerbate the problem of high women's employment in the underground economy (Del Boca, 1988: 124–5; De Marchis, 1995; Grecchi, 1996: 72; Kravaritou, 1997; Romito, 1993; Valentini, 1997: 98).

The issues discussed thus far emphasise the continued exploitation of female sections of the workforce. Bearing in mind Romito's considerations on the use and misuse of maternity legislation, it is important to outline the wider context of women's employment rights in Italy. The Italian Constitutional Court declared Article 2 of the 1971 Law constitutionally invalid only in 1991. More specifically, Article 2 was not deemed to offer adequate protection to women workers because it did not take into account the impact of unlawful dismissal on the psychological wellbeing of the mother to be. This Article proclaimed the inefficiency rather than the illegality of the threat of dismissal to the pregnant worker. For the Court, the focus of the law on health and safety did not take into consideration the special needs of the mother–child relationship. The Constitutional Court thus declared illegal the dismissal of workers who are pregnant. A positive development for the establishment of a framework for the protection of pregnant workers, this ruling fell short of its radical potential on two counts. Firstly, it did not cover the issue of indirect discrimination. Secondly, it reaffirmed the primacy of the current gender order and women's role as carers in the family (De Falco, 1991: 222).

From the discussion outlined above, it appears that Italian legal structures seek to protect working mothers in order to safeguard their role in the social function of reproduction. Drawing upon the reference made by the Constitutional Court about the relationship between mother and child, policy-makers devised a policy that ascribes importance to women's roles primarily in relation to the maternal relationship and the fulfilment of the child's needs. By focusing on the social function of mothering rather than the employment rights element of maternity provisions, the provisions failed to move beyond formal equality. Another ruling by the Constitutional Court (172 of 31 May 1996) highlights the persistence of gender power hierarchies. In this case, the Court found null and void the policy protecting all women employed in the official labour market from unfair dismissal. This ruling allows for the dismissal of workers who become pregnant before the end of their trial period, thus justifying the limitation of women's employment rights on economic grounds. The only concession to equality incorporated in this ruling is the obligation upon employers to explain the motivation of the dismissal if they are aware of the pregnancy (A. Che, 1996). This new imposition by the Constitutional Court increased pressure upon women to conform with the male standard of work and employment. Indeed, women might decide either to postpone maternity or to resort to abortion if they became pregnant during the trial period (Valentini, 1997).

The Constitutional Court's interpretations of the principles established by the 1971 law highlight the idiosyncratic nature of Italian equality legislation, whereby the principle of equality of treatment is disassociated from maternity protection. The 1977 Equal Treatment Law (Legge No. 903) expands the principle of equality between men and women in the workplace. With the implementation of this law, it is finally illegal to refuse to hire a woman because of marital status and/or pregnancy, and establishes the principle of equal pay for work of equal value. This policy also extends the right of maternity leave to adoptive mothers and introduces the principle of parental leave for working fathers, if they have the sole custody of the children, or the other parent (the mother) has surrendered her maternity rights (Articles 6–7). This final issue is particularly interesting because it establishes a right to paternity leave (however limited and constrained). As Landau (1985: 77–9) points out, 'the Act of 1977 covers in one instrument equal treatment in all conditions of work including pay'. It would appear that Italian policy-makers sought to develop one-size-fits-all equality policy, which dealt with all the different issues that determine gender discrimination in the Italian labour market. It is therefore unsurprising that the implementation of this policy did not produce a marked improvement in the allocation of work in the family and/or challenge gender power hierarchies in the labour market.

More recently, the Italian government has sought to streamline the application of equal opportunities and maternity rights. Particularly important in this context is the development of a new body of law on reconciliation between work and family life. The first law to be ratified in this new phase in the development of equal opportunities is the 2000 Law for the Support of Mothering and Fathering, for the Right to Care and Development, and the Coordination of Time in the City (Legge No. 53). The aim of this policy is to encourage enterprises to invest in and support reconciliation between work and family life, as well as a greater balance between work, leisure, and training. As stated in Article 1, the main purpose is to encourage greater social solidarity. Of particular interest for the analysis of reconciliation between work and family life are Article 3 on parental leave, Article 9 on work-time flexibility, and Articles 10–18 on maternity and paternity leave.

Following the 2000 Mothering and Fathering Law, the government issued a variety of measures aimed at consolidating the rights and entitlements established by this policy. Particularly of interest is Legislative Decree 151/2001. The aim of the 2001 decree was to consolidate the provisions for the protection of the rights of working mothers. Based on the provisions outlined in the 1971 Maternity Law, the 1977 Equal Treatment Law and a number of other legislative decrees, this policy outlines the basic statutory rights for the protection of the health and safety of pregnant workers and workers who have recently given birth (Section II). On top of this it regulates the length of maternity and paternity leave, responsibilities over social security contributions and all other economic arrangements related to such leave (Sections I and III). In compliance with European law, it also provides for parental leave (Section V). What is interesting, however, is Section IV dedicated to paternity leave. This policy reiterates the commitments outlined in the 1977 Equal Treatment Law, which established a right for working fathers to be absent from work to fulfil their domestic responsibilities. However, the caveat attached to the original provisions remains: a father is entitled to paternity leave only if the mother defers her rights to maternity leave. Despite some significant weaknesses, this policy is nevertheless an important development as it provides a comprehensive text on the rights of working mothers and fathers.

Recent developments in the area of reconciliation between work and family life highlight a change in policy discourse. However, the conflict between women's aspirations and mothering is still apparent through the analysis of population trends. As Valentini (1997) explains, women's entry in the official labour market has been blamed for many social problems, and particularly the decrease in birth rates. Despite an increasing amount of research that documents the lack of public services and the marginal position of family-friendly policies, the link between sexual discrimination and declining fertility rates has been almost completely ignored. It is in this context that the analysis of substantive equality is useful to highlight the limited impact of current equality provisions (Bonzini Andiñach, 2002; Cianciullo, 1995: 11; Grecchi, 1996: 25; Pringle, 1998: 75; Valentini, 1997).

The influence of EU policies on reconciliation between work and family life on the Italian legal framework

The influence of European policies on Italian equality provisions arises from the horizontal reach of Article 119 and the equality Directives. On several occasions, however, the Italian Constitutional Court tried to challenge this principle by ruling that the plaintiffs cannot base their claim upon European directives, unless the principles of such directives have been implemented within national legislation. This concern with the constitutional repercussion of European directives limits the indirect reach of the legislation within a national framework that has been marred by the inconsistent implementation of these principles (Foglia, 1995: 37, 40–1).

In this framework, it is consequently interesting to note the Italian veto to the maternity directive for failing to uphold the highest possible standards. It was reported that the Council of Ministers was prepared to accept earlier drafts of the Pregnant Worker Directive, 'if Italy did not break ranks with other countries and vetoed the decision calling instead for a maternity leave paid at 80% of the previous salary' (Anon., 1992: 3). Despite the government's protests that the proposal was too limited, it was national interests rather than a concern for women's rights that drove the negotiations. The deadlock caused by the Italian veto almost cost the ratification of the directive altogether. As a direct consequence of this stance, the Council of Ministers ultimately unpicked the work of the Parliament and ratified a directive that effectively equates maternity leave with sick leave (Anon., 1992: 4).

It is interesting to note that European equality policies had their greatest impact in the context of equal treatment and pay, rather than maternity rights and parental leave. Unlike the UK, Italy already had a substantial body of law for the protection of working mothers. However, the presence of a framework for family-friendly policies, as established by the 1971 and 1977 laws, should not be mistaken for a commitment to substantive equality. Given the short-comings of Italian policies in this area, it is possible to conclude that EU policies have contributed to the institutionalisation of equal rights and opportunities within the national framework.

However, the Italian government's resistance towards the equality provisions adopted at the European level is evident in the various cases brought to the European Court of Justice. Starting in the early 1980s, the Commission initiated proceedings against the Italian government over some of the provisions covering parental leave included in the 1977 Equal Treatment Law (Case 163/82). The Italian government defended its regulations arguing that the 1977 Law incorporates a very general principle of equality, and thus fulfils the requirements of the equal pay and equal treatment directives. Citing Article 189 TEC, the Court upheld the right of national authorities to choose the best way to implement European provisions in national law. The ECJ also dismissed the second complaint brought by the Commission against the Italian state on the grounds that the Italian Code of Civil Procedure can be used in the application of the Equal Treatment Directive (Prechal and Burrows, 1990: 139–40).

The third complaint by the Commission against the Italian state is particularly interesting for the analysis conducted in this book. The Commission's grievance revolved around Article 6 of the 1977 Equal Treatment Law. In this particular instance, the Commission argued that the grounds limiting parental leave to the mother in the case of adoption did not comply with the principle of equal treatment as enshrined in European law. The Italian government's defence was based on a fallacious distinction between the principles of maternity rights and equal treatment (Commission, 1986: 58; Ellis, 1991: 169–70; Prechal and Burrows, 1990: 140–2).

The Advocate General sought to establish a link between equal opportunities and maternity protection by arguing that compulsory maternity leave falls under the terms of promotion of women's rights in employment. Unfortunately, once again the Court dismissed the Commission's complaint on the grounds that such discrimination can be *tolerated* if it can be perceived to be in the *best* interest of the child. The Court went on to explain that in the case of adoption, the interest of the child is best fulfilled if all the conditions of entry into the family are as close as possible to those of natural children. Finally, the Court further justified its decision by claiming that at the time of the ruling, Italy was the only country that provided economic and legal protection for parental leave (Commission, 1986: 58; Ellis, 1991: 169–70; McGlynn, 2001b: 331–2; Prechal and Burrows, 1990: 140–2).

The Court's position in the last case is important because it draws attention to the impact of gender power hierarchies on European legal structures. This Court's ruling is exemplary of the complexities that underpin the relationship between social structures and the law. According to Prechal and Burrows (1990: 142), the leave after adoption, however, benefits the child above all in so far as it is intended to foster the emotional ties necessary to settle the child in the family adopting it. Moreover, in the provision of Italian law it appears that the interests of the child to be adopted are predominant. The Advocate General therefore considered adoption leave as a working condition within the meaning of Article 5 of the Directive.

The European Court of Justice justified its position by explaining that the arrival of an adopted and a natural child have to be comparable. In this context, fathers are also extended all the rights provided under Italian law. Unfortunately, despite this qualification, this ruling reinforces assumptions that women are primary carers (Ellis, 1991: 170; McGlynn, 2001b; 331–2).

The analysis of these rulings raises some important questions about the aim and scope of the 1971 maternity provisions. Although compulsory maternity leave is important for the establishment of a framework for work–life balance, it is also important to question the underlying assumptions of this absence from the workplace. Officially, compulsory leave is supposed to allow for a period of rest after childbirth; the interpretations of the Court, however, highlight the process by which this leave reinforces gender roles and divisions of labour (Romito, 1993: 586).

The European Court of Justice was clearly unwilling to interpret policies for the reconciliation between work and family life in a way that could challenge gender power hierarchies. In this context, it is possible to conclude that its rulings reinforced gender power hierarchies, and reaffirmed the role of mothering within traditional socio-economic structures. The next section of this chapter will highlight the discrepancies and inconsistencies of Italian policies on equality and maternity rights.

Leglislative limitations: questions and puzzles

The analysis of the development of maternity rights and family-friendly policies in Italy draws attention to the biases of successive governments, which have sought to enable working women to continue to fulfil their role as primary carers. Family-friendly policies and maternity rights have become a vehicle for the state to sustain gender power hierarchies and divisions of labour (Del Boca, 1988: 120–1). There are several possible explanations for this trend. For Reinecke (1994: 21), however, cultural norms about the role of women in the family and society at large remain a determining factor. As he explains, 'the power of the Catholic Church and its influence on the consciousness of Italian women and their imprisonment within a specific role that was exclusively maternity and family centred are really quite great. All the ideology of the Italian family is based upon the notion of the woman as mother and housewife'.

Despite the social and political changes in the position of women in the last twenty years, cultural norms about mothering appear to be a constant. Women's participation in the labour market has become an important resource for the Italian economy. However, the continued reliance on the family to fulfil care duties is at odds with women's changed expectations and attainment in the public sphere. There has also been only a limited amount of progress in developing the necessary infrastructure to allow women to reconcile work and family life. The failures of equal rights and maternity policies are therefore evident in the employment patterns of the female labour force of this country, which are still characterised by low rates of female participation in the employment market (Bonzini Andiñach, 2002; De Falco, 1991: 222; Grecchi, 1990: 22; Grecchi, 1997: 71–3; Guerra and Pesce, 1991: 22; Romito, 1993; Rubery *et al.*, 1999;).

The increase in women's employment rates over the last ten years has brought the issue of equality back onto the policy-making agenda. As Guerra and Pesce (1991: 26) explain, women's presence in the labour market has become not only noticeable, but it is also 'strong, visible, [and] lasting'. This is undoubtedly an improvement from the past, but what many studies have drawn attention to is the extensive nature of women's double presence. In the 1970s, Balbo (1978 in Guerra and Pesce, 1991: 25) argued that 'the condition of adult women is characterised by a double presence in family work and extra-family employment'. It would appear that thirty years later women's responsibilities for care and domestic work have only marginally changed. The issue of the double presence is particularly important because it is directly linked to social norms about motherhood and women's roles as mothers (Guerra and Pesce, 1991: 25; Valentini, 1997). As Sacchetto (2003) explains, although 'motherhood is not experienced as a life choice that is incompatible with paid work outside the home, ... women in employment are less inclined to have children'.

The increasing deregulation of the employment market and the introduction of flexible working patterns, have also only marginally increased the opportunities for reconciliation between work and family life. Moreover, a traditionally strong emphasis on employment rights and lack of part-time/flexible employment has hampered women's access to employment. Del Boca (1988: 126) argues that 'in most advanced industrialised countries, part-time work or various forms of flexible time schedules are widespread and are especially taken up by women. Not so in Italy'. Because of the lack of alternative forms of employment, women seeking flexible hours are forced into the underground economy (Addis, 2000; Del Boca, 1988: 126–7, 130; Sacchetto, 2003).

Employers' attitudes towards the female workforce also play an important role in limiting the scope and reach of equal rights policies. Various studies have pointed out that, particularly with reference to working mothers, the *overprotection* offered by the legislation makes them less employable because of the costs involved to the employers (Addis, 2000: 124–5; Del Boca,

1988: 134; Romito, 1993: 587). These attitudes towards women result in two trends: firstly the common use of 'blank resignations', and secondly the high percentage of working women without children (Sacchetto, 2003; Valentini, 1997: 123–5).

Employers' reluctance to implement the principles of equality enshrined within the various policies outlined in this chapter is all the more obvious when looking at the difference between women employed in the public and private sectors of the economy. Whereas women employed in the public sector take full advantage of early maternity leave provisions, women employed in the private sector are often denied these 'privileges' (Addis, 2000; Romito, 1993: 587). This analysis highlights the short-sighted nature of this approach. Representations of women primarily as carers have prevented employers from exploiting the full potential of this valuable resource.

Lack of knowledge about employment rights and gender segregation of the official labour market, are the main reasons why the practice of sexual discrimination continues largely unchallenged. A study by Romito and Saurel-Cubizolles (1992: 1488–91) shows gender segregation of the official labour market has left women vulnerable to such practices. Although this problem is particularly acute in the case of women employed at the bottom end of the official labour market, discrimination is endemic within all levels of the labour market. It is also worth noting that the Italian government has been particularly reluctant to publicise the improvements introduced by European legislation. The convergence of these trends is important because it highlights an overarching lack of commitment towards women's rights (Cattaneo, 1996: 15; Del Boca, 1988: 132–3; Romito and Saurel-Cubizolles, 1992).

Some initial conclusions can be drawn from the analysis of Italian labour market structures conducted thus far. Firstly, lack of flexible/part-time employment has meant that there is a relatively high number of women working full-time. Secondly, despite increased female participation in the official labour market, Italian women continue to encounter a number of obstacles to entering and remaining in the official labour market. These trends can be seen to shape women's employment trends, whereby increasing occupational opportunities are in predominantly 'feminised' occupations in the service sector or in the public sector where employment rights are more secure. Finally, the retrenchment of the public sector and the drive to deregulate the employment market, which have been at the heart of economic and welfare reforms of the last decade, are also having a negative impact on women's employment opportunities (Del Boca, 1988: 126–7; Grecchi, 1997: 21–5, 58; Mezzatosta, 1992: 29; Valentini, 1997).

Discrimination remains a defining feature of women's employment experiences. As Cattaneo (1996: 12) explains, when discussing the condition of *woman* as a

social subject, we need to deal with a variegated universe, differentiated amongst geographical areas, because of historical and political reasons, because of economic conditions, because of education and tradition, but with an obvious common denominator: discrimination.

This experience is compounded by the prevalent representation of women as mothers. It is thus remarkable that despite these obstacles, women's employment has increased substantially over the last ten years. There are two identifiable reasons for this growth: the decline in birth rates and the rising educational attainment of women (Cattaneo, 1996: 12; Sacchetto, 2003; Valentini, 1997).

In the last few decades there has been a marked increase in women's participation in the public sphere. However, this trend has been limited by the permanence of traditional norms about mothering and the persistence of gender divisions of labour in the family. Evidence of the importance of gender roles and gender divisions of labour transpires from the application of maternity policies. For example, although equal rights and maternity policies include some limited notion of parental leave, 'this provision is, ... rarely taken up; [because of] deeply rooted social conventions and lack of information [that] keep fathers from taking up child care leave' (Del Boca, 1988: 132). The analysis conducted thus far shows that several factors limit the reach of the legislation and the achievement of substantive equality. In this case study the most important limitations of equal rights policies arise from limited knowledge of available provisions, the limits of the provisions themselves, lacking social and support services for working mothers and the gendered wage differential. The combination of all these factors therefore prevents women from entering the official labour market and the public sphere as equal citizens and full members of the labour force (Cattaneo, 1996: 12; Del Boca, 1988: 129; Mezzatosta, 1992: 29; Valentini, 1997: 59–62).

Specifically with reference to maternity rights policies, Ruggerini (1992: 80–1) suggests that the main problem with the implementation of maternity rights results from the separation of production and reproduction. It is the division between public roles and private duties that ultimately undermines the principles enshrined within the policy and maintains gender power hierarchies. What is missing is the recognition that biological differences should not result in the following: 1. Discrimination against women on the grounds of normative values; 2. The implicit reaffirmation of traditional gender divisions of labour. As Governatori (1992: 171) explains, 'special and adequate protection does not aim at changing a function of important social value such as motherhood to a condition that evokes inferiority, but allows that working mothers maintain their rights'.

These considerations suggest that women's position in the labour market is one of comparative *weakness*. Despite some degree of change in younger generations, traditional representations of mothering are still part of the Italian psyche (Sacchetto, 2003; Valentini, 1997). The application of family-friendly and maternity policies therefore reflects persistent attitudes towards women and work.

In conclusion, traditional gender roles are embedded in the very essence of the Constitutional framework of the state. Although, it is commonly assumed that equality between men and women has now been achieved, particularly through the legislative developments of the last three decades, the analysis presented here draws attention to the continuities that define gender power hierarchies in contemporary Italian society. Finally, the combination of representations of women in the legislation combined with the application of maternity provisions appears to have had mixed outcomes in Italy. Rather than promoting women's rights and substantive equality, it appears to have reproduced the centrality of women's mothering. It is in this framework that many Italian women continue to tolerate various discriminatory practices. It also appears that the European directives have not had a great effect in changing the working conditions of women in Italy. Although women's presence in the labour market is now strong, the relatively small number of women in managerial positions highlights the continued impact of gender structures on employment trends. Women's presence in the official labour market therefore seems marked by contradictions and conflicting interests that prevent the establishment of substantive equality as a working principle (Grecchi, 1996: 13–14; Valentini, 1997).

In 1990, Ada Grecchi called for a wider 'cultural reception' of the role of equality and equal rights policies amongst employers, policy-makers and women themselves. This call is still relevant today and highlights the economic impact of underutilising female labour in an increasingly competitive economy. Reconciliation between work and family life should not be seen solely in terms of providing support for working women. These policies can ensure the long-term participation of highly skilled workers, and in so doing ensure the long-term growth of the Italian economy.

6

Between the family and the market: the case of the UK

There are two main reasons for choosing the UK as the second case study in this book. Firstly, it is traditionally classed as a neo-liberal welfare state, or as a strong male-breadwinner state in gender models of welfare regimes (Duncan, 1995; Duncan, 1996; Esping-Andersen, 1990; Lewis, 1992b). Secondly, British political culture includes a tradition of mooted scepticism towards European social policies (Lovenduski and Randall, 1993: 48). These factors highlight a social, economic and political framework focused on the market and market forces. The overall context within which equal rights and maternity legislation developed is therefore significantly different from that analysed in the case of Italy. This case study will allow an assessment of the impact of a relatively flexible labour market on the pursuit of women's rights and substantive equality.

Simon Honeyball (1991) claims that American influence over the British legal system spurred the development of the basic principles of British equal rights provisions. However, within the context of women's rights, the European Union and its institutions have been instrumental in the development of employment rights within the British legal system. Despite the fact that discussions and negotiations for the 1970 and 1975 Acts preceded membership in the European Economic Community, Meehan and Collins (1996: 224) argue that the prospect of British membership in the EEC provided the necessary impetus for the development of women's employment rights.

The European Union has played a central role in developing comprehensive maternity provisions in the UK. Indeed, the ratification of the Pregnant Worker Directive under the auspices of Article 118(a) of the Treaty of Rome has had far-reaching consequences for the development of women's employment rights in Britain. For the first time women employed in the official labour market were entitled to extensive maternity leave, and part-time workers were protected against dismissal on the grounds of pregnancy.

This chapter will outline the impact of the process of European integration on the development of women's rights and family-friendly polices in the UK. The chapter is divided into three parts. Section one looks at feminist analyses of the family and gender structures within the private sphere. Here I evaluate the impact of the public–private divide on women's access to the official labour market and assess the influence of class on gender power hierarchies. Section two outlines various equal rights policies that have exerted particular influence over the development of maternity rights in Britain. Finally, section three evaluates the influence of the European Union in the development of equal rights and maternity legislation.

The chapter will finally conclude the analysis of this case study by looking at complexities and contradictions of the legislation on the reconciliation between work and family life. This discussion I will focus on employment arrangements available to working mothers, the characteristics of women's employment, and employers and policy-maker's approach to maternity rights and family-friendly policies.

Feminist debates on equality and difference: an analysis of British domestic ideology

In 1976 Oakley argued that the 'myth of motherhood' is based on three basic assumptions. Firstly, it is believed that all children need their mothers; secondly, all women want and strive to be mothers; and finally, all mothers need their children and this relationship is all absorbing (Leonard and Speakman, 1986: 49). As discussed in chapter 1, these assumptions, based on the presumed 'naturalness' of motherhood, lie at the heart of gender power hierarchies. Moreover, as mothering takes place within the private sphere, the family continues to wield a great deal of power in defining gender roles and identities (Leonard and Speakman, 1986: 8–9; Rees, 1992: 8–9). For Elizabeth Roberts (1988: 14–5) the concept of 'domestic ideology' provides the most useful analytical tool to understand gender power hierarchies in British society. This analysis points to two defining features of gender relations in the UK: the division between public and private, and traditional family values. As the focus of the media and public policy on 'de-stabilising social trends' highlights, anything defying this norm is seen as a threat not only to the traditional family, but also to the wellbeing of society (Buxton, 1998; Conway, 1992: 53–4; Levin, 1992: 13–17; Marshall, 1998; Quest, 1992; *see also* Panorama, 1997).

The extensive use of women as a reserve army of labour during the Second World War represents a watershed in changing women's expectations and access to the public sphere. The post-war social and political order was supposed to mark a new beginning for gender relations. Social structures and this new gender order were to be defined by increased female employment rates, greater control of women's fertility and increased equality in marriage. Unfortunately, this social revolution did not substantially alter the social responsibility associated with the biological function of reproduction. Moreover, the failure to develop some kind of infrastructure that would help women to absolve their caring role reinforced traditional gender power hierarchies and divisions of labour. The concentration of women with young children in part-time occupations is further evidence of these trends (Brannen and Moss, 1991: 52–4, 192; Figes, 1995; Leonard and Speakman, 1989; Lewis, 1992; O'Connel, 1994; Rees, 1992: 18; Richardson, 1993).

The values underpinning the 'domestic ideology' served to reinforce the assumption that women's employment is secondary to their role as wife and mother. Central to this vision of family dynamics are gender, the gender division of labour, and the public–private dichotomy. In this context, women's participation in the labour market and contribution to the family income are secondary to those of the male/husband breadwinner. Clearly, these assumptions have served to reinforce the male/husband breadwinner–wife/mother carer dichotomy. And, in turn, this hierarchical division of economic and social roles has been used to justify wage differential and sexual segregation of the labour market (Carter, 1988: 22–3; Duncan, 1996; Hills, 1981: 10; Lewis, 1992b; Tilly and Scott, 1987: 7–8).

Traditional family values about public roles and private duties are still influential in cotemporary British society. Women continue to fulfil the function of primary carers, and the increased frequency with which working mothers are being attacked for challenging such roles, highlights how entrenched such values have become (see for instance Panorama, 1997; Buxton, 1998). The assumptions portrayed in such television programmes and media reports about the detrimental effect of women's employment on child development are not dissimilar from the assertions of nineteenth-century child experts. However, there are three interrelated issues that these reports do not consider: firstly, they ignore the cultural nature of the 'special relationship' between mother and children, hence making the mother the essential carer. Secondly, they fail to recognise the *culturally* ascribed role of the father as breadwinner. Finally, they dismiss the impact that lack of structural support has on women's employment choices.

At the beginning of the 1990s, Brannen and Moss (1991) conducted an extensive study of the effect of mothering on women's employment practices. They found that before parenthood men and women had similar levels of commitment towards paid employment. However, 'with the birth of children women had little choice but to curtail their time in employment to the standard working day or less; they took on or were left with the major responsibility for their children, including taking children to and from carers' (Brannen and Moss, 1991: 86). Although working motherhood has become more common, and consequently more acceptable, the issue of conflicting commitments remains an important factor in determining women's employment trends (Brannen and Moss, 1991; Figes, 1995: 6). More recent studies confirm the persistence of this 'conflict'. The conclusions of these studies highlight the complexities of gender hierarchies in contemporary British society. Whereas the number of dual earner families has increased, there has not been a substantial change in the distribution of labour in the family. In this context, women's workload has substantially increased without being offset by greater democracy in familial gender relations (Rubery *et al.*, 1999).

These studies highlight the endurance of gender divisions of labour. Richardson (1993: 74) explains that 'women are expected to regard motherhood as their most important adult role in life'. Even where both partners are employed full-time, women maintain primary responsibility for childcare, both emotionally and economically. What can be concluded from this analysis is that the rhetoric of equality is not matched by the opportunities available. Under a thin veil of gender neutrality, the recent shift in policy focus towards work–life balance and reconciliation between work and family life is actually aimed at increasing women's participation rates whilst maintaining their position as primary carers (Lovenduski and Randall, 1993: 284; Rees, 1992: 116).

The criticism of lone parents that has taken sway over the last couple of decades highlights the continued importance of traditional family values in the context of social policy. More specifically, it highlights how motherhood is still perceived as the natural extension of marriage. It is in this context that the male-breadwinner model continues to be the defining organisational feature of social and welfare structures in this country (Figes, 1995; Leonard and Speakman, 1986; Lewis, 1992b).

Teresa Rees (1992: 23–4, 116) explains these trends by looking at the Parsonian legacy on British views of the function of the family in the socio-economic system, whereby the family is the basic social unit within which the young are nurtured and cared for. The gendered division of labour therefore serves an important socio-economic function. Rees argues that Parson's theory reflects 'common sense' attitudes that determine the behaviour and decisions of employers and policy-makers. Margaret Thatcher's social reforms were full of these assumptions. Concerned with the kind of changes that were taking place in the 1970s and 1980s, she set out to support and strengthen the traditional family and, in doing so, reaffirmed its position as the necessary foundation for social, political and economic order. Although Thatcher's policies were extensively criticised, they have had an enduring legacy on British society. This legacy is particularly evident in the entrenched nature of the public–private dichotomy (Leonard and Speakman, 1986: 12; Lewis, 1992: 26; Lovenduski and Randall, 1993).

As mentioned previously, the relationship between public and private is particularly important with reference to the development of family-friendly policies. Lack of provisions for working mothers determines women's roles in the private as well as the public. As the state detaches itself from the private, the constant refusal to support working mothers directly shapes gender roles and divisions of labour in the private. Besides making the public–private dichotomy illusory, this relationship between the state and the family determines the framework for the development and implementation of equal rights and maternity provisions.

The next section will discuss how these representations have influenced the development of the equality agenda in the UK. The analysis of the next section will be based upon many of the considerations outlined above, as they provide the socio-economic framework within which family-friendly policies have emerged as part of government rhetoric and policy over the last decade.

Maternity and employment rights today: legislating mothers

As outlined in the previous section, since the end of the Second World War significant socio-economic changes have greatly reduced the time women dedicate to the social and biological function of reproduction. The increase in women's participation in the official labour market, however, has followed a 'bi-modal' structure, whereby employment rates are highest when women are free from childcare responsibilities. In other words, women's employment follows this pattern: entry into the labour market before motherhood, relative absence during the reproductive years to fulfil the function of mothering, re-entry into the labour force when children are older. What emerges from this analysis is that although it has become more acceptable for mothers to combine employment and care, one way in which British women manage these conflicting priorities is through part-time employment (Lewis, 1992; Rees, 1992: 17–18). In this context, part-time/flexible employment has become the main tool used to reconcile women's *different* needs. Unfortunately, this approach fails to address the overall question of gender divisions of labour and power hierarchies either in the labour market and/or in the family (Rees, 1992: 17–18; Thane, 1991: 100).

There were relatively few developments in the area of women's employment rights in the first half of the twentieth century. Despite the ratification of the 1919 Sex Disqualification (Removal) Act, various marriage bars were introduced in the inter-war years that directly contravened the principles enshrined in the Act. In the mid-1940s, the Education Bill (1944) proposed to establish equal pay for male and female teachers. The bill was ultimately withdrawn after a surge of opposition to this principle from all main political parties and the Royal Commission. Despite these setbacks, the fact that the debate was actually taking place draws attention to the impact of the war on changing women's employment patterns. With the end of the labour shortage after the war women were once again forced out of the official labour market; so much so, that by 1947 only 18 per cent of married women were employed in the public sphere. A movement for the recognition of women's role as mothers paralleled this trend, highlighting the nature of the gender order in post war British society (Carter, 1988: 13–15; Lewis, 1992: 79–80).

Lewis (1992: 80) claims that the repercussions of these decisions were almost immediate: 'women's pay as a proportion of men's fell from the early 1950s until the mid-1960s, ... and remained fairly stable until the early 1970s'. Given the level of opposition outlined above, it is unsurprising that the issues of equal rights and equal pay did not return to the policy agenda until the late 1960s. It was only following a series of strikes that the government considered implementing the International Labour Organisation (ILO) Convention No. 100 (1951) on equal pay. (Deakin and Morris, 1995: 482–3; Lewis and Davies, 1991).

With regard to the analysis presented here, one issue that needs to be addressed when examining the legislation is whether or not it bridges the division between public and private. This section will analyse the aims and scope of British policies for the *promotion* of women's' rights. Given the intricate nature of British law, this section will combine an analysis of case law with statue law, with particular emphasis on the latter. The primary statutes that will be looked at are as follows: the Equal Pay Act 1970; the Sex Discrimination Act 1975; the Employment Protection Act 1978; and the development of statutory Maternity Pay, Leave and Allowance (1986) with consideration to the amendments implemented by the Trade Union Reform and Employment Rights Act 1993, and finally the 1999 and 2002 Maternity and Parental Leave Regulations.

Equal rights in Britain have been implemented under the auspices of statute and case law; however their development has to be understood within the framework of common law. Although the Industrial Revolution marked the beginning of debates on employment rights, the British liberal/laissez-faire approach to politics and economics has consistently undermined the adoption of any radical legislation. As Smith *et al.* (1993: 183) explain, common law 'placed no restriction on an employer's freedom to decide whether to hire a particular individual'. Consequently, equal rights and anti-discrimination provisions have traditionally been attributed very little importance (Deakin and Morris, 1995: 480; Smith *et al.*, 1993: 183).

Pressure for the development of equal rights started to mount in the 1960s and culminated with the ratification of the 1970 Equal Pay Act (EPA) and 1975 Sex Dicrimination Act (SDA). It is worth noting that the impending membership of the EEC was instrumental in pushing forward the newly established equality agenda. This can be regarded as a turning point in the development of women's employment rights in Britain. As a matter of fact, the implementation of the 1970 Act must be analysed with reference to the nature of the relationship between European and national law (Deakin and Morris, 1995: 556; Honeyball, 1991: 8; Meehan and Collins, 1996: 223).

Although the Equal Pay Act 1970 can be considered a milestone in the development of women's rights in Britain, there are several weaknesses that limited its scope and reach. The EPA introduced the concept of contractual equality for men and women bascd on the principle of equal pay. Section 1(1) of the act rejects any contractual disadvantage based on the grounds of sex, whereas section 1(2) introduces the concept of equal pay for equal work. The act outlines three necessary conditions for the operationalisation of the law: *equal work, like work,* and *work rated as equivalent.* Sections 6(1)(a), and (b), also introduce the concept of different needs through three exceptions to the overall principle of the act. Of these three exceptions the first two are particularly important. The first exception applies to the wider '*law regulating the employment of women*' (Honeyball, 1991: 20), although the practices targeted here have since been outlawed by the Sex Discrimination Act of 1986 and the Employment Act of 1989. The second exception is '*pregnancy and childbirth*', which allows for 'special treatment' for maternity reasons. The clause allows women to take maternity leave 'with no corresponding terms for men' (Honeyball, 1991: 21). And the third is '*Death* or *Retirement*', which has since been amended in compliance with EU law (Atkins and Hoggett, 1984; Honeyball, 1991; Smith *et al.*, 1993).

Despite establishing the principle of equality within British employment law, this statute also has some significant shortcomings, the most important of which are as follows. Firstly, it regulates only contractual terms. Secondly, the balance of power is skewed in favour of employers. Thirdly, there is no recognition of indirect discrimination. Finally, it does not account for discrimination on the grounds of marital status. These criticisms highlight the lack of recognition by the 1970 Act that equality and equal treatment are concepts far too complex to be dealt with extensively in a single *ad hoc* piece of employment legislation (Atkins and Hoggett, 1984: 21; Honeyball, 1991: 7, 20–5).

The limited scope and reach of this policy gives rise to some important considerations. Firstly, despite some acknowledgement of difference, the emphasis on women's needs shows how the male worker remains the standard. Secondly, the principle of 'special treatment' enshrined within this policy reinforces women's role as carers within the private. To sum up, these limitations greatly restrict the effectiveness of an already limited piece of legislation (Smith *et al.*, 1991).

The second piece of statute that needs to be discussed is the Sex Discrimination Act 1975. The primary objective of this act was to amend the Equal Pay Act 1970, and consequently to broaden the scope and meaning of equality legislation. The introduction of the principle of indirect discrimination and the establishment of the Equal Opportunities Commission were probably the most important achievements of the act. Much further-reaching in scope and aims than its predecessor, this act can be seen as the achievement of Labour women, who, for several years, had been campaigning for equal treatment and brought the subject to the floor for several discussions and debates in the Commons (Carter, 1988: 58–60; Deakin and Morris, 1995: 484–7; Smith *et al.*, 1993: 211).

In terms of the actual provisions, Section 1(1) describes sexual discrimination as any sort of unfavourable treatment towards a female employee. This means that it outlawed indirect discrimination and discrimination on the grounds of marital status, both of which had previously been ignored by the Equal Pay Act 1970. The act thus prohibits discrimination at all stages of employment, including hiring and dismissal procedures. Another important issue addressed is equal treatment and maternity, for the purposes of which, special treatment is not to be considered discrimination (Deakin and Morris, 1995: 493, 523, 539, 545; Smith *et al.*, 1993: 189–90).

The SDA 1975 therefore broadened for the meaning of equality and equal rights. The introduction of the principle of intentionality is particularly important as it outlaws any sort of discrimination, and places the responsibility on employers to ensure that their practices comply with the law. These changes highlight an important shift in policy discourse, which was to be furthered by the Equal Opportunities Commission. The single most important development instituted by this act, the Commission was charged with overseeing the implementation of both the SDA 1975 and the EPA 1970. Both of these achievements are particularly important for the development of comprehensive maternity rights. Firstly, despite having its power greatly limited by various Conservative governments, the Equal Opportunities Commission proved to be an important actor in promoting the equality agenda; secondly, the act outlawed discrimination on the grounds of maternity and pregnancy (Honeyball, 1991: 12, 64).

Some of the most important limitations of this act revolve around the division between the protection and the promotion of women's rights. The first major limitation of the SDA 1975 is its attempt to draw together these new provisions with the Factory Act 1961. These provisions entitled women to special protection such as a limited number of working hours and the prohibition of night work. What the 1975 Act failed to acknowledge was the implicit contradiction between the concept of equal treatment and customary special protection. Secondly, although the act outlaws discrimination on the grounds of marital status, it falls short of its original objective, as it did not recognise the complexities of sexual discrimination. As Honeyball (1991: 70) explains, 'even a dismissal of a single person due to her impending marriage will not come within section 3'. Finally, the act ignores public–private issues and only obliges larger firms to comply with the provisions (Carter, 1988: 60; Smith *et al.*, 1993: 190).

In theory, some of these criticisms were addressed by the claim that these statutes were conceived to work together as a comprehensive code against sexual discrimination. Unfortunately, they are all too often mutually exclusive and are far too limited to achieve such an ambitious goal (Honeyball, 1991: 19, 56–7). This analysis leads to some initial conclusions about these policies. Although they certainly indicate an increase in policy-makers' awareness of the impact of sex discrimination upon women's employment, they fail to address more deep-rooted issues that continue to influence women's participation in the official labour market. The limitations of these acts disassociate the principle of equal pay from that of equal treatment. The 1970 and 1975 Statutes thus advance the principle of formal equality, but fail to promote substantive equality.

The next two statutes that will be considered are the Employment Protection (Consolidation) Act (EPCA) 1978 and the Trade Union Reform and Employment Rights (TURER) Act 1993. These two statutes are particularly important because they aim to extend the scope and reach of the 1970 and 1975 Acts. Moreover, adopted after the UK joined the Common Market, they sought to transpose European provisions within the national law.

The Employment Protection (Consolidation) Act of 1978 is particularly important because it provides the basis for maternity 'protection'. The EPCA is often considered to be the single 'most important remedy' against unfair dismissal (Deakin and Morris, 1995: 582; Honeyball, 1991: 121). Section 60 in particular expands the provisions for special treatment for women workers introduced by the SDA 1975. More importantly, it marks some progress towards the establishment of 'comprehensive' maternity legislation. This act, however, provided minimal protection against dismissal, as it covered only breaches of contracts and a statutory minimum period of notice. Moreover, its application was also limited, in as far as it included a number of restrictive criteria, some of which can be considered in violation of EC law (Deakin and Morris, 1995: 582; Honeyball, 1991: 118, 121).

In terms of the analysis conducted here, probably the most important achievement of the 1978 Act is the institutionalisation of the right to reinstatement after confinement (Section 45.1; Schedule 13.10). Despite various limitations, this act provides women with the basis for claims of unfair dismissal on maternity grounds. Unfortunately, the establishment of a minimum of two years of continuous service severely limits the reach of this policy (Section 58, 19.1 and Schedule 13 EPCA 1978). On top of that, the act allows for exceptions to the rule on unfair dismissal when pregnancy prevents a worker from fulfilling her duties (Section 60.1). Although it also places an onus on the employer to find a suitable alternative (Section 60.2), if such an alternative is not available, then dismissal is permissible. The introduction of restrictive qualifying requirements for protection against dismissal and loopholes that allow for exemptions from the principles enshrined in the act further highlight the continued bias in favour of male norms and the male worker (Deakin and Morris, 1995: 582; Honeyball, 1991; Smith et al., 1993: 233).

The problem with these requirements is the lack of recognition of the gendered nature of employment patterns. Taking the male worker as the standard negatively influences women's opportunity for recourse to the law in case of unfair dismissal and sex discrimination. Moreover, women employed on a part-time basis were excluded from the legislation. By dismissing the impact of gender power hierarchies on labour market practices, this statute fails to *protect* those who are in greatest need of it. Finally, the concept of equality advanced by this statute is very limited and is a far cry from the principle of substantive equality that is needed for the implementation of comprehensive equal opportunities policies and maternity rights (Honeyball, 1991: 123–4; Lewis, 1992: 82–4; McRae, 1991: 67–8, 145).

The analysis of the 1978 Act also reveals the impact of European law on domestic legislation. Amended in 1993 by the Trade Union Reform and Employment Rights Act, it was supposed to implement the provisions established by the 1992 Pregnant Worker Directive. These amendments provided for a minimum fourteen-week maternity leave period 'regardless of length of service', and outlawed all forms of dismissal on the grounds of pregnancy. The extension of these rights was implemented within the existing framework as enacted by the 1978 Act. It is however questionable whether it has achieved this aim. The limitations of these policies arise from the analysis of the *protection* vis-à-vis the *promotion* of women's rights. Whereas these regulations protect women employed in the labour market from unfair dismissal, they do not promote maternity rights as necessary for the accomplishment of substantive equality (Collins, 1994; Deakin and Morris, 1995: 584).

The TURER Act greatly improves working conditions for working women in Britain, and has since been used to highlight an increasing level of commitment towards women's rights. It is, however, worth noting that the act limits itself to the implementation of the basic principles enshrined within the Pregnant Worker Directive. As such, EU law did not prove to be a springboard for further developments, but merely ensured the establishment of minimum standards for the protection of pregnant workers. These shortcomings are all the more obvious when considering the interests that drove the Council negotiations on this policy.

As noted in chapter 3, the 1992 Directive was ratified under the auspices of Article 118(a) of the Treaty of Rome. The focus of this policy was therefore health and safety rather than equal opportunities. Although this move circumvented the possibility of a British veto, it did not overcome the government's objection to this policy. As a matter of fact, the government abstained from the vote in protest. Also implemented within British law under the auspices of health and safety regulations, the principles enshrined within these regulations raise serious questions about the government's commitment to widening the scope of equal opportunities policies. The debates at the European level signalled the government's disregard for women's employment rights through the opposition to extensive maternity rights, and the legislative constraints present at the national level further support these conclusions (Anon., 1992: 3–4; Conaghan, 1993: 82; Millns, 1996: 167; Morris and Nott, 1995: 69).

Consistent with the overall laissez-faire approach characteristic of British welfare structures, the government's strategy in this policy area only partially acknowledged the needs of pregnant workers and the demands of combining motherhood and employment. If the aim was to achieve some degree of balance between public roles and private duties, then this legislation raises serious questions about current norms by which workers are judged. As argued by Morris and Nott (1995: 69–70) maternity legislation has great potential for changing representations and perceptions of women in the labour market. From this initial analysis, however, this does not appear to be one of the aims of this particular policy.

Despite some important criticisms of the TURER Act, it is important to acknowledge that since its full implementation, the rights of working mothers have been substantially expanded. Through various amendments, this policy succeeded in making maternity leave accessible to all women employed in the official labour market. Besides unconditional fourteen weeks maternity leave, it also introduced an entitlement to an additional forty weeks leave subject to length of service and contractual agreement. Section 24 also outlawed dismissal on the grounds of pregnancy irrespective of qualifying criteria or length of service; whereas section 56 provides the right to reinstatement whereby an employer's failure to fulfil this obligation will be considered on a par with dismissal. Unfortunately, this right is subject to a qualifying period: two years continuous service to be completed before the eleventh week prior to the expected date of confinement. Finally, the TURER Act provides for the continuance of employment contracts throughout the maternity leave period (Collins, 1994: 13–15, 19–22; Deakin and Morris, 1995: 584–6; Smith et al., 1993: 233, 238–9).

The ratification of the TURER Act is a clear improvement on past provisions, however there are some issues that need further consideration. Firstly, the conditionality of extended maternity leave and the right of reinstatement severely limit the reach of this policy. Secondly, the question of pay remained largely unresolved. Although all women are entitled to maternity leave, maternity pay was limited by the following qualifying criteria: twenty-six weeks full time employment by the fifteenth week before the expected date of confinement. The separation of leave from pay has important implications for the large number of women employed in part-time or temporary occupations who do not qualify for maternity pay. Aside from the more general issue of justice, this division has the added disadvantage that often prevents working-class women from taking full advantage of their rights. Moreover, it crystallises gender power hierarchies in the family and reinforces the male-breadwinner model (IDS, 1994; McRae, 1991: 69).

The TURER Act was not the only policy implemented by the British government that sought to comply with European maternity provisions. Under the health and safety regulations, European law also provides for a minimum two weeks compulsory maternity leave, which was in the first instance regulated by the 1994 Maternity (Compulsory Leave) Regulations (IS 1994/279). The purpose of these regulations was to protect a woman's right to leave after confinement (IDS, 1994: 14). The 1996 Employment Act completes the process of implementation of European provisions within national law. This policy is important for two reasons: firstly, it highlights a shift in policy by the government; secondly, it strengthens the position of working mothers vis-à-vis employers and the labour market at large (Guerrina, 2001: 33–4; McGlynn, 1996: 233–4).

Following the 1997 elections, the Labour government has sought to reform and expand family-friendly provisions. The 1998 'Fairness at Work' White Paper and 1999 Employment Relations Act are clear examples of such trends. In terms of reconciliation between work and family life, the main aim of these policies was to expand maternity rights and implement the principles of the Parental Leave Directive. This act is important because it reasserts the centrality of maternity rights to the employment rights framework. More specifically, it implements within national law the principles of the Parental Leave Directive by regulating conditions for family leave, including time off for dependants as well as maternity and parental leave (Guerrina, 2001: 33–4). These are provisions that have been subsequently reformed and expanded by the 2002 amendments to the maternity and paternity leave regulations.

The 2000 Green Paper 'Work & Parents: Competitiveness and Choice' provides the backdrop against which the 2002 regulations developed. The Green Paper goes some way towards recognising the impact of conflicting demands on the lives of working parents. It also outlined a series of policy questions about the nature of mothering, the relationship between mothering and work, and the role of fathers in the family. It also sought to test public opinion regarding pay arrangements, flexible employment arrangements and childcare (James, 2001).

This latest development in the field expanded the reach of the policy with the aim of creating a working environment that is more woman/mother friendly. In so doing, the 2002 Maternity Regulations expanded previous statutory entitlements. It reiterated the commitment to two weeks compulsory maternity leave, and increased the minimum entitlement to ordinary maternity leave from eighteen to twenty-six weeks (Article 8). In addition, employees who have completed twenty-six weeks of continuous employment by the fourteenth week before the expected date of confinement are entitled to an additional twenty-six weeks unpaid maternity leave (Article 6). In terms of pay, the 2002 Employment Act also established that the first six weeks of ordinary maternity leave are to be paid at 90 per cent of the employee's ordinary wage, and the remainder of ordinary maternity leave shall be paid at the basic rate of £102.80 set for Statutory Maternity Pay (Inland Revenue, 2004–05 rates) or 90 per cent of an employee's ordinary wage, whichever is less (Section 19 and 20). Although an improvement on previous provisions, this policy still excludes self-employed workers and the unemployed from its provisions (DTI, 2003).

In terms of parental and paternity leave, the 2002 Employment Act expands the rights established by the previous policies. Most importantly, it establishes a right to a minimum two weeks leave to be taken within the first two months (56 days) of the birth of a child (Article 80 A). It ensures that such entitlements are extended to adoptive parents (Article 80 B) and that employers' contractual obligations are maintained during the period of leave (Article 80 C). The 2002 Act also establishes the principle of Statutory Paternity Pay. Subject to qualifying conditions, which are not dissimilar to those established for working mothers (i.e. a worker has to be in employment for a minimum of twenty-six weeks by the fifteenth week prior to the estimated due date), men/fathers are now entitled to a minimum payment that is calculated on the basis of Statutory Maternity Pay (i.e. £ 102.80 per week or 90 per cent of normal wage, whichever is less) (DTI, 2003b).

This brief overview of the development of maternity rights and family-friendly policies in the UK denotes a progressive expansion of the minimum rights/protection working mothers are entitled to under the law. Unfortunately, it is over the issue of pay that the shortcomings of UK policy become evident. Although the establishment a minimum payment of 90 per cent for the first six weeks of leave is an important improvement, the minimal rate provided for under Statutory Maternity Pay is a clear signal that the government is primarily concerned with the short-term economic impact of the costs associated with maternity leave. Given this background, these provisions fall short of providing a statutory right to reconciliation between work and family life. In this context, employees remain subject to the good will of employers; and the rights of working mothers are often curtailed by economic necessity.

This analysis draws attention to the implicit relationship between socio-economic hierarchies/structures and maternity rights. Despite the substantial changes that have taken place since the ratification of the Equal Pay Act in 1970, there has been little convergence of formal rights into substantive equality. As Joshi et al. (1996) further point out, these discrepancies maintain substantial wage differentials, not only between men and women, but also between working mothers and other women employed in the official labour market. The assumption entrenched within all these policies is that women will remain the primary carer, and the legislation should allow women to fulfil that role. Employers, who have become increasingly more involved in the implementation of maternity provisions, have done so with a clear idea of their expectations of women workers and working mothers. These expectations, which are the result of a competitive labour market, however, are often incompatible with the demands of the domestic sphere. Although these arguments have been made before, they need to be restated as such representations influence the shape of the labour market and women's role within it.

UK members of the European Union: a positive outcome for women's rights?

Since joining the Common Market in 1973, successive British governments have had an interesting and sometimes fraught relationship with European institutions. These dynamics have also had significant repercussions on the development of equal rights policies. In many ways, European integration has had a positive impact on the development of a minimum standard of rights and provisions for women in the UK. Moreover, the Equal Opportunities Commission found an ally in European institutions, and the EU has become a stage where it can voice concerns about the domestic framework (Conaghan, 1993: 82; IDS, 1994: 40; Meehan and Collins, 1996: 223–4; Pringle, 1998: 139).

Despite claims that the UK had institutionalised the basic principle of equality before becoming a member of the EEC, its 'pioneering' role in equal rights should not be overestimated. For Meehan and Collins (1996: 223) the prospect of European membership was instrumental in prompting the development of equal rights and social security policies. As outlined in the previous section, the UK adopted the Equal Pay Act 1970 and established the framework for the development of the Sex Discrimination Act of 1975 in preparation for EEC membership. EEC membership subsequently also forced the British government to address some of the weaknesses of its equal rights policies. Following various warnings that British legislation, particularly the EPA 1970, contravened the principle of Article 119, in 198 the Commission initiated proceedings against the government for failing to implement the equal pay provisions established by the Treaty of Rome. The ratification of the 1975 Directive, and various ECJ rulings, led to the 1983 amendment of the EPA 1970. Indeed, since 1972, the European Community, and the European Court of Justice in particular, have played an important role in extending the scope of domestic policies (Deakin and Morris, 1995: 480–7; Figes, 1995: 176; Lewis, 1992: 117–8; Meehan and Collins, 1996; Smith *et al.*, 1993: 185).

The UK has traditionally been amongst the most conservative of member states, and the most sceptical about the development of European social policies. As this ideological resistance has commuted into a wider reluctance to implement European principles in national law, Deakin and Morris (1995: 55–6) argue that European Directives' greatest impact has come through the application of case law. It is important to note that the work of the ECJ has had a key role in steering British policy debates in the area of social affairs. In this context, it is thus worth drawing attention to a few cases in the area of equal opportunities and maternity rights. However, such reliance on case law, and the Court as advocate of women's rights, can produce inconsistent results ultimately preventing the development of a comprehensive framework for equal opportunities and reconciliation between work and family life.

In terms of equal pay, the most important cases were: *Macarthys* v *Smith*, dealing with the issue of equal pay for work of equal value; and *Worringham and Humphrey* v *Lloyds Bank*, in which the ECJ widened the scope of Article 119 to include social security provisions (Honeyball, 1991: 107). Unfortunately, not all rulings have broadened the equality agenda either at the national or European level. In *Jenkins* v *Kingsgate (Clothing Productions) Ltd*, the Court ruled that:

> a difference in pay between full-time workers and part-time workers does not amount to discrimination prohibited by Article 119 of the Treaty unless it is in reality merely an indirect way of reducing the pay of part-time workers on the ground that the group of workers is composed exclusively or predominantly of women. (Honeyball, 1991: 103–4)

The foundations for this action are to be found in the *Clay Cross* case, an important milestone in the development of sex discrimination law in the UK. In *Jenkins'* case, however, the Court's ruling reintroduced the concept of economic advantage, revealing a lack of consideration for gender power hierarchies. Despite the Court's affirmation that part-time employment should not be used to support indirect discrimination, by focusing on the *intentionality* of the act, the Court narrowed the scope of the legislation. What the Court failed to consider is the fact that it is mostly women who are employed in low-paid part-time jobs (Carter, 1988: 156–60; Honeyball, 1991: 102–7; Prechal and Burrows, 1990: 211–6; Rees, 1998: 31; Smith *et al.*, 1993: 224–5).

On the issue of equal treatment, *Barber* v *Guardian Royal Exchange Assurance Group*, and the *R.* v *Secretary of State for Employment, ex p. ECO* were also test trials of UK policy. In the case of *Barber* v *Guardian*, the ECJ interpreted the principle of Equal Pay, as enshrined in Article 119, as inclusive of employment benefits. The exclusion of part-time workers from such benefits thus amounted to discrimination; whereas *R.* v *Secretary of State* reaffirmed the principle of equal treatment established by the previous case. In this instance, Deakin and Morris (1995: 486–7) explain, the Lords applied the principle of European law as defined by the ECJ, ruling that 'qualifying thresholds amounted to indirect sex discrimination on the grounds that they significantly affect women more than men, and could not be justified by reference to wider considerations of social and economic policy'. These cases are important for two reasons. Firstly, they highlight the influence of European law on national equality provisions; and, secondly they emphasise the wider scope and reach of European equal rights legislation as compared to British provisions (Deakin and Morris, 1995: 486–7; Honeyball, 1991: 101–3; Hoskyns, 1996: 85).

Dekker v *VJV Centrum* and *Webb* v *EMO Air Cargo Ltd*, on the other hand, set the stage for current discussions about the rights of working mothers and the scope of reconciliation between work and family life. As discussed in chapter 4, in both cases, the final judgement recognised that discrimination on the grounds of pregnancy is tantamount to direct discrimination. For Deakin and Morris (1995: 497–500) these cases highlight the failure of national law to bring together the principles of equality and 'special' needs. The importance of *Dekker* and *Webb* resides in the ECJ's rejection of 'arguments that direct discrimination in the context of pregnancy could be justified by reference to such factors as the financial expenses incurred by the employer or the practical difficulties caused by the employee's absence' (Deakin and Morris, 1995: 497–500). These cases are important because they recognised, for the first time, that that women's role in the reproductive process is not a valid excuse for discriminatory practices (Hoskyns, 1994: 229–30; Hoskyns, 1996: 159–61; Rees, 1998: 56).

More generally, it is now widely recognised that the 1983 and the 1986 Amendments of the SDA 1975 were a direct result of ECJ rulings and European equality directives. Unfortunately, the achievements of these policies were partial at best, as they attempted to incorporate European principles within the limits of existing regulations. As Figes (1995: 176) explains, 'the matter wasn't addressed afresh; it was simply adapted in order to comply in a haphazard way with the Treaty of Rome. Little consideration was given to how such amendments would work in practice'. Prechal and Burrows (1990: 213–16) developed this critique further arguing that the 1986 Amendments were only a facade aimed at fulfilling the requirement of European legislation, rather than displaying a positive commitment towards increasing the scope of equal rights (Lewis, 1992).

Although European policies have played an important role in creating a more favourable framework for the operationalisation of equal pay and equal treatment, the greatest impact of EU law has been in the field of family-friendly polices. Meehan and Collins (1996: 227–8) point out that 'pregnancy discrimination and maternity rights form one of the most difficult issues under British law'. As outlined in the previous section, in British law the principle of equality implies a comparison between like entities (i.e. sameness), and thus struggles to deal with the concept of equality in difference. The British legal system has struggled to find the 'proper' place or the appropriate terms of reference to deal with 'conditions', such as maternity, that affect only the female workforce. As Meehan and Collins (1996: 227–8) explain, this interpretation of equality, difference and woman has been particularly important for the courts that have struggle to reconcile pregnancy with male patterns of employment and absence from employment.

Unfortunately, this approach not only limits the reach of formal equality, but is diametrically opposed to the principle of substantive equality. In other words, it reinforces traditional representations of women, work and worker, and reaffirms the centrality of the male-breadwinner model. In this framework, the 1992 Directive therefore contributed to the development of a comprehensive framework for the protection of maternity rights in three ways. Firstly, it helped to disassociate pregnancy from disabling illnesses. Then, it provided the backdrop against which the 1993 TURER Act and the

1994 Maternity (Leave) Regulations were adopted. And finally, it provided the rationale for the ECJ ruling in *Webb*, which ultimately extended the reach of this policy area (IDS, 1994: 140–1; Meehan and Collins, 1996: 228). The debate surrounding the ratification of the Parental Leave Directive was even more controversial. The British government was once again vocally opposed the development of parental or paternity leave on economic grounds. According to Prechal and Burrows (1990: 300–1) the roots of this opposition lie in the different aims of these two actors. Given the discussion of current policy developments conducted in the previous section of this chapter, it is worth noting the altogether limited impact of EU policies on the UK policy framework. Despite recent improvements in maternity rights, the British labour market and employers in particular, have remained reluctant to implement fully the values and practices enshrined within the principles of work–life balance, or more specifically reconciliation between work and family life. The Parental Leave Directive and the policy programmes emerging at the European level have introduced a new set of rights, which are largely insignificant as they failed to address the socio-economic concerns associated with the issue of care, such as pay.

It is in this context that Meehan and Collins (1996: 231–4) conclude that the European equality agenda has proved to be instrumental in the development of national equal rights policies, in as far as it prevented the marginalisation of women's rights in national politics and provided a forum within which to raise concerns about domestic policies. They argue that a detailed analysis of how European policies have been transposed into national law also raises important questions about the government's commitment to women's rights. As they further explain,

> in an era in which British governments have tried to minimise rights and the role of regulatory and collective bodies, resort to European law has provided virtually the only enforceable ways of securing improvements to and filling lacunae in domestic legislation. Though further European developments on sex equality, ... may take place under the auspices of the Social Agreement from which the British government has secured exemption, European standards can still be of benefit to women in Britain. (Meehan and Collins,1996: 232–3)

In conclusion, it is clear that the European Union provided a framework for the establishment of reconciliation between work and family life as a principle and in practice. Despite the significant shortcomings of European policies, they have proved to be a force of change. Particularly within a national framework that tends to focus on individual freedoms and equality, as is the case of the UK, the European Union introduced a wider reaching concept of equality and what is necessary to achieve it.

Legislative limitations: questions and puzzles

The legal and economic position of women in the UK has changed dramati-
cally in the last century. However, the analysis presented in this chapter
highlights how economic concerns about the deregulation and competitiveness of the British labour market have taken precedence over the
implementation of substantive equality. Given this background, it becomes
clear why the introduction of a family-friendly agenda in policy discourses
has failed to address fundamental questions about representations of women
and workers, the public–private dichotomy, and the distinction between
formal and substantive equality.

As the evidence presented in this chapter points out, policy-makers have
found it easy to ignore the influence of gender power hierarchies on labour
market structures. The assumption of gender neutrality that underpins the
equal rights framework has allowed policy-makers to ignore the male standard of worker upon which the employment market is based. This approach
to equality has, in turn, only limited scope. It fails to challenge power hierarchies within the family and employment practices that maintain wage
differentials. More importantly, it continues to assume that socio-economic
hierarchies fall outside the scope of equal rights and family friendly policies.
The limits of policies aimed at implementing the principle of reconciliation
between work and family life highlight the difficulties encountered in implementing the principle of substantive equality. As Lovenduski and Randall
(1993: 176) explain, 'for women to escape or alter these conditions, they need
the financial independence which only adequately paid work can provide in a
society such as ours'. Adequate pay and the care infrastructure are only two
of a range of issues that need to be addressed in the analysis of the scope and
reach of equal rights and family friendly policies (Lovenduski, 1996: 5–6, 11;
Lovenduski and Randall, 1993: 176).

There are three preliminary conclusions that emerge from this analysis.
Firstly, the range of employment arrangements available to women is skewed
in favour of atypical and part-time work; a problem that is made worse by the
chronic lack of affordable childcare services. Secondly, women's employment
choices are contingent upon their access to resources. Finally, the approach of
policy-makers and employers to equality and labour market practices highlights the continued preference for workers who abide to traditional male
norms and working patterns.

Despite the increasing amount of women returning to work following
pregnancy, there are still significant discrepancies between political rhetoric
and the establishment of the necessary infrastructure needed to fully implement those provisions. Lack of affordable childcare and the high proportion
of women in part-time employment maintain gendered divisions and sexual
segregation in the official labour market. The new focus on work–life balance,
which revolves around a variety of flexible working patterns, is supposed to

facilitate women's access to the official labour market. Conaghan (1993), however, argues that working mothers' calls for different working arrange-ments have been sabotaged by a market seeking to increase the flexibility of the workforce. The result of this situation is a labour force that is divided between full-time and part-time employment, with a predominance of women in the latter category. It is in this context that Peter Elias (1990: 67–8, 81) argues that ignoring gender divisions between part-time and full-time employment has significant repercussions on women's social and political status and serves to limit women's access to the higher levels of the labour market. As he further explains, these arrangements not only prevent the institutionalisation of substantive equality, but maintain institutional power hierarchies (Brannen and Moss, 1991: 32; Conaghan, 1993: 71–2; Elias, 1990: 67).

Brannen and Moss (1991: 260–1), on the other hand, draw attention to the shortcomings of a labour market based upon full-time employment in which the male model has become the standard of work and worker. In order to achieve substantive equality, they argue, employment patterns need to bridge the gap between the public and the private spheres. They also raise some questions that are fundamental to the analysis of family-friendly poli-cies:

> Does the traditional masculine model of employment continue to be the norm, with alternatives available to a minority at the price of a career advancement and other disadvantages? Or is work restructured on the basis that all employees, men and women, have childcare responsibility – and indeed other social responsibili-ties and relationships – that require long-term recognition? (Brannen and Moss, 1991: 260–1)

The final question is very important as it challenges gender divisions of labour whereby women are the primary carers. Each piece of legislation discussed in this chapter ignored the role of gender in defining employment policies and practices. Even the shift towards flexible working patterns, which it is claimed will provide women with a viable alternative, is only a partial and incomplete strategy. As Lewis (1992: 29–30) further highlights, the 'government determi-nation to minimise its own role and maximise family independence have effectively structured women's choices'. The consequence of this policy is a reassertion of traditional family values and women's role as primary carers (Brannen and Moss, 1991: 31; Lewis, 1992: 29–30; McRae, 1991: 3–4; Rubery et al., 1998).

Differential access to the rights established by the statutes is another important issue that determines women's employment patterns and the scope of family friendly policies. Despite a substantial increase in the percentage of women taking advantage of their statutory rights and various critiques of the gendered nature of employment structures, policy-makers have largely ignored the impact of social and economic factors on women's employment trends (Lewis, 1992: 77; Lovenduski and Randall, 1993: 170; McRae, 1991: xxxv).

The reach of the legislation determines women's interaction with the labour market as well as their position in the private sphere. For Lewis (1992: 119–20) the government's inability to reconcile public and private as the basis for equal rights legislation maintains gender divisions of labour and inequalities: 'because of women's unequal position in the labour market and the inequalities inherent in the marriage contract, such private negotiations tend to be weighted against them'. Provisions for the reconciliation between work and family life now in place strengthen women's position in the public sphere. Unfortunately, the reach of the legislation is limited to women's employment in the official labour market and pays only lip service to the establishment of equality in the private sphere.

The analysis conducted here considered the bias of current policies towards the institutionalisation of formal equality at the expense of structural reforms that would promote substantive equality. Since the end of the Second World War, British women have become an important part of the official labour market. However, women's entry in the public sphere has followed gendered patterns that have restricted their role in the labour force. It is important to recognise that gender power hierarchies are an integral part of the policy-making process, even when the focus is on gender neutral policies. As Lewis (1992: 8) points out, the legislation is based upon a 'well established and remarkably consistent set of assumptions about the proper activities and behaviour of men and women'. In which case, the resulting legislation is a mere reflection of these representations. Within this framework, Lewis (1992: 8) argues that the greatest policy-making dilemma revolves around decreeing the 'right' balance between public and private, and the role the state should play within both of them. The recent shift towards reconciliation between work and family life has been welcomed by some commentators as a positive development. Policy-makers are certainly keen to highlight the radical potential of these developments. Unfortunately, despite all the rhetoric and the gender-neutral language adopted, these policies are ultimately aimed at women. These policies are thus only a superficial attempt at addressing some of the issues raised in this book.

In conclusion, this case study highlights the continued division between formal and substantive equality. The vast amount of development in the area of work–life balance in the last decade and the establishment of a substantial set of rights for working mothers highlight the impact of European integration on widening the scope of equal rights and maternity policies in the UK (Carter, 1988: 164). Feminists, such as Lewis (1992: 5, 117), have argued that a substantial redefinition of the concept of work would lead to substantial social change that could culminate with the institutionalisation of substantive equality. Arguments about the gendered nature of work are very important, as they draw attention to the persistence of gender power hierarchies in contemporary socio-economic structures. However, increased recognition of women's roles in the private does not necessarily lead to a redistribution of responsibilities. For all the campaigns to improve acccss to affordable child-care and flexible working patterns that would allow women to 'reconcile' their role as mother with paid employment, it is important to point out that the function of care remains a maternal responsibility (Lovenduski and Randall, 1993: 185). In this framework, equal rights and maternity provisions are defined by contradicting expectations about women's duties as workers and women's roles as mothers.

Conclusions

The analysis presented in this book examined the scope and reach of maternity rights and family-friendly policies in order to ascertain the impact of gender normative structures on the legislative process. More specifically, it sought to evaluate the relationship between equality, gender roles and work. This discussion was contextualised within the framework of the equal rights debate in feminist theory. This particular debate was chosen because feminist discussions about equality, difference and woman/mother provide important insights into the legislative process. This analysis raised challenging questions about the definitions and implications of different interpretations of the relationship between the public and private sphere as well as the legal and social environment on the overall reach of equal opportunities and family friendly policies. Finally, having identified the strengths and weaknesses of each approach the discussion presented in the book focused on the division between formal and substantive equality in order to assess the biases and values that define the scope of equal rights and maternity legislation in Europe.

In this context, the equal rights debate was used to bring to the attention of the reader important feminist discourses about the impact of equality and equal rights on constructing gender and the concept of woman, and thus provide an analytical framework for the evaluation of policy outcomes. The argument presented in this book is not located within a specific feminist approach in the debate, but has sought to engage with each approach by adopting key concepts at the centre of their analysis. The examination of maternity and equal rights legislation presented here, therefore, draws upon the principles of equality, difference and the deconstruction of the concept of woman. The strengths of each approach highlight possible avenues for the development of maternity legislation. Their weaknesses, on the other hand, emphasise the limitations of the legislation. As the analysis conducted here has shown, this combination of feminist approaches is necessary to develop an extensive critique of maternity legislation and equal rights policies that is sensitive to the social, economic and political framework within which such rights are developed and implemented.

In the process of discussing the socio-political and legal issues surrounding the ratification and implementation of family-friendly policies, I have therefore raised some questions about the impact of gender roles and gender divisions of labour upon the scope of equality provisions. The two case studies considered in this book proved to be an important source of comparison for the analysis of the impact of gender on the policy-making process; whereas the analysis of the European policies provides an overarching framework of reference for the development of women's employment rights in Europe. It highlights the influence of current socio-economic trends on policy outcomes and the policy-making process at large.

In chapter 1 I asked the following questions with reference to the concept of equality: 1. What is the standard by which equality is measured? 2. Who falls within the scope of equality? 3. What are its theoretical limitations, and how do they affect its policy effectiveness? The analysis presented in the empirical chapters of this book lead us to the following conclusions: 1. Despite current political rhetoric about the need to foster a work–life balance, equal rights and maternity policies remain heavily reliant on the principle of formal equality. 2. Equality continues to be disassociated from social justice and, as such, it continues to be perceived as a women-only issue. 3. The focus on substantive equality ultimately constrains the reach of current developments in the area of reconciliation between work and family life.

Given this context, my concluding remarks will assess the implications of the analysis of the empirical material presented here in terms of Nancy Chodorow's (1978) theory of gender and mothering outlined in chapter 1.

Questions and puzzles: how important is gender?

Drucilla Cornell's (1992) discussion of equality, difference and woman highlights the importance of feminist deconstructions of the legislation and the legislative process. She argues that

> the deconstruction of the *conventional* structures of gender identity as either biologically necessary or as culturally desirable not only does not erase the 'reality' of women's suffering, but demands instead the affirmation of feminine sexual difference as irreducible to the dominant definition of the feminine within the gender hierarchy as man's other or as his mirror image. In other words, sexual difference and more specifically feminine sexual difference, is not being erased; instead, the rigid structures of gender identity which have devalued women and identified them with the patriarchal conventions of the gender hierarchy are being challenged. (Cornell, 1992: 281)

In a similar fashion, the analysis conducted in this book raised some questions that have important implications for future developments in the area of reconciliation between work and family life. This analysis challenged the hierarchical nature of the public and the private dichotomy, and called into question the ability of the principle of formal equality to bring about social change. In so doing, it brought to light social practices and values that have thus far produced and maintained gender power hierarchies.

The survey of maternity legislation and family-friendly policies presented in this book draws attention to some of the issues raised by various feminist discourses about the relationship between social policy and gender structures. More importantly, it showed the unique position of maternity legislation. Whilst focusing primarily on women's employment rights, this body of law raises important questions about the institutional set up of European welfare states and the impact of gender hierarchies upon European and national political structures.

The analysis presented in this book has not sought to provide a prescriptive answer for the mainstreaming of equality; however, as equality remains a disputed subject amongst feminists as well as policy-makers, it has sought to contribute to current debates about the nature and outcomes of the equality discourse. In doing so, it endeavoured to highlight the biases and gaps present in policy-making structures, and their possible impact on the position of women in the European labour market. More specifically, it argued extensively that traditional divisions between the public and the private sphere are founded upon, and in turn reinforce, a concept of equality that is based upon male norms of work and worker. As such, the policies that emerge from this socio-political framework are not only insensitive to women's interests, but they also work against the establishment of substantive equality as a working principle.

Given this background, the analysis of current policy developments in the area of reconciliation between work and family life has concentrated on three issues. Firstly, it looked at equal rights and maternity legislation in terms of substantive rather than formal equality. Secondly, it assessed the impact of assumptions about gender and gender roles on the scope of the legislation. And thirdly it evaluated the concern of the legislation with reconciling women's public and private roles. The questions that have emerged from this discussion revolve around the social construction of gender power hierarchies and the concepts of 'woman' and 'mother' in the policy-making process. The argument that ensues highlights how the analysis of the legislation and the deconstruction of the concept of woman raise important questions about women's position and roles in contemporary European society.

If we recap the findings of the empirical analysis it is possible to conclude that despite an important shift in political rhetoric towards creating a more inclusive labour market, what is lacking is the political commitment to create the necessary infrastructure to support this shift in policy. This division is particularly evident in the case of European legislation for the reconciliation between work and family life. Developments in this policy area, such as the Pregnant Worker Directive, have played an important role in creating a framework for the establishment of minimum standards for the protection of working mothers. This shift in policy focus can also be seen to encourage fathers to take on a greater role in sharing family responsibilities, particularly through the Parental Leave Directive. Unfortunately, a number of different interests converged during the negotiations that served to limit the radical potential of these policies. The failure of European policy-makers to recognise the impact of maternity and parental leave on gender relations is reflected in the absence of serious consideration for the issue of pay.

The analysis of current policy developments in the UK further highlights the failures of European law. In line with the principles of European law, in principle UK policies have sought to encourage a more equitable distribution of care work in the family. However, limited consideration for the impact of socio-economic hierarchies on gender power structures has led to the creation of a policy framework that reinforces women's role as carers in the family. Whereas the gender-neutral language of the legislation implies a shift in discourse, the practical implication of the policies outlined in chapter 6 highlights the values entrenched within the legislation. Rather than being family-friendly, these policies seek to be women-friendly.

This discussion brings us back to one of the key issues addressed in this book: the link between gender norms and family-friendly policies. At the heart of this investigation is an evaluation of values and representations of gender become embedded within maternity policies. The analysis of the European policy framework and the national case studies provides two possible explanation for these trends. Firstly, equal rights and maternity legislation implicitly accept male norms of work. This is particularly evident through the approximation of maternity or pregnancy to invalidity schemes. Secondly, the legislation reveals a bias in favour of traditional gender roles and gender division of labour. The assumption that family-friendly policies are indeed women-friendly, presume some degree of continuity in the current gender order. Given this background, it is possible to conclude that the principle of reconciliation between work and family life is predominantly concerned with improving women's access to the labour market, not challenging traditional gender power hierarchies and divisions of labour.

On those occasions when the legislation has attempted to account for women's *special* needs, it has done so as a way of protecting women's role in the social function of reproduction. In this context, the uncritical acceptance of women's role in the social function of reproduction has ultimately served to reinforce, rather than challenge, gender power hierarchies. Women's needs are therefore defined in terms of traditional representations about women's roles in the family. An example of these trends is the continued categorisation of childcare as a matter of women's rights. Although a restructuring of services is an important step towards women's greater access to the official labour market, the focus on childcare as part of women's right reaffirms women's role as carers. It is thus clear that the politics of care are directly linked to those of gender.

Taking Monique Wittig's (1997: 220) assertion that 'one is not born a woman' as a starting point, it is thus possible to conclude that the concept of woman is constructed through the association of gender and sexual differences, and culminates in the idea that 'the capacity to give birth (biology) is what defines a woman' (Wittig, 1997: 220). It is these values that permeate the legislation. Concerns about health and safety, and more prominently assumptions about motherhood, care and the gender order have become embedded within national and European legislation. More importantly, this process highlights the impact of traditional values about gender roles and divisions of labour on the policy-making process.

Assumptions about the current gender order also transpire in the standard of work and worker incorporated within legislative texts. The official labour market is structured according to the division between public and private work. The male standard therefore transpires as the official measure by which women need to conform to make a 'substantial' contribution to the official labour market. Current economic trends towards market flexibility have strengthened, rather than challenged, gender power hierarchies. Reliance on atypical work has not yet led to a shift towards greater redistribution of care in the family, but has increased women's double burden.

Whereas more women are now expected to make a contribution to the family income, albeit as secondary to that of the main/male breadwinner, men have not taken on board a greater share of the care 'burden'. Women's work in the private not only continues be ignored and unaccounted for by employment/work statistics, but it remain essential for the operation of the official labour market and the welfare state. The difficulties experienced in reconciling work and family life become evident for women who seek to remain employed in the official labour market on a full-time basis following pregnancy. The economic penalties for such women come in the form of high childcare costs, whereas the psychological costs of dealing with the pressures of employment and care are noticeable in the substantial decrease in personal/leisure time available to those women.

There are wider considerations that also need to be considered. The impact of the dichotomisation of care and employment has become increasingly noticeable in relation to the sharp decline in fertility rates in contemporary Europe. The case study of Italy is particularly interesting in this context. Having adopted some of the most wide-reaching and radical maternity laws in Europe, it continues to have some of the lowest fertility rates in Europe. A possible explanation for this trend advanced in chapter 5 is that although women's expectations about employment have changed drastically in the last thirty years, the expectations of the state, and the family, vis-à-vis their role as carers, has remained virtually unaltered. The increasing burden of women's double presence has ultimately resulted in the postponement of motherhood. Couple this with employers' attitudes towards women's mothering, and it then starts to become clear why Italian women have started to reject mothering altogether. In many ways, to choose not to become a mother is a quicker way of challenging gender structures than fighting for an overhaul of gender power hierarchies in the family and the labour market.

What becomes evident from this analysis is that women's and men's needs have been disassociated. For some feminists and policy-makers the aim of the legislation is to target women's *special* contributions and establish a framework for the *protection* of women's roles and rights. The focus on women's *special* needs, however, presumes that the male standard is, and should remain, the norm. Such assumptions impact upon the construction of woman as a subject and worker. As the feminist debates presented in this book highlight, if there is no universal woman, then assumptions about women's needs also need to be deconstructed and re-elaborated. This discussion therefore raises important questions about the role of gender norms in the policy-making process. A second conclusion that can be drawn from the analysis presented here is that the legislation is not gender neutral, but is the product of gender hierarchies. As such, deconstructing the gendered foundations of the policy-making process is a necessary step in the analysis of the scope and reach of the legislation. In other words, assumptions about gender determine the scope of equal rights, maternity legislation and family-friendly policies.

Implications for the policy-making process

Clearly the acknowledgement of the impact of gender on the policy-making process has important implications for the analysis of equal rights and maternity legislation. The division between formal and substantive equality is one of the most important and recurrent issues addressed in this book. This division raises important questions about the meaning and value of the principle of equality, both as incorporated in the policy-making process and as the subject of feminist debate. This uncertainty over the meaning and applicability of this concept raises one final question: can equality, the deconstruction of woman, and social policy come together in a partnership capable of promoting substantive social change in the public and private sphere? In other words, can the legislation address the division between substantive and formal equality, without drastically changing society and social structures?

Ada Grecchi (1996: 46–7), in her analysis of Italian equality legislation, argues that

> formal equality between men and women was undoubtedly reached in Italy, however, the goal of substantive equality was still far from being achieved and

this is shown by the fact that .. inequalities of treatment based on sex had not disappeared in the working world.

What Grecchi's analysis, however, does not account for, is that inequalities in the official labour market are not an isolated phenomenon; rather, they are the by-product of gender hierarchies in the private. As long as the legal framework does not account for women's position in society and the overarching influence of gender power hierarchies on the allocation of care work in the family, the resulting legislation will continue to focus solely on the public sphere and will only superficially address the issues raised by the analysis of substantive equality, as the case of family friendly policies shows.

Unlike Italy, which has had a well established framework of maternity rights since the early 1970s, in the case of the UK the establishment a body of legislation in the area of work–life balance has been the result of current developments in this area at the European level. As a consequence, national provisions have incorporated, and in many ways amplified, the weaknesses of European regulations. Despite a recent surge of interest in this particular area, which goes beyond the minimum standards set by European policies, the British approach to work–life balance is still driven by economic concerns. Far from challenging gender power hierarchies, reconciliation between work and family life becomes a vehicle for the deregulation of the employment market in favour of atypical or flexible employment. In this context, work–life balance serves the economic interests of the state and employers, not those of working mothers. More importantly, it fails to establish a framework for the operationalisation of substantive equality.

The assumptions surrounding the incorporation of formal equality in the legislative process presume that employment in the official labour market is necessary for emancipation. In the context of the European social, economic and political framework, employment in the official labour market continues to be instrumental for the acquisition of formal rights. However, such rights are dependent upon the fulfilment of traditional criteria of work and worker. Within this framework full-time employment becomes central to emancipation and equality. This position is consistent with the equality approach that seeks to remove all obstacles to women's participation within mainstream politics and employment (Evans, 1995: 15; Lovenduski and Randall, 1993: 47). Unfortunately, this approach does not account for the gendered nature of official labour markets and political systems at large. Within this framework, the principle of equality is not deconstructive, and women remain the *other*. As the working group on equal opportunities of the European Foundation for the Improvement of Living and Working Conditions points out, 'equality may not be the answer to all problems facing society. Legislative changes are necessary and fundamental, but cannot succeed without changes in attitude which require a different approach' (EFILWC, 1996: 14).

An alternative approach to equal rights legislation is to focus upon women's *special* needs and role in society (Cavarero, 1992: 37; Hare-Mustin and Marecek, 1994: 63). This position, however, feeds into the traditional divisions between public and private, and it reinforces traditional assumptions and stereotypes about gender roles and the gendered division of labour. The introduction of family-friendly policies has gone some way towards addressing the calls of difference feminists in this area. However, a more detailed analysis of the overall aims of these new developments highlights three issues that, as of yet, remain unresolved. Firstly, as discussed extensively in chapters 2 and 4, despite the apparent gender neutrality of the policies in question, they are essentially women-friendly. Secondly, the association between family-friendly policies and women's employment rights reasserts the assumption that gender is a matter that concerns only women. Finally, because of these assumptions, this new policy development remains ineffectual in challenging gender power hierarchies. At best it provides a framework for the facilitation of women's entry into the official labour market; it certainly does not establish a more 'democratic' model of care in the family. It is thus possible to conclude that far from challenging gender divisions of labour, this approach helps to reinforce the gender hierarchies it originally sought to undermine.

The analysis presented in this book has focused upon the concept of substantive equality. This principle is based on a marriage between public rights and recognition of the pressures women have to face when seeking to juggle the demands of mothering and employment. The argument presented here has called for a re-elaboration of the norms associated with the concepts of work, employment and worker. Whereas the male standard of worker has often been used to force women to subscribe to strict employment patterns, the analysis presented here highlights how these values are incompatible with those of care, thus forcing women to choose between their aspirations and social function of mothering. Such employment patterns, it has been argued, limit women's access to the official labour market, they highlight the shortcomings of the principle of formal equality and the pervasive nature of the male-breadwinner model. Although recent economic trends favour atypical employment patterns, such as flexible employment and part-time work, these arrangements have only had a superficially beneficial impact. Far from challenging gender divisions of labour, they have crystallised the gender segregation of the official labour market. Moreover, the availability of atypical work is also reinforcing the male breadwinner model, whereby there is a primary (full-time) and a secondary (part-time) breadwinner. In this context, women's income only serves to supplement the overall family income. Rather than being an insight into women's increased opportunities for employment, it should be seen as a reflection of the economic pressures families are increasingly becoming subjected to. The underlying assumption of this analysis is that the labour market should be structured so as to allow women to fulfil their function of carers as well as participate in the official labour market.

Criticisms of this approach have been raised by various feminists, who argue that increased participation in the official labour market has the effect of producing what has been defined as the double burden. The analysis presented here highlights the limitations of a legal approach that accepts such divisions as the norm, and simply tries to accommodate them in order to meet the challenges of the market. In this context, EU family-friendly policies fail to establish a framework that encourages a more even distribution of responsibilities between men and women. Although it has been argued that the Parental Leave Directive of 1996 goes some way towards reddressing these issues, the unwillingness of member states and the Social Partners to attach pay to the right to leave ultimately undermines the radical potential of this policy.

In conclusion, substantive equality needs to account for a wide range of factors that cut across the public–private dichotomy. The analysis presented here has addressed only some of the complexities associated with the relationship between women's rights and deconstruction of gender power hierarchies. The principle of substantive equality is not flawless, but it has the widest-reaching implications for the policy-making process. The analysis of the scope of equal rights and maternity legislation in Italy, the UK and the EU highlights the effect of gender hierarchies and assumptions about motherhood on current definitions of equality. The considerations on the welfare regimes also show the continued importance of gendered division of labour for the survival of the European social model. Finally, the combination of these considerations with the traditional focus on the economic aspects of equality goes some way to explain current trends in the European equality agenda, such as the rhetoric of work–life balance and reconciliation between work and family life. Far from being a sign of a growing commitment to women's rights, substantive equality and a redefinition of the function of care, this shift in policy rhetoric and practice is representative of an increased awareness of the needs of the market and the economic impact of inequality and discrimination.

BIBLIOGRAPHY

A. Che (1996) 'Durante il Periodo della Prova Licenziabile la "Futura" Mamma: Per la Consulta il Datore di Lavoro Non Ha l' Obbligo di Assumere la Dipendente Incinta'. *Il Sole 24 Ore.* 1 Giugno 1996.

Addis, E. (2000) 'Gender Reform of the Italian Welfare State' in González, M.J., Jurado, R. and Naldini, M. (eds) *Gender Inqeualities in Southern Europe: Women, Work and Welfare in the 19902.* Frank Cass: London and Portland.

Aldinger-Tziovas, M. (ed.) (1984) *Working Towards European Unification: Women and the Family in Europe.* European People's Party: Strasbourg.

Angelilli, R. (1991) 'Il Lavoro nelle Fabbriche: le Leggi Fasciste Non Dimenticano le Donne' in Centro Studi Futura, *Gli Angeli e la Rivoluzione.* Edizioni Settimo Sigillo: Roma.

Anon. (1992) 'Maternity Directive Gets Last Minute Go-Ahead'. *Crew Reports,* Vol. 12 (10).

Anon. (2001) 'The Court Develops its Case-Law on the Prohibition of Dismissal of Pregnant Women'. Available at: www.curia.eu.int/en/actu/communiques/cp01/aff/cp0147en.htm.

Arribas, G.V. and Carrasco, L. (2003) 'Gender Equality and the EU: An Assessment of the Current Issues', *Eipascope,* 2003/1.

Atkins, S. and Hoggett, B. (1984) W*omen and the Law.* Basil Blackwell: Oxford and New York.

Bacchi, C. (1990) *Same Difference: Feminism and Sexual Difference.* Allen & Unwin: Sydney.

Balbo, L. (1978) 'La doppia presenza', *Inchiesta* No. 32 (Marzo/Aprile).

Bailyn, L, Drago, R. and Kochan, T.A. (2001) *Integrating Work and Family Life: A Holistic Approach – A report of the Sloan Work-Family Policy Network.* MIT, Sloan School of Management. Available at: http://lsir.la.psu.edu/workfam.WorkFamily.pdf.

Bakker, Isabella (1988) 'Women's Employment in Comparative Perspective' in Jenson J., Haggen, E. and Reddy, C. (eds) *Feminisation of the Labour Force: Paradoxes and Compromises.* Oxford University Press: New York.

Barnard, C. (1996) 'The Economic Objectives of Article 119' in Hervey, T. and Shaw, J. (eds) *Sex Equality Law in the European Union.* John Wiley & Sons: Chichester.

Barrett, M. and Phillips, A. (1992) 'Introduction' in Barrett, M. and Phillips, A. (eds) *Destabilising Theory: Contemporary Feminist Debates.* Polity Press: Cambridge and Oxford.

Beechey, V. (1988) 'Rethinking the Definition of Work: Gender and Work' in Jenson, J., Hagen E. and Reddy, C. (eds) *Feminization of the Labour Force:*

Paradoxes and Promises. Oxford University Press: New York.

Bercusson, B. and Dickens, L. (1996) *Equal Opportunities and Collective Bargaining in Europe: 1. Defining the Issues.* European Foundation for the Improvement of Living and Working Conditions. Office for Official Publications of the European Communities: Luxembourg.

Bimbi, F. (1993) 'Gender, gift relationship and Welfare States Cultures in Italy' in Lewis, J. (ed.) *Women and Social Policies in Europe: Work, Family and the State.* Edward Elgar: Aldershot and Brookfield.

Birke, L. (1986) *Women, Feminism and Biology: the Feminist Challenge.* Harvester Press: Brighton.

Bland, L. (1985) 'In the Name of Protection: The First Policing of Women in the First World War' in Brophy, J. and Smart, C. (eds) *Women-in-Law: Explorations in Law, Family, Sexuality.* Routledge & Kegan Paul: London, Boston Melbourne and Henley.

Boch, C. (1993) 'The European Community and Sex Equality: Why and How?' in MacQueen (ed.) *Sex Equality: Law and Economics.* Hume Papers on Public Policy, Vol. 1 (1). Edinburgh University Press: Edinburgh.

Bock, G. and James, S. (1992) 'Introduction: Contextualizing Equality and Difference' in Bock, G. and James, S. (eds) *Beyond Equality and Difference: Citizenship, Feminist Politics and Female Subjectivity.* Routledge: London and New York.

Bock, G. and Thane, P. (1994) 'Introduction' in Bock, G. and Thane, P. (eds) *Maternity and Gender Policies: Women and the Rise of European Welfare States 1880s–1950s.* Routledge: London and New York.

Bonzini Andiñach, M. (2002) 'Working Women-Mothers in Southern Europe: Reconciling Female Roles in the Turn of the Twentieth Century', *EPIC Conference Papers.* Available at: www.lse.ac.uk/collections/EPIC/documents/C2W2.htm.

Borchorst, A. (1994) 'Welfare State Regimes, Women's Interests and the EC' in Sainsbury, D. (ed.) *Gendering Welfare States.* Sage: London, Thousand Oaks and New Delhi.

Boudard, J. (1986) 'Community Law and National Laws of the Member States Relating to the Principle of Equal Pay Between Male and Female Workers' in Verwilghen, M. (ed.) *Equality in Law Between Men and Women in the European Community: Vol. 1.* General Reports. Presses Universitaires de Louvain: Louvain-la-Neuve.

Bowers, J. and Moran, E. (2002) 'Justification in Direct Discrimination Law: Breaking the Taboo', *Industrial Law Journal,* Vol. 31 (4).

Bowers, J., Moran, E. and Honeyball, S. (2003) 'Justification in Direct Sex Discrimination: A Reply', *Industrial Law Journal,* Vol. 32 (3).

Brannen, J. and Moss, P. (1991) *Managing Mothers: Dual Earner Households After Maternity Leave.* Unwin Hyman: Boston, Sydney and Wellington.

Bridgeman, J. and Millns, S. (1995) 'Introduction' in Bridgeman, J. and Millns, S. (eds). *Law and Body Politics: Regulating the Female Body.* Dartmouth Publishing Company: Aldershot, Brookfield, Singapore and Sydney.

Bryson, V. (1992) *Feminist Political Theory: an Introduction.* Macmillan: London.

Buckley, M. and Anderson, M. (1988) 'Introduction: Problems, Policies and Politic' in Buckley, M. and Anderson, M. (eds) *Women, Equality and Europe.* Macmillan Press: Basingstoke and London.

Burrows, N. (1993) 'The Future of Sex Equality in the EC', *Hume Papers on Public Policy,* Vol. 1 (1).

Bussemaker, J. and van Kersbergen, K. (1994) 'Gender and Welfare State: Some Theoretical Reflections' in Sainsbury, D. (ed.) *Gendering Welfare States.* Sage: London, Thousand Oaks and New Delhi.

Buxton, J. (1998) *Ending the Mother War: Starting the Workplace Revolution.* Macmillan: Basingstoke and New York.

Byre, A. (1988) 'Applying Community Standards on Equality' in Buckley, M. and Anderson, M. (eds) *Women, Equality and Europe.* Macmillan Press: Basingstoke and London.

Caldwell, L. (1991) 'Italian Feminism: Some Considerations' in Baranski Z.G. and Vinall S.W. (eds) *Women & Italy.* Macmillan and the Graduate School of European and International Studies University of Reading: London.

Cairns, W. (1997) *Introduction to European Union Law.* Cavendish Publishing Limited: London.

Cappiello, A.A. Del Bufalo, M., Marinucci, E., Remiddi, L. and Saulle, M.R. (eds) (1984) *Codice Donna: Norme Interne e Atti Internazionali.* Presidenza del Consiglio dei Ministri (Direzione Generale delle Informazioni): Rome.

Caracciolo, E. (2001) 'The "Family-Friendly Workplace": the EC Position' *The International Journal of Comparative Labour Law and Industrial Relations,* Vol. 17 (3).

Caracciolo di Torrella, E. (2000) 'A Place for Maternity in the European Union' in McGlynn, C. (ed.) *Legal Feminisms: Theory and Practice.* Ashgate: Dartmouth.

Carter, A. (1988) *The Politics of Women's Rights.* Longman: London and New York.

Case C-184/83, *Ulrich Hofmann* v *Barmer Ersatzkasse,* [1984], ECR 03047.

Case C-170/84, *Bilka-Kaufhaus Gmbh* v *Karin Weber von Hartz,* [1986], ECR 01607.

Case C-177/88, *Elisabeth Johanna Pacifica Dekker* v *Stichting Vormingscentrum voor Jong Volwassenen (VJV-Centrum) Plus,* [1990], ECR I-03941.

Case C-179/88, *Handels-og Kontorfunktionaerernes Forbund I Danmark* v *Dansk Arbejdsgiverforening,* [1990], ECR I-03979.

Case C-262/88, *Douglas Harvey barber* v *Guardian Royal Exchange Assurance Group,* [1990], ECR I-01889.

Case C-271/91, *M. Helen Marshall* v *Southampton and South-West Hampshire Area Health Authority,* [1993], ECR I-04367.

Case C-32/93, *Carole Louise Webb* v *EMO Air Cargo (UK) Ltd.,* [1994], ECR I-03567.

Case C-450/93 *Eckhard Kalanke* v *Freie Hansestadt Bremen,* [1995], ECR I-03051.

Case C-135/96, *UEAPMA* v *Council of the EU,* [1998], available at: www.curia.eu.int/.

Case C-394/96, *M. Brown* v *Rentokil Ltd.,* [1998], ECR I-04185.

Case C-411/96, *Margaret Boyle and Others* v *Equal Opportunities Commission*, [1998], ECR I-06401.

Case C-249/97, *G. Gruber* v *Silhouette International Scmied GmbH & Co. KG*, [1999], ECR I-05295.

Case C-333/97, *Lewen* v *Denda*, [1999], ECR I-07243.

Case C-207/98, *Silke-Karin Mahlburg* v *Land Mecklenburg-Vorpommern*, [2000], ECR I-00549.

Case C-109/00, *Tele Danmark* v *Handels-og Kontorfunktionaerernes Forbund, acting on behalf of Marianne Brandt-Nielsen*, [2001], ECR I-06993.

Case C-109/00, *Tele Danmark* v *Handels-og Kontorfunktionaerernes Forbund, acting on behalf of Marianne Brandt-Nielsen*, [2001], Advocate General Colomer, opinion delivered on 10 May 2001.

Case C-320/01, *Bush* v *Klinikum Meustadt GmbH & Co. Betriebs-KG*, [2002], Advocate General Colomer, opinion delivered on 21 November 2002.

Case C-476/99, *Lommers* v *Minister van Landbouw, Natuurbeheer en Vissrij*, [2002], ECR I-02891.

Case C-320/01, *Bush* v *Klinikum Meustadt GmbH & Co. Betriebs-KG*, [2003], ECR I-02041.

Cattaneo, M. (1996) 'Donna, Discriminazione e Politica del Lavoro' (Woman, Discrimination and Labour Politics), *Le Scienze*, No. 330 (Febbraio).

Cavarero, A. (1990) 'Il Modello Democratico nell' Orizzonte della Differenza Sessuale', *Democrazia e Diritto*, No. 2.

Cavarero, A. (1992) 'Equality and Sexual Difference: Amnesia in Political Thought' in Bock, G. and James, S. (eds) *Beyond Equality and Difference: Citizenship, Feminist Politics and Female Subjectivity*. Routledge: London and New York.

Cavarero, A. (1993) 'Towards a Theory of Sexual Difference' in Kemp, S. and Bono, P. (eds) *The Lonely Mirror: Italian Perspectives on Feminist Theory*. Routledge: London and New York.

Cianciullo, A. (1995) 'Quei Figli Partoriti a Premio', *La Repubblica*, Thursday 23–2–1995.

Charpentier, L. (1998) 'The European Court of Justice and the Rhetoric of Affirmative Action' *European University Institute Working Papers RSC*, No. 98/30. Available at: www.iue.it/RSCAS/WP-Texts/98_30.html.

Chodorow, N. (1978) *The Reproduction of Mothering: Psychoanalysis and the Sociology of Gender*. University of California Press: Berkeley, Los Angeles and London.

Collins, H. (1994) *The EU Pregnancy Directive: A Guide for Human Resource Managers*. Blackwell: Oxford (UK) and Cambridge (USA).

Collins, H. (1988) *The Equal Opportunity Handbook: A Guide to Law and Best Practice in Europe*. Blackwell Business: Oxford (UK) and Cambridge (USA).

Commission of the European Communities (1981) *A New Community Action Programme on the Promotion of Equal Opportunities for Women 1982–1985*. COM (81) 758 Final. Reported in Supplement No. 9 to *Women of Europe*, Brussels, 9 December 1981.

Commission of the European Communities (1986) 'Community Law and

Women', *Women of Europe*, Supplement No. 25. Brussels.

Commission of the European Communities (1990) *Community Charter of the Fundamental Social Rights of Workers.* Office for official publication of the European Communities: Luxembourg.

Commission of the European Communities (1991) *Third Medium-Term Community Action Programme on Equal Opportunities for Men and Women (1991–1995).* Official Journal of the European Communities C 142, 31 May 1991. Available at: http://europa.eu.int/comm/sg/scadplus/leg/en/cha/c10915.htm.

Commission Proposal for a Council Directive on Parental Leave and Leave for Family Reasons. *Official Journal of the European Communities* C. 333, 9 December 1983.

Amended Commission Proposal for a Council Directive on Parental Leave and Leave for Family Reasons. COM (84) 631 Final. *Official Journal of the European Communities* C. 316, 27 November 1984.

Communication from the Commission to the Council, the European Parliament, the Economic and Social Committee and the Committee of the Regions Towards a Community Framework Gender Equality (2001–2005) COM (2000) 335 Final; 2000/0143 (CNS) Available at: http://europea.eu.int/comm/employment_social/equ_opp/strategy/comm2000_335_en.pdf.

Conaghan, J. (1993) 'Pregnancy and the Workplace' in Bottomley, A. and Conaghan, J. (eds) *Feminist Theory and Legal Strategy.* Blackwell Publishers: Cambridge (USA) and Oxford (UK).

Conroy Jackson, P. (1990) 'The Labour Market Effects of 1992 on Women' in van Prondzynski, F. (ed.) *Women and the Completion of the Internal Market: Report and Conclusions.* Department of Labour, Dublin and the Commission of the European Communities: Dublin.

Conway, D. (1992) 'Do Women Benefit from Equal Opportunities Legislation?' in Quest, C. (ed.) *Equal Opportunities: a Feminist Fallacy*, Health and Welfare Series no. 11. IEA Health and Welfare Unit: London.

Cornell, D.L. (1992) 'Gender, Sex, and Equivalent Rights' in Butler, J. and Scott, J.W. (eds), *Feminists Theorise the Political.* Routledge: London and New York.

Costituzione della Repubblica Italiana (Entrata in vigore 1948) *Gazzetta Ufficiale* 27 Dicembre 1947, n. 298, S.O. Also available at: www.palazzochigi.it/Governo/Costituzione/costituzione.pdf.

Council Decision 95/593/EC of 22 December 1995 Concerning a Medium-Term Community Action Programme on Equal Opportunities for Women and Men (1996–2000). *Official Journal of the European Communities* L 335, 30 December 1995. Available at: http://europa.eu.int/comm/sg/scadplus/leg/en/cha/c10918.htm.

Council Directive 2000/78/EC of 27 November 2000 establishing a General Framework for Equal Treatment in Employment and Occupation. *Official Journal of the European Communities* L 303/16–22, 2 December 2000.

Council Directive 93/104/EC of 23 November 1993 concerning certain aspects of the organization of working time. *Official Journal of the European Communities* L 307, 13 December 1993.

Council Directive 97/81/EC of 15 December 1997 concerning the Framework

Agreement on part-time work concluded by UNICE, CEEP and the ETUC – Annex: Framework agreement on part-time work. *Official Journal* L 014, 20 January 1998.

Council Directive 75/117/EEC of 10 February 1975 on the Approximation of the Laws of the Member States Relating to the Application of the Principle of Equal Pay For Men and Women, *Official Journal of the European Communities* L 45/20, 19 February 1975.

Council Directive 76/207/EEC of 9 February 1976 on the Implementation of the Principle of Equal Treatment for Men and Women as Regards Access to Employment, Vocational Training and Promotion, and Working Conditions. *Official Journal of the European Communities* L 39, 14 February 1976.

Council Directive 79/7/EEC of 19 December 1978 on the Progressive Implementation of the Principle of Equal Treatment for Men and Women in Matters of Social Security. *Official Journal of the European Communities* L 6, 10 January 1979.

Council Directive 86/378/EEC of 24 July 1986 on the Implementation of the Principle of Equal Treatment for Men and Women in Occupational Social Security Schemes. *Official Journal of the European Communities* L 225, 12 August 1986.

Council Directive 86/613/EEC of 11 December 1986 on the Application of the Principle of Equal Treatment Between Men and Women in an Activity, Including Agriculture, in a Self-Employed Capacity and in the Protection of Self-Employed During Pregnancy and Motherhood. *Official Journal of the European Communities* L 359, 19 December 1986.

Council Directive 92/85/EEC of 19 October 1996 Concerning the Implementation of Measures to Encourage Improvements in the Safety and Health at Work of Pregnant Workers and Workers Who Have Recently Given Birth or Are Breast-Feeding. (Tenth Individual Directive within the Meaning of Article 16(1) of Directive 89/391/EEC). *Official Journal of the European Communities* L. 348, 28 November 1992.

Council Directive 96/34/EC of 3 June 1996 on the Framework Agreement on Parental Leave Concluded by UNICE, CEEP and the ETUC. *Official Journal of the European Communities* L. 145, 10 June1996.

Council Directive 96/97/EC of 20 December 1996 Amending Directive 86/378/EEC on the Implementation of the Principle of Equal Treatment for Men and Women in Occupational Social Security Schemes. *Official Journal of the European Communities* L 46, 17 February 1997.

Council Directive 97/80/EC of 15 December 1997 on the Burden of Proof in Cases of Discrimination Based on Sex. *Official Journal of the European Communities* L 014, 20 January 1998.

Council Resolution of 21 January 1974 Concerning a Social Action Programme [374Y0212(01)]. http://europa.eu.int/eur-lex/en/lif/dat/en_374Y0212_01.html (Last update 27 July 1998); or *Official Journal of the European Communities* C 013, 12 February 1974.

Council Resolution of 21 May 1991 on the Third Medium-Term Community Action Programme on Equal Opportunities for Women and Men (1991–95).

Official Journal of the European Communities C 142, 31 May 1991.

Daly, M. (1994) 'Comparing Welfare States: Towards a Gender Friendly Approach' in Sainsbury, D. (ed.) *Gendering Welfare States.* Sage: London, Thousand Oaks and New Delhi.

Deakin, S. and Reed, H. (2000) 'The Contested Meaning of Labour Market Flexibility: Economic Theory and the Discourse of European Integration' in Shaw, J. (ed.) *Social Law and Policy in an Evolving European Union.* Hart: Oxford and Portland.

Deakin, S. and Morris, G.S. (1995) *Labour Law.* Butterworths: London, Dublin and Edinburgh.

De Falco, F. (1991) 'La Corte Costituzionale e la Nullitá del Licenziamento della Lavoratrice Madre' (The Constitutional Court and the Invalidity of Dismissal of Working Mothers), *Il Diritto del Lovoro,* Anno LXV (No. 3–4).

De Grazia, V. (1992) *How Fascism Ruled Women: Italy, 1922–1945.* University of California Press: Berkeley, Los Angeles and London

De Lauretis, T. (1994) 'The Essence of the Triangle or, Taking the Risk of Essentialism Seriously' in Schor, N. and Weed, E. (eds) *The Essential Difference.* Indiana University Press: Bloomington and Indianapolis.

Del Boca, D. (1988) 'Women in a Changing Workplace: the Case of Italy' in Jenson J., Hagen E., and Reddy C. *Feminization of the Labour Force.* Oxford University Press: New York.

Del Boca, D. Locatelli, M. and Pasqua, S. (2000) 'Employment Decisions of Married Women: Evidence and Explanations', *Labour,* Vol. 14 (1).

Del Boca, D., Pasqua, S. and Pronzato, C. (2003) 'Analyzing Women's Employment and Fertility Rates in Europe: Differences ad Similarities in Northern and Southern Europe', *Centre for Household Income, Labour and Demographic Economics.* Available at: http://iserwww.essex.ac.uk/activities/conferences/epunet-2003/docs/pdf/papers/pronzato.pdf.

De Luca, L. (1994) 'La Famiglia Oggi' (The Family Today) in *Il Diritto di Famiglia e delle Persone,* Anno XXIII, April–June.

De Marchis, C. (1995) 'La Maternitá Negata: La Corte Constituzional Attenua la Speciality del Rapporto di Lavoro Domestico'. *Il Diritto del Lavoro,* Anno LXIX (no. 5), September–October.

Department of Trade and Industry (2000) *Work & Parents: Competitiveness and Choicem – a Green Paper.* Available at: www.dti.gov.uk/er/g_paper/pdfs/wpgreen.pdf.

Department of Trade and Industry (1998) 'Fairness at Work', cm 3968. Available at: www.dti.gov.uk/er/fairness/.

Department of Trade and Industry (2000) *New Options to Support Parents and Employers at the Time of Birth – Green Paper.* Available at: www.dti.gov.uk/er/individual/workparents_hist.htm.

Department of Trade and Industry (2003) *Maternity Rights: A Guide for Employers and Employees (PL958).* Available at: www.dti.gov.uk/er/individual/maternity.pdf.

Department of Trade and Industry (2003b) *Working Father (PL517) Rights to Leave and Pay: A Guide for Employers and Employees.* Available at:

www.dti.gov.uk/er/individual/patrights-pl517.htm.

Directive 2002/73/EC of the European Parliament and of the Council of 23 September 2002 amending Council Directive 76/207/EEC on the implementation of the principle of equal treatment for men and women as regards access to employment, vocational training and promotion, and working conditions *Official Journal of the European Communities* L 269. Available at: http://europa.eu.int/smartapi/cgi/sga_doc?smartapi!celexplus!prod!CELEXnu mdoc&lg=en&numdoc=32002L0073.

Di Stefano, C. (1990) 'Dilemmas of Difference: Feminism, Modernity, and Postmodernism' in Nicholson, L.J. (ed.), *Feminism/Postmodernism.* Routledge: London and New York.

Douchet, A. (1995) 'Gender Equality and Gender Differences in Household Work and Parenting', *Women's Studies International Forum*, Vol. 18 (3).

Draft Charter of Fundamental Rights of the European Union. Brussels, 28 September 2000. CHART 4487/00, CONVENT 50 in K. Feus (ed.) *The EU Charter of Fundamental Rights: Text and Commentaries.* Federal Trust: London.

Draft Treaty Establishing a Constitution for Europe (2003) CONV 850/03, 18 July 2003.

Duchen, C. (1992) 'Understanding the European Community: A Glossary of Terms', *Women's Studies International Forum*, Vol. 15 (1).

Duncan, S. (1995) 'Theorising European Gender Systems', *Journal of European Social Policy*, Vol. 5 (4).

Duncan, S. (1996) 'The Diverse Worlds of European Patriarchy' in García-Ramon, M. and Monk, J. (eds) *Women of the European Union: The Politics of Work and Daily Life.* Routledge: London and New York.

Eisenstein, Z.R. (1993) *The Radical Future of Liberal Feminism.* Northeastern University Press: Boston.

Elam, D. (1994) *Feminism and Deconstruction: Ms an Abyme.* Routledge: London and New York.

Elias, P. (1990) 'Part-Time Work and Part-Time Workers: Keeping Women In or Out?' in McRae, S. (ed.), *Keeping Women In: Strategies to Facilitate the Continuing Employment of Women in Higher Level Occupations.* Policy Studies Institute: London.

Ellis, E. (1991) *European Community Sex Equality Law.* Clarendon: Oxford.

Elshtain, J.B. (1992) 'The Power and Powerlessness of Women' in Bock, G. and James, S. (eds) *Beyond Equality and Difference: Citizenship, Feminist Politics and Female* Subjectivity. Routledge: London and New York.

Employment Rights Act 1996 (c. 18) Available at: www.legislation. hmso.gov.uk/acts/acts1996/1996018.htm.

Employment Relations Act 1999 (c. 26) Available at: www.legislation. hmso.gov.uk/acts/acts1999/19990026.htm.

Employment Act 2002 (c. 22) Available at: www.legislation.hmso.gov.uk/ acts/acts2002/20020022.htm.

Employment Protection (Consolidation) Act 1978 (c. 44) in *Current Law Statutes Annotated* 1978. Sweet Maxwell, Stevens and Sons: London and Edinburgh.

Enloe, C. (1990) *Banana, Beaches and Bases: Making Feminist Sense of*

International Relations. University of California Press: Berekely and Los Angeles.

Esping-Andersen, G. (1990) *The Three Worlds of Welfare Capitalism.* Polity: Cambridge and Oxford.

European Commission (Directorate General for Employment, Industrial Relations and Social Affairs) (1994) *European Social Policy: A Way Forward for the Union* (A White Paper). Office for the Official Publications of the European Communities: Luxembourg and Brussels [COM (1994) 333] 27 July 1994.

European Commission Directorate General for Employment, Industrial Relations and Social Affairs (1995). *The Medium Term Social Action Programme: 1995–97.* (Adopted by the Commission on 12 April 1995.) www.cec.lu/en/comm/dg05/soc_prog/chap_5.htm. (Last updated: 19 May 1995; downloaded: 25 January 1996.)

European Commission (1996) *Incorporating Equal Opportunities for Women and Men into All Community Policies and Activities,* COM (1996) 67 Final. Available at: http://europa.eu.int/comm/employment_social/equ_opp/com9667.htm.

European Commission (Employment and Social Affairs) (1996b) *A Code of Practice on the Implementation of Equal Pay For Work of Equal Value for Men and Women.* Office for the Official Publications of the European Communities: Luxembourg.

European Commission (1996c) *Code of Practice on the Implementation of Equal Pay for Men and Women for Work of Equal Value* COM (1996) 36.

European Commission (1997) *Equal Treatment for Women and Men: Equal Pay.* Available at: http://europa.eu.int/comm/sg/scadplus/leg/en/cha/c10905.htm. (Downloaded 9 May 1997.)

European Commission (Employment and Social Affairs) (1997b) *Equal Opportunities for Men and Women: 1996.* Office for the Official Publications of the European Communities: Luxembourg.

European Commission (2003) *Proposal for a Council Directive Implementing the Principle of Equal Treatment Between Men and Women in the Access to and Supply of Goods and Services,* COM (2003) 657 Final. Available at: http://europa.eu.int/scadplus/leg/en/cha/c10935.htm.

European Foundation for the Improvement of Living and Working Conditions, and the European Commission (1996) *A Report on the Forum: Working on European Social Policy* (Brussels, 27–30 March, 1996). Office for the Official Publications of the European Communities: Luxembourg.

European Foundation for the Improvement of Living and Working Conditions (1998) 'ECJ Reject UEAPME's case against the parental leave directive'. *Eironline,* available at: www.eiro.eurofound.ie/1998/07/inbrief/EU9801121N. html.

European Foundation for the Improvement of Living and Working Conditions (2002) *Reconciliation of Work and Family Life and Collective Bargaining – An Analysis of EIRO articles.* Dublin. Available at: www.eurofund.eu.int/.

European Parliamentary Labour Party. *The 1990's: The Decade for Women.* (Publication date unavailable.)

European Social Statistics, Labour Force Survey Results 2002 (2003) Office for the

Official Publications of the European Communities: Luxembourg.

European Women's Lobby (2002) 'The Future of the Union'. Available at: www.womenlobby.org/Document.asp?DocID=414&tod=3291.

European Women's Lobby (2003) 'EWL Convention Assessment'. Available at: www.womenlobby.org/htmldoc\convAss.htm.

Evans, J. (1995) *Feminist Theory Today: An Introduction to Second Wave Feminism.* Sage: London, Thousand Oaks and New Delhi.

Fagan, C. and Burchell, B. (2002) *Gender, Jobs and Working Conditions in the European Union.* European Foundations for the Improvement of Living and Working Conditions: Dublin. Available at: www.eurofund.eu.int/.

Falkner, G. (1997) 'Corporatist Governance and Europeanisation: No Future in the Multi-level Game?' *European Integration online Papers,* Vol. 1 (11), 1997. Available at: http://eiop.or.at/eiop/texte/1997–011a.htm.

Falkner, G. (1998) *EU Social Policy in the 1990s: Towards a Corporatist Community.* Routledge: London and New York.

Figes, K. (1995) *Because of Her Sex: The Myth of Equality for Women in Britain.* Pan Books: London and Basingstoke.

Flax, J. (1990) 'Postmodernism and Gender Relations in Feminist Theory' in Nicholson L. (ed.) *Feminism/Postmodernism.* Routledge: New York and London.

Flax, J. (1992) 'Beyond Equality: Gender Justice and Difference' in Bock, G. and James, S. (eds) *Beyond Equality and Difference: Citizenship, Feminist Politics and Female Subjectivity.* Routledge: London and New York.

Flax, J. (1997) 'Postmodernism and Gender Relations in Feminist Theory' in Kemp, S. and Squires, J. (eds) *Feminisms.* Oxford University Press: Oxford and New York.

Foglia, R. (1995) 'Efficacia del Diritto Communitario nell' Ordinamento Italiano e Paritá di Trattamento tra Uomini e Donne', *Il Diritto del Lavoro,* Anno LXIX (No. 1) Gennaio–Febbraio 1995.

Gill, T. and Monaghan, K. (2003) 'Justification in Direct Sex Discrimination Law: Taboo Upheld' *Industrial Law Journal,* Vol. 32 (2).

Gittins, D. (1992) 'What is the family? Is it Universal?' in McDowell, L. and Pringle, R. (eds), *Defining Women: Social Institutions and Gender Divisions.* Polity Press and The Open University: Cambridge and Oxford.

Gomá, R. (1996) 'The Social Dimension of the European Union: A New Type of Welfare System?' *Journal of European Public Policy,* Vol. 3 (2).

Governatori, L.R. (1992) 'Uguaglianza e Differenza Sessuale nel Diritto' in Besenghi, E. and Telmon, V. (eds). *Educazione al Femminile: dalla Paritá alla Differenza.* La Nuova Italia: Firenze.

Grant, J. (1993) *Fundamental Feminism: Contexting the Core Concepts of Feminist Theory.* Routledge: New York and London.

Grecchi, A. (1990) 'Women's Working Conditions in Italy: Positive Action in Practice' in von Prodzynki F. (ed.) *Women and the Completion of the Internal Market* (European Community Seminar 14–16 February 1990). Department of Labour: Dublin.

Grecchi, A. (1996) *Men and Women Equal Opportunities: A Goal Achieved? A*

General Overview from a Legal and Cultural Standpoint. Franco Angeli: Milano.

Guerra, E. and Pesce, A. (1991) 'Lavoro e Differenza Sessuale' (Employment and Sexual Difference), *Inchiesta*, No. 94.

Guerrina, R. (2001) 'Constructing Gender in the EU: The case of Equality and Maternity Rights' *Current Economics and Politics of Europe*, Vol. 10 (1).

Guerrina, R. (2003) 'Gender, Mainstreaming and the EU Charter of Fundamental Rights' *Policy, Organisation & Society*, Vol. 22 (1).

Guerrina, R. (2003b) 'Employment Policy and the Family in the European Union' in Ackers, P. (ed.) *Employment Relationship and Family Life*. Cross-National Research Papers 6 (4).

Hantrais, L. (2000) *Social Policy in the European Union* (2nd edn). Palgrave: Basingstoke and New York.

Hardy, S and Adnett, N. (2002) 'The Parental Leave Directive: Towards a "Family-Friendly" Social Europe?', *European Journal of Industrial Relations*, Vol. 8 (2).

Hare-Mustin, R.T. and Marecek, J. (1994) 'Gender and the Meaning of Difference: Postmodernism and Psychology' in Herrmann, A.C. and Stewart, A.J. (eds) *Theorising Feminism: Parallel Trends in the Humanities and the Social Sciences*. Westview Press: Boulder, San Francisco and Oxford.

Hartsock, N. (1990) 'Foucault on Power: A Theory for Women?' in Nicholson, L. (ed.), *Feminism/Postmodernism*. Routledge: London and New York.

Held, V. (1983) 'The Obligations of Mothers and Fathers' in Trebylcot, J. (ed.) *Mothering: Essays in Feminist Theory*. Rowman and Littlefield: Savage.

Hertogs, B. (1990) 'Working Women in Europe' in van Prondzynski, F. (ed.) *Women and the Completion of the Internal Market: Report and Conclusions*. Department of Labour, Dublin and the Commission of the European Communities: Dublin.

Hervey, T. and Shaw, J. (1998) 'Women, Work and Care: Women's Dual Role and Double Burden in EC Sex Equality Law', *Biblio Europe*, No. 2.

Hills, J. (1981) 'Britain' in Lovenduski, J. and Hills, J. (eds) *The Politics of the Second Electorate: Women and Public Participation*. Routledge & Kegan: London, Boston and Henley.

Honeyball, S. (1991) *Sex Employment and the Law*. Blackwell Law: Oxford.

Hoskyns, C. (1985) 'Women's Equality and the European Community', *Feminist Review*, No. 20 (Summer).

Hoskyns, C. (1991) 'Working Women and Women's Rights: The Development and Implications of EC Policy'. *Workers' Rights in Europe: Cross National Research Papers*, November 1991.

Hoskyns, C. (1992) 'The European Community Policy on Women in the Context of 1992', *Women's Studies International Forum*, Vol. 15 (1).

Hoskyns, C. (1994) 'Gender Issues in International Relations – The Case of the European Community', *Review of International Studies*, Vol. 20.

Hoskyns, C. (1996) *Integrating Gender: Women, Law and Politics in the European Union*. Verso: London.

Hoskyns, C. (2003) 'Gender Equality and the Convention: A comment' *Federal Trust Online Paper*, 08/03. Available at: www.fedtrust.co.uk/eu_constitution.

Humm, M. (1989) *The Dictionary of Feminist Theory*. Harvester Wheatsheaf: New York.

Income Data Services (1994) *Maternity Rights*. Series 2 No. 5. Income Data Services Ltd: Surrey.

Inland Revenue (2004) 'SMP Calculator – Important News'. Available at: www.inlandrevenue.gov.uk/news/smpcalc_news.htm.

James, G. (2001) '"Work and Parents: Competitiveness and Choice" Green Paper (Cmnd 5005 December 2000): A Policy to Promote Parenting / Workplace Harmony?' *Web Journal of Current Legal Issues*, [2001] 2. Available at: http://webjcli.ncl.ac.uk/2001/issue2/james2.html.

Johnson, B. (1980) *The Critical Difference: Essays in the Contemporary Rhetoric of Reading*. Johns Hopkins University Press: Baltimore.

Joshi, H. Pace, P. and Waldfogel, J. (1996) *The Wages of Motherhood: Better or Worse?* Discussion Paper. Welfare State Programme. Toyota Centre, Suntory and Toyota International Centres and the London School of Economics: London.

Kaplan, G. (1992) *Contemporary Western European Feminism*. UCL Press: London.

Kitzinger, C. (1996) 'Therapy and How it Undermines the Practice of Radical Feminism' in Bell, D. and Klein, R. (eds) *Radically Speaking: Feminism Reclaimed*. Zed: London.

Kravaritou, Y. (1997) *Equal Opportunites and Collective Bargaining in the European Union: 2. Exploring the Situation*. European Foundation for the Improvement of Living and Working Conditions. Office for the Official Publications of the European Communities: Luxembourg.

Lacey, N. (1993) 'Theory into Practice? Pornography and the Public/Private Dichotomy' in Bottomley, A. and Conaghan, J. (eds) *Feminist Theory and Legal Strategy*. Blackwell: Oxford (UK) and Cambridge (USA), pp. 93–113.

Landau, E.C. (1985) *The Rights of Working Women in the European Community*. Commission of the European Communities: Luxembourg.

Landes, J.B. (1998) *Feminism in the Public and Private*. Oxford University Press: Oxford.

Lasok, K.P.E. (2001) *Law & Institutions of the European Union* (7th edn). Butterworths: London.

Legge 30 Dicembre 1971, n. 1204 Tutela della Lavoratrici Madri (Law on the Protection of Working Mothers). *Gazzetta Ufficial della Republica Italiana*, No. 14, 13 January 1972.

Legge 8 Dicembre 1977, n. 903 – Paritá di Trattamento tra Uomini e Donne in Materia di Lavoro (Equality of Treatment between Men and Women in Matters of Work). Cappiello *et al.*, *Codice Donna*.

Legge 8 Marzo 2000, n. 53 – Disposizioni per il Sostegno della Maternitá e della Paternitá, per il Diritto alla Cura e alla Formazione e per il Coordinamento dei Tempi della Cittá. (Rules for the support of mothering and fathering, for the right to care and training, and for the coordination of the city's time.) Available at: www.palazzochigi.it/GovernoInforma/Dossier/tutela_maternita/legge_8_marzo.

Leonard, D. & Speakman, M.A. (1986) 'Women in the Family: Companions or Caretakers?' in Beechey, V. and Whitelegg, E. (eds) *Women in Britain Today.* Open University Press: Milton Keynes and Philadelphia.

Levin, M. (1992). 'Women, Work, Biology, Justice' in Quest C. (ed.) *Equal Opportunities: A Feminist Fallacy.* Choice in Welfare No. 11. IEA Health and Welfare Unit: London.

Lewis, J. (1992) *Women in Britain Since 1945: Women, Family, Work and the State in the Post-War Years.* Blackwell: Oxford (UK) and Cambridge (USA).

Lewis, J. (1992b) 'Gender the Development of Welfare Regimes' *Journal of European Social Policy,* Vol. 2 (3).

Lewis, J. and Davies, C. (1991) 'Protective Legislation in Britain, 1870–1990: Equality, Difference and Their Implications for Women', *Policy and Politics,* Vol. 19.

Lovenduski, J. (1996) 'Sex, Gender & British Politics' in Lovenduski, J. and Norris, P. (eds) *Women in Politics.* Oxford University Press and The Hansard Society for Parliamentary Government: Oxford.

Lovenduski, J. and Randal, V. (1993) *Contemporary Feminist Politics: Women and Power in Britain.* Oxford University Press: Oxford.

Macedo van Overbeek, J.P. (1995) *Handbook on Equal Treatment for Men and Women in the European Community.* European Commission: Brussels and Luxembourg.

Marshall, B. (1998) 'The Boy Can't Help it' *Guardian* (The Guide), 20 June 1998.

Marshall, B.L. (1994) *Engendering Modernity: Feminism, Social Theory and Social Change.* Polity Press: Cambridge and Oxford.

Maternity and Paternity Leave (Amendment) Regulations, 2002. No. 2789. Available at: www.legislation.hmso.gov.uk/si/si2002/20022789.htm.

Maternity (Compulsory Leave) Regulations, 1994. No. 2479. Available at: www.legislation.hmso.gov.uk/si/si1994/Uksi_19942479_en_1.htm.

Maugeri, M. (1991) 'Il Fascismo Femminile Antemarcia' in Centro Studi Futura, *Gli Angeli e la Rivoluzione.* Edizioni Sigillo: Roma.

Mazey, S. (2001) *Gender Mainstreaming in the EU: Principles and Practice.* Kogan Page: London.

Mazey, S. (2002) 'The Development of EU Gender Policies: Towards the Recognition of Difference', *EUSA Review,* Vol. 15 (3).

McCrudden, C. (1993) 'Access to Equality Between Men and Women in the European Community: The Lessons of the Lovain-la-Neuve Conference' in Verwilghen (ed.) *Access to Equality Between Men and Women in the European Community.* Presses Universitaire de Louvaine: Louvaine-la-Neuve.

McDowell, L. and Pringle, R. (1992) 'Defining Public and Private Issues' in McDowell, L. and Pringle, R. (eds) *Defining Women: Social Institutions and Gender Divisions.* Polity Press and the Open University: Cambridge and Oxford.

McGlynn, C. (1996) 'Pregnancy Dismissals and the *Webb* Litigation', *Feminist Legal Studies,* Vol. IV (2).

McGlynn, C. (2000) 'Ideologies of Motherhood in European Community Sex Equality Law', *European Law Journal,* Vol. 6 (1).

McGlynn, C. (2001) 'Reclaiming a Feminist Vision: The Reconciliation of Paid Work and Family Life in European Union Law and Policy', *Columbia Journal of European Law*, Vol. 7.

McGlynn, C. (2001b) 'European Union Family Values: Ideologies of "Family" and "Motherhood" in European Union Law', *Social Politics*, Vol. 8 (3).

McRae, S. (1991) *Maternity Rights in Britain: the PSI Report on the Experience of Women and Employers*. Policy Studies Institute: London.

Meehan, E. (1992) 'Women's Rights in a Citizenship Europe', *A Manchester Paper*. Charter 88: London.

Meehan, E. and Collins, E. (1996) 'Women, the European Union and Britain' in Lovenduski, J. and Norris, P. (eds) *Women in Politics*. Oxford University Press and the Hansard Society for Parliamentary Government: Oxford.

Meyer, T. (1994) 'The German and British Welfare States as Employers: Patriarchal or Emancipatory?' in Sainsbury, D. (ed.). *Gendering Welfare States*. Sage: London, Thousand Oaks and New Delhi.

Mezzatosta, T. (1992) 'La Cultura della Parita', *Nuova Paideia*, Vol. 1.

Millns, S. (1996) 'Legislative Constructions of Motherhood' in Lovenduski, J. and Norris, P. (eds) *Women in Politics*. Oxford University Press and The Hansard Society for Parliamentary Government: Oxford and New York.

Mitchel, J. (1987) 'Women and Equality' in Phillips, A. (ed.) *Feminism and Equality*. Basil Blackwell: Oxford.

Moller Okin, S. (1989) *Justice, Gender and the Family*. Basic Books: USA.

Morris, A. and Nott, S. (1995) 'The Law's Engagement with Pregnancy' in Bridgeman, J. and Millns, S. (eds) *Law and the Body Politics: Regulations of the Female Body*. Dartmouth Publishing Company: Aldershot and Brookfield.

Nielsen, R. (2001) 'Burden of Proof in Equality Cases' *Málþing SA um Evrópuvinnurétt og jafnréttislöggjöf, 9–10 March 2001*.

Nielsen R. and Szyszczak, E. (1993) *The Social Dimension of the European Community* (2nd edn). Hendlshojskolens Forlag: Copenhagen.

O'Connel, H. (1994) *Women and the Family*. Zed Books Ltd.: London and New Jersey

Pace, L., Di Lello, A., Accame G. and Poli Bertone, A. (1991) 'Il Dibattito' in Centro Studi Futura, *Gli Angeli e la Rivoluzione*. Edizioni Settimo Sigillo: Rome.

Panorama Programme *Missing Mom*. BBC1, 1997.

Pascall, J. (1997) *Social Policy: A New Feminist Analysis*. Routledge: London and New York.

Pateman, C. (1992) 'Equality, Difference, Subordination: The Politics of Motherhood and Womens' Citizenship' in Bock, G. and James, S. (eds), *Beyond Equality and Difference: Citizenship, Feminist Politics and Female Subjectivity*. Routledge: London and New York.

Pateman, C. (1991) *The Sexual Contract*. Polity Press: Cambridge and Oxford.

Pateman, C. (1989) *The Disorder of Women: Democracy, Feminism and Political Theory*. Polity: Cambridge.

Paul, F.E. (1992) 'Fetal Protection, Women's Rights and Freedom of Contract' in IEA Health and Welfare Unit, *Equal Opportunities: A Feminist Fallacy* (Choice in Welfare No. 11). IEA Health and Welfare Unit: London.

Peterson, S.V. and Runyan Sasson, A. (1993) *Global Gender Issues.* Westview Press: Boulder, CO.

Phillips, A. (1987) 'Introduction' in Phillips, A. (ed.) *Feminism and Equality.* Basil Blackwell: Oxford.

Pillinger, J. (1991) *Feminising the Labour Market: the Single European Market and Women's Employment.* CRESR Lecture Series: Sheffield City Polytechnic, 30 October 1991.

Pochet P., Barbuerm C., Moro E., Raulier A., Turloot L. and Vernay, C. (1996) 'European Briefing', *Journal of European Social Policy,* Vol. 6 (2).

Polatnick, R. (1983) 'Why Men Don't' Rear Children: A Power Analysis' in Trebilcot, J. (ed.) *Mothering: Essays in Feminist Theory.* Rowman & Littlefield: Savage.

Pollack, M.A. and Hafner-Burton, E. (2000) 'Mainstreaming Gender in the European Union' *Jean Monnet Working Papers* 00/32. Available at: www. jeanmonnetprogram.org/papers/papers00.html.

Poole, M. and Isaacs, D. (1997) 'Caring: a Gendered Concept', *Women's Studies International Forum,* Vol. 20 (4).

Prechal, S. and Burrows, N. (1990) *Gender Discrimination Law of the European Community.* Dartmouth: Aldershot and Bookfield.

Primicerio, B. (1976) 'Maternitá' in Giuffré (ed.) *Enciclopedia del Diritto,* vol. XXV. Giuffré Editore: Varese.

Pringle, K. (1998) *Children and Social Welfare in Europe.* Open University Press: Buckingham and Philadelphia.

Quest, C. (1992) 'Introduction', in Quest, C. (ed.) *Equal Opportunities: a Feminist Fallacy* (Health and Welfare Series No. 11). IEA Health and Welfare Unit: London.

Quintin, O. (1986) 'Treatment Equality of Men and Women in the European Community' in Verwilghen (ed.) *Equality in Law Between Men and Women in the European Community* Vol. 1 General Reports. Presses Universitaire Louvain-la-Neuve: Louvain-la-Neuve.

Quintin, O. (1988) 'The Politics of the European Communities with Special Reference to the Labour Market' in Buckley, M. and Anderson, M. (eds) *Women, Equality and Europe.* Macmillan Press: Basingstoke and London.

Ramazanoglu, C. (1989) *Feminism and the Contradictions of Oppression.* Routledge: London and New York.

Ranti, I. (1991) 'La Donna Nuova del Fascismo nella Stampa Periodica degli Anni Venti e Trenta' in Centro Studi Futura. *Gli Angeli e la Rivoluzione.* Edizioni Sigillo: Roma.

Rees, T. (1992) *Women and the Labour Market.* Routledge: London and New York.

Rees, T. (1998) *Mainstreaming Equality in the European Union: Education, Training and Labour Market Policies.* Routledge: London and New York.

Reinicke, K. (1994) 'Le Donne Italiane Deboli ma Forti'. *Internazionale,* 3 Decembre 1994, Anno 2 (56).

Remiddi, Laura (ed.) (1993) *Pagine Rosa: Guida ai Diritti delle Donne* (3rd edn).

Commissione Nazionale per la Realizzazione della Paritá tra Donna e Uomo: Roma.

Remuet Alexandrou, F., Gonzales, M.J. and Honrado, F. (1986) *Community Law and Women.* Supplement No. 25 to *Women of Europe.* Commission of the European Communities: Brussels.

Rhode, D.L. (1992) 'The Politics of Paradigms: Gender Difference and Gender Disadvantage', in Bock, G. and James, S. (eds), *Beyond Equality and Difference: Citizenship, Feminist Politics, Female Subjectivity.* Routledge: London and New York.

Richardson, D. (1993) *Women, Motherhood, and Childrearing.* Macmillan: Basingstoke and London.

Roberts, E. (1988) *Women's Work 1840–1940* (Studies in Economic and Social History). Macmillan: London.

Romito, P. (1993) 'The Practice of Protective Legislation for Pregnant Women Worker in Italy: Limit, Problems and Contradictions', *Women's Studies International Forum,* Vol. 16 (6).

Romito, P. and Saurel-Cubizolles, M.J. (1992) 'Fair Law, Unfair Practices? Benefiting from Protective Legislation for Pregnant Workers in Italy and France'. *Social Science and Medicine,* Vol. 35 (12).

Ross, R. and Schneider, R. (1992) *From Equality to Diversity: a Business Case for Equal Opportunities.* Pitman: London.

Rozes, S. (1986) 'Discrimination on Grounds of Sex: Rights and Facts' in Versilghen (ed.) *Equality in Law Between Men and Women in The European Community,* Vol. 1 General Reports. Presses Universitaires de Louvain: Louvain-la-Neuve.

Rubery, J., Grimshaw, D., Fagan, C., Figueiredo, H. and Smith, M. (2003) 'Gender Equality Still on the European Agenda – But for How Long?', *Industrial Relations Journal,* Vol. 34 (5).

Rubery, J., Smith, M. and Fagan, C. (1999) *Women's Employment in Europe: Trends and Prospects.* Routledge: London and New York.

Ruggerini, M. (1992) 'Donne e Cariere: Quel Maledetto Senso di Responsabilitá'. *Politica ed Economia.* No. 10–11.

Sacchetto, D. (2003) 'Work and family flexibility: an interpretation of Italian transformation' in Ackers, P. (ed.) *The Employment Relationship and Family Life – Cross National Research Papers,* Vol. 6 (4).

Sainsbury, D. (1994) (ed.) *Gendering Welfare States.* Sage: London, Thousand Oaks and New Delhi.

Saraceno, C. (1978) *Dalla Parte della Donna: la 'Questione Femminile' nelle Societá Industriali Avanzate.* Club Italiano dei Lettori: Milano.

Scott, J.W. (1994) 'Deconstructing Equality-Versus-Difference: or, The Uses of Poststructuralist Theory for Feminism' in Herrmann A.C. and Stewart, A.J. (eds) *Theorising Feminism: Parallel Trends in the Humanities and Social Sciences.* Westview Press: Boulder, San Francisco and Oxford.

Sex Discrimination Act 1975 (1975 c. 65) in *Current Law Statutes Annotated* 1975. Sweet Maxwell, Stevens and Sons: London and Edinburgh.

Shaw, J. (1999) 'Gender and the Court of Justice' Available at:

http://eucenter.wisc.edu/Conferences/Gender/shaw.htm; also available as Shaw, J. (2001) 'Gender and the Court of Justice' in de Búrca, G. and Weiler, J.H.H. (eds), *The European Court of Justice*, Oxford University Press: Oxford.

Shaw, J. (2002) 'Gender Mainstreaming and the EU Constitution', *EUSA Review*, Vol. 15 (3).

Showstack Sasson, A. (1992) 'Introduction: the Personal and the Intellectual, Fragments and Order, International Trends and National Specificities' in Showstack Sasson, A. (ed.), *Women and the State: the Shifting Boundaries of Public and Private*. Routledge: London and New York.

Siaroff, A. (1994) 'Work, Welfare and Gender Equality: A New Typology' in Sainsbury, D. (ed.) *Gendering Welfare States*. Sage: London, Thousand Oaks and New Delhi.

Smart, C. and Brophy, J. (1985) 'Locating Law: A Discussion of the Place of Law in Feminist Politics' in Brophy, J. and Smart, C. (eds) *Explorations in Law, Family and Sexuality*. Routledge & Kegan Paul: Boston, London, Henley and Melbourne.

Smith, I.T., Wood, J. C. and Thomas, G. (1993) *Industrial Law* (5th edn) Butterworth: London, Edinburgh and Dublin.

Terranova, A. (1991) 'Madri e Massaie in Camicia Nera: le Organizzazioni del Fascismo-Regime' in Centro di Studi Futura *Gli Angeli e la Rivoluzione*. Edizioni Settimo Sigillo: Roma.

Tesoka, S. (1999) 'Differential Impact of Judicial Politics in the Field of Gender Equality: Three National Cases under Scrutiny' *European University Institute Working Paper RSC*, No. 99/18. Available at: www.iue.it/RSCAS/WP-texts/99_18t.htm.

Thane, P. (1991) 'Visions of Gender in the Making of the British Welfare State: The Case of Women in the British Labour Party and Social Policy, 1906–1945' in Bock, G. and Thane P. *Maternity & Gender Policies: Women and the Rise of the European Welfare States 1880s–1950s*. Routledge: London and New York.

Tiessalo, P. (1996) 'Equality between Women and Men in the European Union'. Available at: www.helsinki.fi/valttdk/neusem/tiessalo/index.html [downloaded 27 August 1996]. Also published in Jan-Peter, P. (ed.) (1996) *Europe and its Citizens*. Edita: Helsinki.

Tillotson, J. and Foster, N. (2003) *Text, Cases and Materials on European Union Law* (4th edn). Cavendish: London.

Tilly, L. and Scott, J. (1987) *Women, Work and Family* (2nd ed.). Routledge: New York and London.

Trade Union Reform and Employment Rights Act 1993 (1993 c. 19). Available at: www.legislation.hmso.gov.uk/acts/acts1993/Ukpga_19930019_en_1.htm.

Treaty Establishing the European Community (Signed 25 March, 1957). Available at: http://europa.eu.int/abc/obj/treaties/en/entoc05.htm.

True, J. (2003) 'Mainstreaming Gender in Global Public Policy', *International Feminist Journal of Politics*, Vol. 5 (3).

Valentini, C. (1997) *Le Donne Fanno Paura*. Il Saggiatore: Milano.

Warner, H. (1984) 'EC Social Policy in Practice: Community Action on Behalf of

Women and its impact in the Member States', *Journal of Common Market Studies*, Vol. 13 (2).

Waters, K. (1996) '(Re)Turning to the Modern: Radical Feminism and the Post-Modern Turn' in Bell, D. and Klein, R. (eds) *Radically Speaking: Feminism Reclaimed*. Zed: London.

Weber, M. (1981) 'Italy' in Lovenduski, J. and Hills, J. (eds) *The Politics of the Second Electorate: Women and Public Participation*. Routledge & Kegan Paul: London.

Webster, J. (2000) *Reconciling Adaptability and Equal Opportunities in European Workplaces*. Report for DG-Employment of the European Commission. Available at: http://europa.eu.int/comm/employment_social/equ_opp/documents/reconcil_webster.pdf.

Wheat, K. (1998) 'The Sick Men and Women of Europe: (Case C-400/95) Handes-Og Kontorfunktionaerernes Forbund, acting on behalf of Larsoon v Dansk Handel & Service, acting on behalf of Fotx Supermarked A/S [1997] IRLR 643' *Web Journal of Current Legal Issues*, [1998], 1. Available at: http://webjcli.ncl.ac.uk/1998/issue1/wheat1.html.

Wheelehan, I. (1995) *Modernist Feminist Thought: From the Second Wave to 'Post-Feminism'*. Edinburgh University Press: Edinburgh.

Williams, R. and Lamb, M. (1997) *European Social Policy: Fact Sheet*. European Commission in the United Kingdom: London.

Whitworth, S. (1994) *Feminism and International Relations: Towards a Political Economy of Gender in Interstate Institutions*. Macmillan: Basingstoke and London.

Wittig, M. (1997) 'One is Not Born a Woman' in Kemp, S. and Squires, J. (eds), *Feminisms*. Oxford University Press: Oxford and New York.

Wobbe, T. (2003) 'From Protecting to Promoting: Evolving EU Sex Equality Norms in an Organisational Field', *European Law Journal*, Vol. 9 (1).

Wynn, M. (1999) 'Pregnancy Discrimination: Equality, Protection or Reconciliation?' *The Modern Law Review*, Vol. 62.

Zalewski, M. (1993) 'Feminist Theory and International Relations' in Bowker and Brown (eds) *From Cold War to Collapse: Theory and World Politics in the 1980s*. Cambridge University Press: Cambridge.

INDEX

1974 Social Action Programme 46
3rd Action Programme on Equal
    Opportunities (1991–95) 68–9
5th Equality Programme 56, 58–9
Agreement on Social Policy 66, 77
Amendment to the European Equal
    Treatment Directive 96/97/EC
    56–7
atypical work 79–81, 146–7, 154
    see also flexible employment patterns

Barber Case 52, 143
Beijin Platform for Action 54
birth rates 1, 117–19, 122
Brown Case (1998) 102–4, 109–10
Burden of Proof Directive 97/80/EC
    56–7

Cavarero, A. 26, 28
Charter for the Fundamental Social
    Rights of Workers 53, 66
Child-Care Recommendations 11, 65–6,
    73–5, 106
Code of Practice on the Implementation
    of Equal Pay for Work of Equal
    Value 48, 56
collective bargaining 48
Commission vs. Italy 94–5, 123–4
Community Programme for the
    Promotion of Equal Opportunities
    for Women 75–6

Defrenne cases/judgements 41, 44–6,
    87–8
    Gabrielle Defrenne 44
Dekker Case 98–100, 102, 109, 143–4
demographic transition 1
demographic trends 1, 117–18, 154
difference 7–9, 19–20, 25–31
    critiques of 29–31
    feminism 19

motherhood 26
    sexual difference 17, 24, 26–7, 29–30
direct discrimination 45

Elshtain, J.B. 22
equal pay 89
    for equal work 45
    principle of 42–4, 86
    for work of equal value 47
Equal Pay Directive 75/117/EEC 41,
    46–9
Equal rights debate 3, 7–10, 14, 18–20,
    150
equal treatment 48–9, 58
Equal Treatment Directive
    (76/207/EEC) 48–51, 90, 98–102,
    107–10, 112
Equal Treatment Framework Directive
    (2000/78/EC) 56–9
Equal Treatment in Occupational Social
    Security Schemes Directive
    (79/7/EEC) 52
Equal Treatment in Occupational Social
    Security Schemes for Self-Employed
    Occupations (86/613/EEC) 52–3
Equal Treatment in Social Security
    Directive (86/378/EEC) 51
equality 3, 7–9, 14, 19–25, 32, 151–2
    critiques of 27
    in difference 19
    feminist theory 19, 23–5
    formal equality 7, 22, 37, 48, 50, 53,
        63, 87–9, 112, 156
    formal vs. substantive 3–5, 15–16,
        21–4, 43, 51, 60, 83, 89, 111, 146,
        150, 155
    substantive equality 5, 15, 23–5, 36,
        50–3, 55, 65, 67–8, 71–2, 74,
        81–2, 84, 89, 92, 106, 112, 127,
        147
equality–difference debate 8, 17–18

equality feminism 22
EU Charter of Fundamental Rights 7,
    53, 58, 60, 62–3
European Commission White Paper on
    Social Policy 66–7
European Constitution 54, 60–3
European Convention on the Future of
    the Union 60–1
European Court of Justice 11, 44–6, 52,
    57, 70, 76–7, 86–9, 72, 74–5, 77, 84,
    86, 96, 103–4, 112
    childcare 106–9, 113
    equal pay 89
        see also Defrenne cases/judgements
    equal treatment 89–92, 111
    family-friendly policies 89, 91–6,
        107–8, 110
    judicial activism 88
    maternity rights 97–104, 110
    parental leave 104–6, 110
    security and pension 89
European Equality Agenda 11–12, 41,
    44, 48, 50–1, 59–60, 63, 68–9, 72,
    74–5, 77, 84, 86, 96, 103–4, 112
European Foundation for the
    Improvement of Living and
    Working Conditions 156
European Social Dimension 1, 53, 66–8
European Social Model 11–12
European Women's Lobby 61–2

family-friendly policies 1, 14–16, 66, 68,
    72, 84, 146–8, 150, 152–5, 157
    family structures 17
    post-structuralist critiques of 34–5
flexible employment patterns 70, 79–81,
    84
        see also atypical work

gender divisions of labour 4–6, 9, 15, 17,
    23, 31, 50, 66, 73, 75, 77, 80, 82
gender power hierarchies 1, 3–5, 8, 11,
    14, 34, 48, 61, 68, 72, 80, 83–4, 96,
    111, 113, 148–9

Hertz Case 98, 101–3, 109

indirect discrimination 47
Italy 12–13, 70–1, 154–6

1971 Maternity Law 12–13, 118–22
1977 Equal Treatment Law 120–3
2000 Mothering and Fathering Law
    13, 121–2
2001 Legislative Decree for the
    Protection of Mothering and
    Fathering 13, 121–2
birth rates 117–18, 122
constitution 116
family-friendly policies 118–19
Fascist Regime 115–16

Kalanke Case (1995) 90–1

mainstreaming 11, 53–5, 59, 61, 63–4, 152
male breadwinner model 9, 12, 72, 83,
    95–6, 111, 113
male norms 8, 27, 152
    equality feminism 22
Marshall Case (1993) 90–1, 111
maternity leave
    EU 69–70
    Italy 118–22
    UK 140–1
Medium Term Action Programme
    (1995–97) 68–9
mothering/motherhood
    European Court of Justice 93–6
    social construction of 37–8
    social function of 50

Open Method of Coordination 64

Parental Leave Directive (94/34/EC)
    11–13, 65–6, 75, 79–82
Part-Time Worker Directive (97/81/EC)
    11, 81–2
Pateman, C. 23, 28, 38
patriarchy 28
post-structuralist feminism 7–9, 15, 19,
    30–6
pratica e pensiero della differenza
    sessuale (philosophy and practice of
    sexual difference) 28–9
Pregnant Worker Directive (92/85/EEC)
    11, 13, 15, 65, 68–73, 75, 77,
    99–100, 103, 104, 109–11, 122, 129,
    138, 144, 153

public–private dichotomy 2–5, 8, 12–13, 15, 19–20, 22–4, 27, 38, 48, 51–2, 74, 87, 95–6, 111, 130–3, 146
  post-structualist critique of 33

radical feminism 27, 29
  critiques of 29–31
reconciliation between work and family life 1, 11, 13–14, 17, 60, 65–85, 148, 151–2

second wave feminism 17, 21, 37
sexual contract 28
social construction of gender 17, 33
social exclusion 59, 62
Social Partners 72, 82
Social Protocol 77

Treaty of Amsterdam 54–5, 57, 79
Treaty of Maastrich 1, 82
Treaty of Rome 7, 39–41, 63, 70–1
  Article 119 10, 41–8, 52, 87, 90, 142–3

UK 12–13
  2002 Employment Act 13, 141
  2002 Maternity Regulations 140
  domestic ideology 13, 130–3
  Employment Protect (Consolidation) Act 1978 137–8
  Equal Pay Act 1970 13, 134–5, 141–2
  lone parents 132
  Sex Discrimination Act 1975 134–5, 144
  TURER Act 1993 134, 137–9, 144

Webb Case (1994) 98, 100, 109–10, 143–5
woman
  concept of 31
  post-structuralist deconstructions of 31–3
Working-Time Directive (93/104/EC) 11, 65, 75, 79–82
work–life balance 1, 11, 17, 66, 82–3, 145–6, 156

Date Due